Strength & Speed's

Guide to Elite Obstacle Course Racing

Strength & Speed's

Guide to Elite Obstacle Course Racing

EVAN PERPERIS

BREAKAWAY BOOKS
HALCOTTSVILLE, NEW YORK
2016

ISBN: 978-1-62124-023-5
Library of Congress Control Number: 2016935644

Published by Breakaway Books
P.O. Box 24
Halcottsville, NY 12438
www.breakawaybooks.com

FIRST PRINTING

PREFACE

Starting line of the team competition of the first Obstacle Course Racing World Championships.

You stand on the starting line. Hands are sweaty. You nervously await the gun signaling the start of the race. A hype man is nearby spouting motivational phrases: "Every day of work has brought you to this point"; "This is the culmination of a lifetime of effort"; "Prepare for the hardest day of your life." Some of these phrases hit home for you, while others are just words spoken to motivate the masses. Today *is* in fact a culmination of a lifetime of effort, and every day of work has indeed brought you to this point. However, today will be very hard, but it will not be the hardest day of your life. You have spent the last year cycling periods of exercise focused on this goal. Months of prepping by building a huge aerobic base and then focusing on VO_2max and lactate threshold workouts. The hardest part was the months and years of preparation that built your body to its current capability.

You take one last look at your double-knotted shoes, adjust your arm sleeves, and make sure your compression pants are tied closed. You lean over into a semi-crouched starting position. *BANG!* and you are off. Welcome to the world of elite obstacle racing.

Obstacle racing is a massive sport that has been growing at an exponential rate over the last few years. Every year new companies appear promising harder challenges, more obstacles, and a better experience. Every year the birth of new companies coincides with the death of those that failed to deliver on promises from the year before.

Typically, obstacle races range in length from 3 to 13 miles and consist of twenty to thirty military-style obstacles designed to challenge participants along the way. To accommodate the large numbers of racers and prevent lines at obstacles, the day of the race is broken into waves. The first wave of the day is the elite or the competitive wave, a semantic difference depending on the event. Usually the waves later in the day are untimed and focus more on team building, camaraderie, and a fun atmosphere.

This book is for racers competing in the first wave, or those who are currently in the later waves but looking to make the leap into the first one. It is for the competitive obstacle racer, the elite obstacle racer. While the non-competitive waves and the elite wave run the same course, their goals, preparation, and mind-set are different. This book explores all aspects of elite obstacle racing. If you are looking to improve, this book will help guide you along your path. With any serious sporting endeavor, your improvement in your chosen sport occurs twenty-four hours a day, not just during the hour or two you spend in the gym or on the trail. By taking a holistic approach, which includes diet, rest, exercise, and mental preparation, you will maximize your ability to race fast. If you are the type of person looking to win, I recommend following all or most of the suggestions listed in this book. However, on a case-by-case basis, parts can be modified to fit your life. For example, if you are already a top-level runner and need to work on upper-body strength, you might modify the plans to be more upper-body-focused. If you are a vegan, the diet section will be largely invalid but the principles can still be applied to your diet. To assist with this, I included interviews with other elite obstacle racers at the back of the book. These other racers will provide their own opinions and will even contradict some of the statements I make in the book. This section is here to help, and show that there is no single way to succeed. Furthermore, it emphasizes that depending on your athletic background, you may have to take a slightly different approach to training.

If you are a non-elite or non-competitive obstacle racer, this book can still be helpful. However, you don't have to follow all of it. Feel free to choose the parts that suit your lifestyle. If you aren't interested in trying to win, then go ahead and have that free beer post-race. Want to eat a fatty, unhealthy meal the night before the race because you're racing in a new city? Go for it. This book will still provide you with some information you can integrate into your training. After all, who doesn't want to be able to conquer a hill without having to stop and rest? Who doesn't want to climb over an obstacle with greater ease? Maybe you're reading this book because you are required to race as part of a team-building competition and don't want to embarrass yourself in front of co-workers. Take the information here and use it so you are the one waiting for your co-workers to catch up.

Regardless of your level or goals, this book has information that will make you a better obstacle racer. From elite to recreational, I guarantee you will learn something over the next chapters. It's time to put on your trail shoes and get ready.

Let's get started, because hard work can beat genetics . . .

The first Obstacle Course Racing World Championships begins with the elite male wave.

CONTENTS

Preface 5

Introduction 13

1. Exercise 15

Specificity 16

Periodization and Prioritization 21

Peaking 24

2. Diet and Supplements 30

Macronutrients 33

Eating Clean 37

Supplements 52

3. Rest and Recovery 61

Rest 61

Recovery 63

4. Getting Started and the Competitive Drive 71

5. Obstacle Race Training: The Obstacles 76

6. Obstacle Race Speed Training 109

Training Chart Terminology 113

Other Notes 119

Strength Training for the Workout Plans 121

8-Week Easy 5K Training Plan for a PR (Peaking at 21 Miles a Week) 126

8-Week Medium 5K Training Plan for a PR (Peaking at 30 Miles a Week) 128

8-Week Hard 5K Training Plan for a PR (Peaking at 40 Miles a Week) 130

8-Week Easy 8-Mile Training Plan for a PR (Peaking at 25 Miles a Week) 132

8-Week Medium 8-Mile Training Plan for a PR (Peaking at 33 Miles a Week) 133

8-Week Hard 8-Mile Training Plan for a PR (Peaking at 40 Miles a Week) 135

12-Week Easy 13-Mile Training Plan for a PR (Peaking at 28 Miles a Week) 137

12-Week Medium 13-Mile Training Plan for a PR (Peaking at 35 Miles a Week) 139

12-Week Hard 13-Mile Training Plan for a PR (Peaking at 45 Miles a Week) 141

16-Week Easy 26-Plus-Mile / Ultra Plan (Peaking at 38 Miles a Week) 143

16-Week Medium 26-Plus-Mile / Ultra Plan (Peaking at 50 Miles a Week) 145

16-Week Hard 26-Plus-Mile / Ultra Plan (Peaking at 75 Miles a Week) 148

Common Questions, Complaints, and Statements 151

Accessories for Speed Training: Shoes, Electronics, Masks, and Vests 158

Racing 165

Ultra-Distance Racing Considerations 176

7. Strength Training: Off-Season Cross-Training and Improving Your Weaknesses 186

8-Week Bodybuilding / Strength Gaining Split 189

8-Week Bodybuilding / Strength Gaining Split with Leg Days Divided Up Because You're Still Doing Some Cardio 196

Strength Training Principles 200

Best Exercises for OCR 203

Common Questions, Complaints, and Statements 209

8. Learning from Other Sports 213

A Lesson from Bodybuilding: Control Your Diet 214

A Lesson from Bodybuilding: Improvements Occur Twenty-Four Hours a Day, Not Just During Training 216

A Lesson from Elite Runners: Athletes Strength Train 217

A Lesson from Power Lifters: Use Low Reps to Increase Maximum Strength 218

A Lesson from Triathletes and Baseball Players: Practice Individual Sections Before Combining Them 218

A Lesson from Cyclists: Ounces Make Pounds 219

A Lesson from Adventure Racers: The Drag Method for Team Competitions 220

A Lesson from Rock Climbers: Improve Grip Strength 221

9. Obstacle Racing Accessories and Equipment 223

Building Your Own Obstacle Racing Equipment 223

Building Your Personal Fitness Mecca 227

10. More Ways to Gain an Edge 231

Mental Training 231

Drugs 233

Motivation 235

11. Finding Your Ideal Race 241

The Different Race Series 241

The Various Obstacle Race World Championships 246

An Interview with the Founder of the OCRWC: Adrian Bijanada 251

12. Interviews with Elite Obstacle Racers 257

Marc-André "Marco" Bédard 258

Hobie Call 263

Corinna Coffin 270

Claude Godbout 279

Evan Perperis 285

Kevin Righi 292

Cassidy Watton 298

Lindsay Webster 304

Elite Athlete Conclusions 311

Conclusion 312

Join Strength & Speed 313

Acknowledgments 316

Photo Credits 320

INTRODUCTION

Improving physical fitness level is a twenty-four-hour-a-day activity. Just because we only stress our bodies by exercising for an hour or two a day doesn't mean the rest of the day isn't important. I like to break things down into categories to make them easier to understand. When I'm teaching physical fitness to people, I usually use the following categories:

1. Exercise

2. Diet and supplements

3. Rest and recovery

These elements are listed in decreasing order of complexity and importance, but they are all crucial for success. A deficit in one of the categories will cause your performance to suffer. Most people don't realize how linked these topics are. For example, if you work out hard and do not recover properly, you won't improve at an optimal rate. Your body won't build new muscle or grow stronger in the gym or on the track. The stress on your body occurs at that time, but then your body needs nutrients (diet and supplements) and downtime (rest and recovery) to grow properly. Muscle growth and fitness improvement occur thanks to all three of these categories working in conjunction.

Chapter 1

EXERCISE

Multi-lap Mudders and Strength & Speed athletes Jordan Smith and Evan Perperis finish an obstacle during a 40-plus-mile training weekend.

Exercise is the most complicated section of this book—and the most important. Without proper stimulus, aka exercise, your body will not adapt or grow. However, as I've emphasized before, it is crucial that you also incorporate proper diet and rest to ensure your exercise is not in vain. What is the point of killing yourself working out every day if you're going to ruin it every night by drinking alcohol or not getting adequate rest?

To improve as an obstacle racer, you must adhere to several principles:

1. Specificity
2. Periodization and prioritization
3. Peaking

Specificity

Specificity is a simple concept. It means that to get better at a certain activity, you must practice it. The more you practice it, the better you'll become. Let's break this down scientifically to see why it works. (I always understand things better when I know *why* they work rather than just *that* they work.)

I'll use running as an example, because running is the foundation on which elite obstacle course racing (OCR) is built. Regardless of how good you are at the obstacles, in order to win you must be a good runner. This is because the majority of time spent in an obstacle course race is spent running. Even on the densest of obstacle races—the ones that boast of having the most obstacles per mile—not having a strong cardiovascular base will cause you to lose. If you want to win, you need to practice running, and the more you run the better you get. The question is: Why do you get better from running more?

The first improvement comes from neurological adaptations. Your body adapts fastest to neurological changes. Your neurological pathways are like a tall field of grass. The first time you try an activity, there are all kinds of tall blades of grass and plants in your way. Pushing them down will make it easier to walk through the field. Practicing an activity thousands, hundreds of thousands, then millions of times creates a beaten path. It allows messages to flow to their intended target in a smoother, faster, and easier way. This why you can type without looking at the keys of a computer. It's also the reason you can operate your cell phone one-handed while driving—which you should not do because it is extremely dangerous. Both driving and cell phone operation are skills you have practiced repeatedly separately. Putting them together is easy because you already have beaten paths for both. If I told you to operate two complicated things you have never used before, it would seem almost impossible.

Neurological adaptation is why you cannot take a world-class cyclist, tell him to run a marathon, and expect him to win. He has many of the other adaptations that come with endurance training, but his specific pathway for running has not been developed to the same degree that his pathway for biking has. He will still perform better than the average runner, but he won't perform at the elite level. There are other reasons, too, mostly having to do with body structure and with different muscles developing, but the neurological pathway is one of the major reasons the switch in sports will not be perfectly effective.

Practicing means that less of a neurological impulse is required to get the same response out of your body, making the activity seem easier. Since less of a signal produces a greater response, when you want to increase performance a greater signal will cause an even bigger response. The bottom line is that your body learns, and it does so by improving the efficiency of your neurological system. The initial improvement associated with your first few days and weeks in any sport, lifting activity, or obstacle comes solely from neurological adaptation and not changes in your muscles.

The second improvement is at the cellular level. Mitochondria are the powerhouses of cells; they help the body process energy. The more you run, the more your body understands that it needs more mitochondria. The stress caused by running creates a response in your body, and it identifies the need for more mitochondria. Add in proper rest and nutrition, and the body will produce more. Your mitochondria will increase in numbers and density, allowing your body to better utilize energy. This, in turn, makes you faster and improves endurance.

A third improvement comes from your body's ability to transport,

2015 Female 30–34 Age Group World Champion, Conquer The Gauntlet Pro Team member and Strength & Speed athlete Ashley Jeanne Samples races through the Platinum Rig.

carry, and extract oxygen from red blood cells. Red blood cells carry oxygen for use throughout your body. None of us can use all the oxygen we take in when we breathe. (This is why rescue breathing works. If your body consumed all the oxygen it took in, then blowing CO_2 into the lungs of someone who'd stopped breathing would not help.) The ability to extract oxygen can improve through training. The more you practice running and stressing your cardiovascular system, the better your body will become at extracting oxygen from the hemoglobin that's carrying it through your body. By being able to extract more oxygen from hemoglobin, it will be able to process higher quantities within the body. Overall, this results in greater aerobic capacity.

A fourth improvement is your body's ability to deal with waste products in the blood. The more you exercise, the better your body becomes at clearing lactate from the blood. This removal of lactate allows you to perform at a higher level of activity for longer. Without going into a complicated biology lesson, it is important to understand that lactate starts to build up faster than it's cleared when you're operating above your aerobic zone. Lactate itself is not bad for your body, but its rise is linked to other factors that require slowing your pace. Being able to clear lactate faster means you can extend your aerobic zone.

Finally, your heart physically gets stronger. The sports clichés about having a strong heart are surprisingly accurate, but this comes from months of training built upon years of training and not from one day of hard effort. These sports clichés often use the heart as a metaphor for how much effort you are putting into a certain activity, but realistically if you have a bigger heart, it will help you perform better. Although its function is controlled involuntarily, the heart is still a muscle. Muscles can grow larger and stronger through exercise. The heart muscle increases the size of its left ventricle via periods of exercise and rest. The walls get thicker, making for a stronger heart that can push more blood harder through the body. The left ventricle's volume gets bigger, too, allowing more blood to fill up the space before it's pushed to the rest of the body. The greater circulation of blood improves health in a variety of ways, resulting in an overall cardiovascular gain. Therefore, when you hear coaches or speakers say you need more heart, they're not just referring to your motivation level.

The same principles can be applied to the obstacle portions of the race. The first time you try an obstacle that requires significant strength such as climbing a wall above your height or traversing a long set of monkey bars, it feels difficult. When you repeat these movements in practice or at races, though, your body creates the neurological pathway to perform those specific motions. The first change your body experiences when learning these new muscle movements is neurological adaption.

Cody Peyton and Nathan "Napalm" Palmer of Strength & Speed–Mid-America cross Skull Valley.

This also explains the rapid strength gain seen in new weight lifters. Many feel highly motivated when they first start lifting because every time they go to the gym they hit a new personal record (PR). However, after a couple of weeks they appear to plateau. This is their neurological system making initial rapid changes; the rest of the body's systems then require time to develop. This does not mean that the neurological system stops improving, however; it will continue to make improvements by learning to send stronger impulses, learning to contract the muscles harder, and learning to use fewer muscle fibers to produce the same amount of force. Just as when you're completing a new obstacle, the more times you practice a motion the easier it will become thanks to this neurological path. (Note: As an OCR athlete, this quick neurological adaptation can be used to your advantage. If you already have the required strength from the off season and/or your strength training sessions, it means you can learn a new obstacle relatively quickly.)

The Fugitive Run in Rolla, Missouri, begins.

Periodization and Prioritization

Periodization and prioritization are keys to success if you want to be able to race at an elite level. Many obstacle racers try to stay at a certain high level of physical fitness year-round instead of focusing on one specific season, changing their goals and peaking. This lack of focus is a common mistake among obstacle racers. Instead of dividing the year up with specific goals in mind, they are of the mind-set that *If I just keep running 4 miles a day, every day, I will improve.* The body responds better, however, if you give it a specific goal to work toward. For example, when I am going to run a longer obstacle race such as a Spartan Beast (13-plus miles), then I use that as base training to run a fast Warrior Dash (5K length) two months later. By building a strong aerobic base first, then using my training to peak for speed, I get better results.

Prioritization refers to focusing on your weaknesses first. This will ensure that you improve where you need it most. If you ran in high school and/or college, then your weakness is probably upper-body strength. If you didn't run in school, your weakness most likely lies in your cardio-vascular ability. Therefore, you should schedule your important runs when freshest such as after a rest day or as the first workout of the day if you are doing two workouts each day. People who don't prioritize often end up focusing on their strengths because that's what they feel comfortable doing. This means their weaknesses continue to get worse and hold them back.

If you plan on working out twice a day, scheduling can become an issue. I use a morning/lunch split or a lunch/evening split. For the morning/lunch split, I will exercise first thing in the morning and then again at lunch. Typically, I use this split the majority of the year, but definitely if I am doing high-mileage training. It allows me to finish my run right away and not have to worry about scheduling other things around it. This is especially useful because the run training is what takes the longest. Then instead of going out to lunch, I go to the gym for my second work-out. My second workout emphasizes strength training and possibly ad-ditional cardio for obstacle racing. I am able to do this because I pack my own lunch daily. After going to the gym at lunch, I eat at my desk. I often take a pre-workout caffeine-based drink prior to going to the gym, which also increases my focus for the last thirty minutes before lunch.

The same method works for a lunch/evening split. I use lunchtime for my first training session of the day, then do cardio later in the day after dinner. This is especially good if your weakness is upper-body strength. Typically, lunch isn't long enough to get in a good cardio work-out on most days. I typically don't like to do strength training first thing in the morning because I feel like my body isn't fully awake yet. When I take caffeine in the morning, it takes me from sleepy to normal, but when I have it at lunchtime it takes me from normal to excessive energy. This is why I prefer lunchtime for strength training. I have gotten around this morning sleepiness in the past by getting up over an hour prior to heading to the gym. This allows my body to wake up and heat up naturally. Then I take my pre-workout drink to kick things into high gear.

However, I caution against working out too close to bedtime, because it can disturb your sleep. If you are taking a pre-workout drink before lifting at night, chances are you will be up another five hours past the time you took the drink. If you're doing high-intensity cardio near bedtime, don't plan on going to bed within two hours of the end of your workout. Your body will still be producing a lot of heat from the exercise, making it difficult to fall asleep.

Something I hear a lot is, "I don't have time to work out each day." As an elite obstacle racer, this should not be you, but there are times when the other parts of your life cause conflicts in your schedule. It's all about making time for what's important to you. How do I have time to work out twice a day? I cut out things I deem less important, such as watching TV, or I incorporate them into my workouts (treadmill in front of the TV). Some people enjoy the social atmosphere of going to lunch with their co-workers every day. If you want to work out once or twice a day, something has to give. Without looking at your specific schedule, I cannot tell you what to cut out, but list what you do each day by priority and figure out where there is free space. Chances are you are not using every minute of every day to its maximum effectiveness.

If working out twice a day is good, is working out three times a day better? I have tried this logic before and generally do not recommend it. Just as with two workouts a day, the second—or in this case third—workout of the day will get shortchanged. I found that if I try three workouts a day, during the third one I have so little energy that it's usually a waste of time. Furthermore, this violates my principle of rest and recovery. Your muscles do not improve unless you provide stress followed by adequate time to recover. If for some reason you end up doing a three-a-day workout, definitely take the following day off to ensure adequate recovery. The bottom line is you should be able to squeeze all your training into two workouts effectively.

Troy Bruns of Mid-America Obstacle Course Racers (MAOCR) crosses the final obstacle during a Conquer the Gauntlet event.

Peaking

Another key to success is peaking your fitness level. *Peaking* refers to using large periods of time to build up a fitness level and then only trying to perform at your best for a short period of time. Not using peaking is a mistake often made by recreational obstacle racers, who sign up for a variety of races throughout the year without a focus or specific goal in mind. When stressed over time, the body responds best to increasing amounts of stress for several weeks or months. Then as the competition date approaches, the amount of stress is reduced, allowing the body to recover and overcompensate.

Many serious endurance athletes are familiar with this concept, but if you are just getting into obstacle racing, or have just changed from recreational racer to competitive athlete, it may be new. Following a full training plan is hard work, and if you don't decrease the stress on your body as the competition grows closer, you won't be properly recovered for race time and will not perform at your best.

This presents conflicting internal feelings. As those final two or three weeks of training before a race wind down, your mind is telling you to do more work. In reality, however, you should do *less* work to allow for a proper recovery and maximize your performance on race day. Furthermore, because you are recovering more, your body feels like it can go harder and train more. The feeling of wanting to do more is hard to shake. Even after seeing the positive effects of peaking, I still get worried those last three weeks and wonder if I should be doing more. However, I know that this is a calculated plan thought out months in advance, so I try not to let my feelings get the best of me. If you have never tried peaking for a race, then you need to start.

Part of peaking is your focus. While it's okay—even encouraged—to race multiple times through the year, you should have one to three main races as your priority. I often run in many races throughout the year, but I do not do a full multi-week taper for all of them; my overall goal comes later in the year. Typically, I try to align my intermediary races with the end of a recovery week or a week with lower volume than my typical training week.

I often use the other races as hard workouts rather than true races. By that I mean I take only a single rest day before the race and do not conduct a multi-week peak or taper leading up to it. I still care about my performances at these other races and try my best, but the main goal is to support training for a different race. These smaller races can also keep you motivated during a long four-month training period. They allow you to enjoy your fitness level a little more and can be used as a check on your current fitness. Understand, though, that without a proper taper and peaking period, you won't perform at the same level as you would for your main race of the season.

The specifics regarding how to lay out your training plan and what activity you should be performing come later, in chapter 6. Within that chapter, you will find several training plans for races of various distances and ability levels. You will also find ways to improve your performance by making small changes to your fitness regime.

What does the peaking concept look like in practice? Let's say you want to compete in one or more of the world championship events for obstacle racing, which typically take place in October and November. Last year you were able to complete the majority of obstacles in your races, but your lack of upper-body strength led to one or two failures and a couple of close calls. Since performing at the world championships is your goal for the year, you should plan backward from those dates. However, to get to the world championships, you have to qualify.

First, you will need to improve your strength by following a strength-focused training plan for a few weeks. Starting in mid-November of the previous year, begin one of the strength training programs for one to three months while doing a lower volume of cardiovascular training. This ensures that you will have the upper-body and leg strength to complete all the required tasks/obstacles. The lower-volume cardiovascular training is designed to build your aerobic base. All cardio activity should therefore be done at an easy intensity. This will allow speed work to be more effective once you add it later in the year. The lower-volume cardio allows for maximum strength gain but keeps the neurological reinforcement required for running. Moreover, it provides a mental reset to allow future hard training.

Starting in mid-November and continuing for one to three months, you would be strength-focused and probably doing a reduced 5K-style training plan, performing one to three easy runs a week from one of the 5K plans. Depending on how much strength you need to gain, a bulking/strength gain diet might also be beneficial to ensure your body is properly fueled.

Once that is complete, switch your priority to running by following a speed-focused training plan appropriate to your race distance or longer. A longer distance will provide you enhanced aerobic capability that will lead to a faster short-distance race time. I am an advocate of high-volume training since all my personal records in short distances occurred when I was training for higher-mileage races. This phase will last from the end of your strength phase until the start of your first *important* race. Switch to a maintenance diet to ensure you have adequate energy to train but are not consuming so much food that you are gaining weight. You can follow a cutting diet for a month if you want to drop weight, but don't follow it for the entire cycle. You can sprinkle some road, trail, or OCR events into this phase to keep motivation high. Any races done prior to your first important race of the year should be used as training events or hard workouts with minimal or no taper. This means using your low-volume week as the week leading up to race week and taking one or two days off before the race but not modifying your training plan completely. The problem when people race every weekend is that they fall into a cycle of taper for race, race, and recover from race. This means that they never put in a strong training block to reach their full potential.

Now that you have followed one of the speed training plans (listed in chapter 6) entirely and peaked for your first important race of the year, you can continue to race throughout the rest of the year.

The rest of your year should continue to involve building and tapering for races. So build volume and intensity for two to three weeks, conduct a one-week taper, and race again. You can use one of the other training plans and follow it for three weeks before jumping to the last

Conquer the Gauntlet Pro Team member Cody Peyton climbing over an 8-foot wall at Conquer the Gauntlet.

week of the plan for your taper. After the race, go back to where you left off on the training plan and continue along. When you are two to four months out from your ultimate goal for the year (probably a world championship event), try to limit the races you run; you want to put in a solid block of training in order to peak for your ultimate goal for the year. If you are not racing frequently, then you can just follow each plan until completion and race every two to four months throughout the year.

Trying to maintain your highest level of fitness all year long is mentally and physically exhausting. Focusing your efforts into small portions of the year will yield better results. Use periodization to plan your year, use prioritization along with specificity to determine where to put your strongest effort, and use peaking to race fast at your most important races.

OCR World Champion from 2015 Lindsay Webster clearing a tire obstacle.

Chapter 2

DIET AND SUPPLEMENTS

Conquer The Gauntlet Pro Team member Nathan "Napalm" Palmer completing Savage Race's Pipe Dreams obstacle.

Often the most overlooked aspect of training is diet. When I use the word *diet*, I am referring to the way you eat year-round—specifically, the proper eating habits that are, in effect, a lifestyle. Too often people use the term *diet* to refer to what they plan on following for the next couple of weeks before returning to their normal, terrible eating habits. There is a saying: "Working out is easy; controlling what goes on your plate the other twenty-three hours of the day is the hard part." Since diet is often neglected, I chose to put it toward the front of this book. Once many people get to the training plans in books, they disregard the rest and begin exercising. This is fine if you already have a thorough understanding of nutrition and the importance of rest, but too often that's not the case.

People assume that because they are training for a race along with doing high levels of cardio, they can eat whatever they want and still perform at their best. It's just not true. Seconds can become the difference between a new PR and missing your goal. Seconds can also be the difference between first and third place. It is important to take advantage of every tiny benefit that you can. This concept of many tiny changes leading to a big transformation is applicable to both time and weight. During adventure races, my friends and I have a saying: "Ounces make pounds." If you shave off a couple of ounces from every piece of gear you carry, it will add up to several pounds. Overall, the less weight you are carrying, the faster you will be able to move.

This is a popular concept among cyclists, who are very concerned about the weight of everything from their body, to the frame of their bike, to the rotating weight of the pedals. I have a cyclist friend who was training for an adventure race. He would go through the effort of cutting off excess fabric, removing rivets from equipment, and shaving things down to reduce weight in the hope that removing those ounces would have a measurable effect over hours of racing. While it seems excessive, the concept is right on point. If you shave off enough ounces of weight, it will lead to an overall reduction in pounds, which equates to less time. Why *wouldn't* you apply the same logic to your body?

If you have two people with the same fitness level and same amount of muscle that are exact clones except one is 150 pounds with 15 pounds of non-essential fat, and the other is 145 pounds with 10 pounds of non-essential fat, who will be faster? The one carrying less weight is the clear answer. Why not trim your body down to maximize performance?

The unstoppable Ryan Atkins showing that a lean athlete is a fast athlete on his way to another victory.

If you are training hard, will that be enough to slim down? While hard training does result in fat loss, a large portion of your body fat comes from diet. I have participated in both endurance training and bodybuilding-type training over my athletic career. The main difference when I switch from endurance sports to bodybuilding mode is a change in diet. Most of the fat loss is a direct result of a strict diet and not exercise. I actually exercise less while cutting weight for bodybuilding than I do when training for endurance training. Yet my weight loss for bodybuilding is significantly greater because of my diet.

The same logic is applicable to people training to gain upper-body strength for races. Many of them think that if you just take in as many calories as you can handle, you'll gain muscle. The problem is that if the calories you are taking in are not useful, then your body won't be able to use them effectively. Furthermore, if you're filling your body with garbage calories, you won't be able to eat healthy protein and healthy carbohydrates in a timely manner. This in turn will slow down protein synthesis and reduce your ability to perform at your peak level.

As with all diets and supplement plans, consult with a doctor to be sure that you don't have any unusual requirements or health conditions. Any changes in diet or supplements that you make are at your own risk.

Macronutrients

Let's start with the basics of nutrition. There are three main types of macronutrients: protein, carbohydrates (carbs), and fat. Both carbs and protein are 4 kcal per gram; fat is 9 kcal per gram. (The term we know as *calories* is actually *kcal*.) Total caloric intake is often the focus of people changing their diet. This is a common mistake, because not all calories or kcals are equal. Kcals are calculated by burning food and nutrients and seeing how much energy they provide by measuring the resulting change in water temperature. This process isn't exactly the same chemical process your body uses, but it's a good approximation. However, a better way of monitoring food intake would be to watch your macronutrient intake.

All three macronutrients are essential to a healthy diet and essential to a diet focused on performance. If your diet is lacking one of these three macronutrients, your body isn't getting the nutrition it requires to function properly. Here is some basic information regarding each of the three macronutrients.

Protein: Muscle is primarily made of protein. The building blocks of protein are amino acids, which you will typically see written as *L-something*—for instance, L-glutamine or L-tryptophan. There are also essential amino acids, meaning that your body cannot disassemble other proteins to make them; they must be ingested via diet. The essential amino acids that have positive anabolic effects for building muscle (according to re-search) are leucine, isoleucine, and valine (also sometimes written with an *L-* in front of them). These come from whole foods such as any type of meat (chicken, beef, turkey, fish) as well as some vegetarian products like soy and beans with rice. Protein is the building block of muscle. You want more muscle? Eat more protein. Protein can be used for energy production but only when carbohydrates are very low.

Carbohydrates are the main source of energy for the body. When ingesting carbohydrates your body will typically first store them as glycogen in various places, including the muscles and the liver. Glycogen is simply stored carbohydrates in the body. When your glycogen gets very low, your muscles appear smaller (because they do not have as much carbohydrate or water inside) and you are typically lethargic. Carbohydrates are used or stored as fuel; excess carbohydrates are stored as fat in the body. People switching to a low-carbohydrate diet often see an immediate weight loss of a couple of pounds in a couple of days. Do not be fooled into thinking this is fat disappearing; it's just glycogen and water leaving your muscles. Carbohydrates can be classified by how fast your body can break them down and absorb them. This leads them to be classified as fast-burning carbohydrates (high on the glycemic index or having a large glycemic load) or slow-burning carbohydrates (low glycemic index or having a low glycemic load). To be specific, glycemic index is a measure of how much your blood sugar or insulin increases when you ingest the specified carbohydrate. Glycemic load is a combination of the type of carbohydrate and the quantity you ingest. Therefore, ingesting a small piece of candy may have less of an effect on your blood sugar than eating a plateful of a slow-burning carbohydrate like brown rice. In that example, the candy has a high glycemic index but a low glycemic load, while the plate of brown rice has a higher glycemic load but a lower glycemic index. As a rule, to minimize fat gain we want to stick with low-glycemic carbohydrates—with the exception of post-workout. After a workout you want high-glycemic carbohydrates to refill glycogen stores and build muscle by spiking your insulin levels.

Strength & Speed athlete and ultra-runner Jordan Smith emerges from a pipe obstacle.

Fats can be broken into many categories, but the two big ones I will cover are saturated and unsaturated. Generally, saturated fats are bad and unsaturated fats are good. Saturated fats are found in processed foods or fatty cuts of meat. Unsaturated fats are in foods such as almonds, guacamole, and olive oil. If a label tells you the food inside has 10g of fat, that may still be a healthy food as long as the saturated fat content is low. Your body needs some saturated fat to help produce testosterone, but that amount is low and most people get more than enough saturated fats through their daily diet. Unsaturated fats are often referred to as healthy fats. These fats improve heart health and help your body perform optimally by allowing the absorption of fat-soluble vitamins.

Typically, most people have a diet based heavily around carbohydrates. I often see friends or clients who go half the day without any protein. How is your body supposed to maintain its muscle if you are not feeding it? If you are into lifting weights, you are probably familiar with the importance of protein and base your diet around it. However, many endurance or obstacle racing athletes neglect protein because they don't want a lot of muscle. Protein is still important for endurance athletes, however, because it repairs muscle, allowing for another hard workout the following day. Besides building muscle, protein has other benefits: It adds satiety to meals, meaning you will feel less hungry, and it typically requires more energy to break down protein than it does carbohydrates. This is useful if you are trying to slim down. Think of this as your stomach exercising and using energy to break down protein.

If you are trying to create the leanest racing physique possible, you want to burn off fat but maintain your muscle. Through diet and exercise, fat will melt away, creating an ultra-lean racing machine. This must be carefully balanced with race preparation. You should never be actively trying to cut weight during final preparations for a race. When people try to lose weight and prep for a race, most of them end up restricting their food intake too much, resulting in not having the proper nutrition to recover or train to the best of their ability.

BattleFrog Pro Team member Lindsay Webster carrying a Wreck Bag across a balance beam.

If you are planning to cut weight, do so before you begin your race preparation by reducing your intake of carbs and increasing your intake of protein. There is a balance to maintain, though, because if you reduce your carbohydrates too much, your energy levels will drop, making it harder to work out. This, in turn, will result in burning fewer calories.

Eating Clean

Eating clean is a common phrase in the bodybuilding community but it has crossover applications to elite obstacle racing. It generally refers to eating a low-saturated-fat diet but still maintaining healthy fats and generally consuming slow-burning carbohydrates. I recommend trying to eat clean year-round and only adjusting the number and type of carbohydrates during phases of training. This creates the leanest athlete possible, both strong and fast. You can go through cycles in which you purposely bulk or purposely cut weight, but this is for non-race-preparation only. Any weight loss that occurs during race season should be a result of high levels of exercise and not diet manipulation.

Racing and Training Phase

What follows is a suggested diet for elite obstacle racers during racing and training phases. To best improve your fitness and maintain energy levels, I recommend eating five to six meals a day. Eating often provides a constant flow of nutrients, allowing your body to maximize fitness improvement. It also prevents any extreme hunger, which often results in overeating of unhealthy food. A further benefit is that if you are participating in ultra-distance obstacle races like Spartan Ultra Beast, World's Toughest Mudder, or Shale Hell, it gets your body used to eating lots of smaller meals rather than the typical three gigantic ones. Eating small amounts frequently is a requirement for ultra-distance success.

The first step is getting your body used to eating five or six meals each day. The multiple meals will result in better protein synthesis, so you'll build more muscle or strength. Furthermore, eating more meals a day will allow you to consume more protein spread out more evenly throughout the day. It creates a constant flow of both protein for building muscle and carbohydrates for steady energy. Start with smaller portions than you normally eat until your body adjusts to eating every three hours throughout the day. Generally eat healthy, because the healthy food will allow you to take in more quality foods more often. Each meal needs to have carbs, protein, and healthy fats to optimize your performance.

These are the optimal types of food for fitness improvement.

Acceptable carbs: Brown rice, quinoa, sweet potatoes, Ezekiel bread (sprouted grain bread), oatmeal, and fibrous vegetables or greens (any green vegetable such as broccoli, spinach, kale). However, smothering a salad in high-fat or high-sugar dressing is not okay. I recommend salad with maybe some olive oil or guacamole (both healthy fats) on top but no dressing, since most salad dressings have a lot of fat or sugar.

Post-workout acceptable carbs: Nonfat chocolate milk, nonfat Greek yogurt, all fruits, honey, and other sugary substances as long as they are low in fat.

Acceptable fats: Avocado, guacamole, almonds, olive oil, nuts, natural nut butter (almond butter is lower in saturated fat but more expensive than peanut butter), unsweetened almond milk, and flax milk.

Acceptable protein: Egg whites, chicken, white fish, lean cuts of red meat or salmon. I recommend two times a week at most for lean red meat and another two times a week at most for salmon, each served at the end of the day only. I generally stick to between zero and one lean steak a week, and one to two salmon pieces.

Sample Meal Plan

6 AM meal 1: Egg whites, 1 yolk, oatmeal or Ezekiel bread with nut butter. Always eat as soon as possible upon waking. Your body is starving for protein and carbs from the long night without eating (an hour before cardio workout).

9 AM meal 2: Chicken, Ezekiel bread, and guacamole.

Noon meal 3: Chicken, sweet potato, broccoli (pre-workout).

Snack: Apple on the way to the gym/road (workout).

3 PM meal 4: Chicken, sweet potato or white potato (okay because post-workout).

6 PM meal 5: Salmon or white fish, sweet potato, greens (broccoli, spinach, salad, et cetera).

9 PM meal 6: Casein protein shake (slow-digesting protein shake) made with unsweetened almond or flax milk and a handful of almonds.

Your last or second-to-last meal of the day can be fattier fish like salmon, the occasional steak (leanest cuts possible), or another clean protein. Fast-digesting carbs or white carbs are okay post-workout only. The fast-digesting carbs will cause a spike in insulin, which helps spur muscle growth and refills glycogen stores. Remember, you want all three food categories in every meal (fat, carb, protein) with the exception of the last meal of the day. Generally, I stay away from carbohydrates in that last meal since carbs eaten late in the day are more likely to be stored as fat (people do not move around much at night). If you have a long hard run the next day, you may want to eat carbs with your last meal to ensure that your glycogen levels are high.

How much of each macronutrient should you eat? The general rule is you want 20 to 30g of protein, and a minimum of 10g of healthy fat; then add as many of the acceptable carbs as you need in every meal. As long as you continue to eat five to six meals throughout the day, you are doing well. If you cannot eat five to six meals, reduce the quantity of food at each meal until you can eat them all. Depending on your body weight, gender, and age, you can add more protein, carbs, and fat. Each person is different, which is why I avoid giving specific numbers for quantities.

Demetrios "Sty" Karellas climbing over the Destroyer.

Other General Guidelines

• Fast-digesting carbs (white carbs or sugar) are okay post-workout. If you want candy or other sugary foods, post-workout is the time to eat them.

• Cheat meals are okay once a week. Cheat meals are anything other than the healthy options listed above. Furthermore, a cheat meal is also something reasonable such as eating a burger and fries from your favorite place. A cheat meal is not a pig-out fest where you eat a whole pizza and then half a carton of ice cream. A good recommendation to maintain body weight is to have your cheat meal count as two meals due to its high caloric and macronutrient content.

• If you have a shake post-workout, drink it as soon as possible and then eat a full meal within the hour. This ensures that the shake fuels the muscles quickly; the full meal provides all the necessary nutrients post-workout. This takes some getting used to, because if you wait too long after the protein shake to eat, you will feel full and not optimize your gains from training or be ready to train again the next day.

• For liquids, sticking with water the majority of the time is your best bet. To optimize performance, you should stay hydrated at all times. If you need a better explanation, imagine reducing the amount of liquid in your blood but keeping all the red blood cells and white blood cells. This will make your blood more viscous and harder to pump, meaning your body will work harder to maintain the same level of effort. Stay away from liquids other than water; they just provide empty calories and are often high on the glycemic index. If you need your soda, drink it immediately post-workout and go with the regular version, not the diet. If I plan to drink milk, I drink it post-workout or first thing in the morning. I try to drink coffee black; if I want sugar or flavor in it, I try to have it post-workout, or at least to put in the least sugar or creamer possible so I get the flavor without too many additional high-glycemic carbs.

• Supplements are covered at the end of this chapter.

For some people, this diet may be too regimented and too extreme. The bottom line is that the best diet is the one you can easily follow and is still healthy. Use the diet above as a starting point and adjust it until you find something that works for you. Another option is to follow the 90/10 rule, which states that 90 percent of what you eat should be natural, unprocessed foods; the other 10 percent can be other foods that are less healthy. Realistically, most of the time my diet looks very similar to what I described above but with one or two exceptions during the day—maybe a café latte with nonfat milk, or the occasional serving of ice cream post-workout.

Again, take notice that everything on this diet is whole food; there isn't a lot of processed stuff in there. If this diet is too complicated

Devin Roberts and the rest of Strength & Speed–Mid-America at the OCR World Championships.

for you, another suggestion is to just avoid processed foods and eat carbs, protein, and healthy fat at every meal. This simple solution will result in a lean athlete.

You may find your weight dropping as you follow this food plan, and that's fine. If you feel your performance is suffering, you can add in more carbohydrates or more meals to ensure your body has adequate nutrients. Still, you're unlikely to reach such a depleted state without actually trying to.

Bulking / Strength Gaining: Optional for the Off-Season

When I'm hoping to bulk or gain large amounts of strength, I follow the same diet but increase carbohydrates while reducing cardio. I also usually change my rep scheme for the gym to try to maximize strength gain. Bulking is not mandatory for the elite obstacle racer, but if you're looking for a big improvement in strength, then I do recommend a bulking diet. There are also athletes who enjoy lifting weights and don't want to be obstacle-racing-focused year-round. If this sounds like you, bulking may be a good option.

I often hear people complain about not being able to put on muscle weight when they are only eating three meals a day. As with your racing diet, eating healthy food will allow you to take in more quality foods more often. If you have a burger or something fatty, you will not be hungry again for another four to six hours. If you can still get the required amounts of protein, carbs, and healthy fats along with eating a cheat food, then you can leave the cheat meal in your diet plan for the bulk / strength gaining phase. I personally find that eating cheat foods makes it significantly harder to eat my next planned meal, throwing my diet off for the day. Just to reiterate: Each meal needs to have carbs, protein, and healthy fats to optimize your performance.

Here are the optimal foods for gaining mass. Note that they are essentially the same foods we've already discussed, but in higher quantities.

Acceptable carbs: White/brown rice, sweet/regular potatoes, quinoa, beans, Ezekiel bread, oatmeal, greens (broccoli, spinach, asparagus, lettuce). You can generally eat a lot of greens without issues. Fruits are good, too, but try to limit their consumption to mornings or to pre-/post-workout. They're high in sugar, but your body absorbs them more slowly than you might think because of the amount of fiber they contain. Other carbs are acceptable for bulking, too, but you generally want to stay away from processed foods. Your body will respond better to foods that are not processed. Foods like potato chips, doughnuts, candy bars, and protein bars do not get digested as efficiently as natural foods and—as I've said previously—will often fill you up with empty calories.

Healthy fats: Avocado, guacamole, almonds, natural peanut butter, almond butter, olive oil, unsweetened almond milk, flax milk.

Protein: Whole eggs, egg whites, chicken, white fish, salmon, lean steak.

Sample Meal Plan

The quantities of each food here will vary based on your body composition, weight, and goal.

6 AM meal 1: Egg whites, 1 yolk, oatmeal or Ezekiel bread. Always eat as soon as possible upon waking. Your body is starving for protein and carbs from the long night. Eating as soon as possible will kick-start your body, letting it know that it can continue burning calories and building muscle.

9 AM meal 2: Chicken, Ezekiel bread, and guacamole.

Noon meal 3: Chicken, sweet potato, broccoli (pre-workout).

Snack: Apple on the way to the gym/road (workout).

3 PM meal 4: Chicken, sweet potato, or white potato. You definitely want a fast-acting carbohydrate post-workout—anything sugary or anything that digests like sugar, such as white bread, white potatoes, or fruits.

6 PM meal 5: Salmon or steak, potato or rice, broccoli or spinach or salad. Your last or second-to-last meal of the day for bulking should be something with fat in it, such as salmon or a lean steak. This will help slow digestion throughout the long night.

9 PM meal 6: Casein protein shake (slow-digesting protein shake) or cottage cheese (which is high in casein) and a handful of almonds (fat helps slow digestion further). You can also add in some flaxseed for even more healthy fats to slow digestion.

Similar rules apply: Fast-digesting carbs are good post-workout. Cheat meals are okay once a week or at the end of each day if you don't mind putting on a little more fat. Drink primarily water; if you want fruit juice, soda, or other high-glycemic beverages, drink them post-workout only. If you are using protein shakes, be sure to eat a whole-food meal within an hour post-workout.

Cutting: Optional for the Off-Season

The cutting phase is very similar to clean bulking but with fewer carbs—and only those that are slow digesting—as well as no cheat meals. Don't do this while you're preparing for a race; it is okay during the off-season if you feel your weight is too high. I like bulking and cutting in the off-season, because I think it results in better strength gain. When I bulk, I feel like it's easier to gain strength. Furthermore, when I cut, I tend to retain almost all the strength from bulking, but at a significantly lighter body weight. If you plan on bulking and cutting, allow equal time for each. So if you spend four weeks bulking, plan on spending four weeks cutting to get back to your normal weight before starting your obstacle race training. If your normal weight is a higher body fat percentage than you want, allow more than four weeks for cutting. For cutting, the weight loss is a result of diet and not an increase in quantity of exercise. Typically, during cutting I continue to lift heavy and do a minimal amount of cardiovascular training. The cardiovascular training is high-intensity workouts similar to the VO_2max workouts listed later in the book.

Cutting may also be useful if you feel your weight is too high. In this case, skip the bulking diet during your off-season and go right to a cutting diet. The weight loss will help make you faster because you'll be carrying less body weight during your races. However, to reiterate, this is not mandatory but specific for those looking for a change in body weight, composition, or strength.

Your saturated fats for the day should be low. The saturated fat should only be from whole foods (meat, nuts, etc) and be around 10-20g (this can vary depending on body weight, age, and gender). When you start cutting, you can drop carbs to about 1g per pound of body weight. This type of eating is generally not sustainable year-round because your body is eating itself for fuel by breaking down fat.

Acceptable foods are listed below and are remarkably similar to the other diets listed in this book.

Acceptable carbs: Brown rice, quinoa, sweet potatoes, Ezekiel bread (sprouted grain bread), oatmeal, greens, fibrous vegetables.

Acceptable fats: Avocado, guacamole, almonds, olive oil, natural nut butter, unsweetened almond milk, flax milk.

Acceptable protein: Egg whites, chicken, white fish, lean cuts of red meat or salmon (once or twice a week).

What about seasonings or sauces? I have a few guidelines. Seasonings generally have no caloric value, and almost all of them are okay. For cutting, eating spicy seasonings that contain capsaicin is recommended because it's known to increase metabolism. Hot sauces are fine as long as they do not have sugar in them. In fact, stay away from any sauces that contain sugar—which most do.

Sample Meal Plan

6 AM meal 1: Egg whites, oatmeal, or Ezekiel bread with natural nut butter. Always eat as soon as possible upon waking. Your body is starving for protein and carbs from the long night (pre-cardio-workout; if you are doing evening cardio, your 6 PM meal would be pre-cardio).

9 AM meal 2: Chicken, Ezekiel bread, and guacamole.

Noon meal 3: Chicken, sweet potato, broccoli (pre-workout).

Strength workout.

3 PM meal 4: Chicken, sweet potato.

6 PM meal 5: Salmon or white fish, greens (broccoli, spinach, salad).

9 PM meal 6: Casein protein shake (slow-digesting protein shake) and a handful of almonds.

Your last or second-to-last meal of the day can be fattier fish like salmon or the occasional steak (leanest cuts possible), or you can go with another clean protein. Fast-digesting carbs (white carbs) are okay post-workout only. For best results, stick with all low-glycemic carbs (the acceptable carbs I listed above). In general, try to push the majority of your carbs to the first half of the day. If you work out in the evening, then obviously this is not possible, but regardless the majority of your carbs should be centered on your workout. The pre-workout carbs provide fuel for the workout; the post-workout carbs assist in muscle building and replenish muscle glycogen.

The important thing to remember when cutting is not to starve yourself. Eat regularly throughout the day. This will prevent you from feeling like you are starving. It is easy not to overeat if you are constantly eating, because you don't get those terrible hunger pains. The only time I crave cheat meals is if I've missed a meal and I feel like I'm starving. This is when people usually cheat concerning the type or amount of food.

Sometimes people who are cutting try to reduce their calories super low. What is *super low*? I consider anything below 1,200 calories super low regardless of your weight, age, or gender. This is a bad idea for several reasons. The first is that if your calories get too low, you will start burning muscle and fat. Even those who are working out solely to look better don't want to burn muscle: When you lose fat, muscle is what makes you look like you're in shape and not actually malnourished.

The second reason is your body will eventually go into starvation mode. This means that while you may see drastic weight loss at the beginning, as time progresses you'll find it significantly harder to lose weight because you can't cut any more calories without causing health problems. Your body will think you're starving (because you are), and will begin to hold on to fat instead of burning it.

The final reason is the rebound effect after the dieting period ends. If your body gets used to operating on 900 calories a day, the second you start eating like a normal human at 2,000 calories or more a day, what do you think is going to happen? All that weight you lost will immediately be regained, and then some. Now that you are getting enough food, to prevent future starvation situations your body will hold on to more fat than it previously did.

Strength & Speed athlete Jordan Smith, the man who ran across the state of Michigan, racing during the OCR World Championships.

Cleanse diets also fall into the super-low-calorie category. Drinking only lemon juice and cayenne pepper—or whatever else is required for your ridiculous fad diet—isn't effective. You may see a significant initial weight loss, but that is from glycogen along with water leaving your muscles and your large intestine emptying. Do not be fooled; this weight loss has nothing to do with a change in body fat percentage. If you continue a cleanse diet you will be subject to all the problems discussed above: Your body will go into starvation mode; you'll suffer a rebound effect after you stop dieting; and your body will burn everything, including fat and muscle, something you do not want as a competitive athlete.

This same logic can be applied to other fad diets that sweep through public media every year. Diets that involve eating only one "magical" item will not work. Diets that involve simply adding something—*eat this grapefruit* or *take this pill*—to your usual meal plan are not effective. If the pill is blocking fat absorption, it will stop your body from absorbing healthy fats and fat-soluble vitamins along with the unhealthy fats.

Weak Excuses for Not Eating Healthy

Making a change in diet isn't easy, as most of America knows. Real change requires months and years of incremental adjustments. If you do not want to eat healthy, that's your choice; just don't complain about your appearance or lagging race performance. As a personal trainer who helps people prepare for races and competitions, I hear a lot of complaints. Here are some of the most frequent.

"Eating healthy is too expensive": This excuse is not only weak but also untrue. The problem is that eating healthy requires preparation if it's going to be cheaper. If you do prepare properly, though, it will be much cheaper. Even if you only pay $8 for an average lunch, compare that with buying a week's worth of chicken breasts ($10) and brown rice ($10 to $20 depending on the size of the bag) from a supermarket. Buying food from the grocery store is significantly cheaper than spending money every day on lunch. Eating healthy only becomes more expensive when you are eating at restaurants or do not prepare your meals ahead of time. For example, a burger is going to be much cheaper than a fillet of salmon. I personally prepare my food the majority of the time; that way when I do eat out, I don't feel bad about spending a little extra money to get the healthy option.

"I don't have time to prepare healthy food": Once I've shown folks that eating healthy is cheaper with prior preparation, this is the fallback excuse I usually hear. Eating healthy does not take more time than not eating healthy, but again the key is preparation. I will break it down by meal.

Breakfast: I cook breakfast every morning: egg whites, Ezekiel toast or oatmeal, and almond butter or natural peanut butter. This takes a little bit of time but it has become routine. My second breakfast after cardio is typically stuff I carry in a cooler: milk, chocolate milk, Greek yogurt, Hammer Nutrition's Recoverite carb/protein shake, or cherry juice mixed with L-glutamine powder. Typically, my co-workers will go out and eat breakfast, which takes thirty or forty minutes. My two breakfasts with food prep take about twenty-five minutes.

Lunch: I prepare the majority of my lunches one to two weeks in advance. I do this by cooking chicken, sweet potatoes, and brown rice then storing them in the fridge. My co-workers go out to eat, which takes forty-five minutes to an hour every day. My food prep takes about ten minutes; baking time is another one to two hours, on one day. My co-workers spend seven times longer on their meals than I do per week— and I am sitting on my couch for most of my hour of cooking. I am also eating two lunches daily. The extra time available frees up my lunch hour for training.

Dinner: For dinner, I often eat healthy chili (made with 99 percent lean ground turkey, chicken, and/or extra-lean ground beef) or other dishes that I prepared days or weeks prior and froze. Anytime I cook, I just make sure to prepare more food than I need and use the leftovers for a few days. Preparation is the key to eating healthy without spending a lot of money, and as I have proven it definitely does not take more time to eat healthy.

"Eating healthy doesn't taste good": I will give this one some credit because occasionally I agree with it. When I first started eating healthy, it was a large shock to my system; my body still craved the high-fat foods and high-glycemic carbohydrates it was used to eating. It took a while to get used to the change, and indeed any change in diet is best accomplished slowly. By changing only small parts of your diet over a long period of time, you can completely turn your diet from unhealthy to healthy foods. Over time, your body will stop craving high-fat foods.

I had trouble not ordering french fries at every restaurant I went to when I first decided to clean up my diet for racing. After occasionally getting vegetables over several years, I stopped craving french fries. Now when I eat high-fat foods like french fries or fast-food burgers, it makes me feel sick. This didn't happen overnight, but it did happen and I have talked to many other people who feel the same way. It takes months to get to this point, however, so don't say this isn't true if you eat healthy for a week and then still crave fast food.

Healthy foods can be made tastier through spices, rubs, and sauces. I eat chicken for lunch (lunches, technically . . . meals 3 and 4) every day of the year. I can vary the taste through spices and sauces, which makes things a little more exciting. I enjoy the food, but I enjoy the results I get from eating this way more. As I stated already, avoid sauces that contain sugar.

I am not going to sit here and tell you I'm perfect, because I'm not. I, too, have the occasional weakness for high-fat foods—a particular brand of pizza from Delaware called Grotto Pizza, Girl Scout Thin Mint cookies, and few others. I don't think everyone needs to eat healthy every day of the year. Again, though, realize that your body is a direct reflection of how you eat. Don't get mad about extra fat on your body if you are unwilling to put in the effort to eat healthy.

Erin Brooks of Strength & Speed–ERA carrying the Wreck Bag to a top ten elite team world finish.

Losing fat is a slow process that often occurs over months and/or years. If it took you ten years of eating crappy to gain all your undesired extra fat, don't get upset if a month of healthy eating doesn't result in the positive change you're looking for. Slow changes are more easily accomplished and have more staying power. Keep on eating healthy, because a lean athlete will outperform one carrying excess fat.

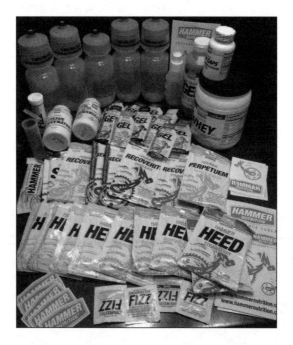

The different types of supplements can be confusing to someone who isn't familiar with the ingredients of each product.

Supplements

The supplement industry is a big business bringing in billions of dollars a year. To compete with one another, supplement companies are prone to making aggressive statements about their products' effectiveness. Furthermore, the Food and Drug Administration does not regulate these products or statements, so companies can make bold claims that have little or no basis in reality. However, some supplements do provide close to their advertised benefits. The important thing is to understand what products contain by reading labels. Once you understand what the companies are putting into their products, you will realize many of the products are very similar and will be able to understand what they are actually doing inside your body.

The biggest benefit supplements provide is convenience. After I've been training in the gym, sometimes I don't want to eat a chicken breast right away; it's easier to have a protein shake. I can store the protein powder in my unrefrigerated gym bag all day, too, unlike the chicken breast.

Anytime you get to choose between a supplement and a whole food meal, always go with the whole food meal. There are two exceptions, however. The first is pre-workout drinks that provide concentrated caffeine—they're a better choice than drinking a large cup of coffee. The second is endurance fuels like gels and drink mixes specially designed for ultra-endurance. Carrying gels is just easier than carrying whole food with you while running. Drink mixes like Hammer Nutrition's Perpetuem provide carbs, fat, and protein in one bottle, covering all your fueling needs for ultra-endurance events.

Improving in obstacle racing requires improving your strength, improving your speed, or improving both. I've listed some of the major types of supplements below. Each one has a rating for improvements in strength, one for improvements in speed, and one for improvements if you're conducting both strength *and* speed training simultaneously. If you have a strong running background and want to improve your ability to complete obstacles, you should be strength-focused. Strength improvement is also great for all athletes in the off-season. For those with a non-running background, your goal should be improving your speed. Finally, if you are in a training period when you are trying to peak or improve one while maintaining the other, look at the rating for strength & speed. Ratings are as follows:

++ Great for the goal stated

+ Good for the goal stated

o Neutral for the goal stated

- Bad for the goal stated

— Really bad for the goal stated

Gels

Strength: **+**

Speed: **++**

Strength & Speed: **++**

Gels contain carbohydrates to fuel your energy while you exercise or race. Ideally, you want a gel that has a mix of complex and simple carbohydrates, which will provide you with a constant stream of energy. Having a small amount of amino acids in the gel can also help prevent your body from using muscle for fuel, especially for events lasting two hours or more. Without amino acids, you are essentially trying to eat your engine while racing. The racing section of this book will go into more details about how to use gels, but it's important to have some fuel in the tank if you're racing. Gels provide that fuel, especially when your exercise exceeds an hour. Gels are typically not used for strength training, unless you want to use them to spike your insulin levels post-workout.

Electrolyte Drink Mix

Strength: **o**

Speed: **+**

Strength & Speed: **+**

Think of electrolyte drink mix as you would oil for your car. When your body has enough electrolytes everything is fine, so adding more will not enhance performance. However, when your body is low on electrolytes, painful cramping is often the result. When the weather gets hot and sweating rates increase, the probability of needing an electrolyte supplement increases. Electrolyte supplements are often available as just pure electrolytes or a mix of electrolytes and carbohydrates. A great natural source of electrolytes is coconut water like Vita-Coco, if you are not interesting in purchasing supplements.

Protein

> Strength: ++
>
> Speed: +
>
> Strength & Speed: ++

A variety of protein products are on the market, and the number grows almost daily. There are generally three categories of protein available: whey, casein, and soy. Other products are available that contain derivatives of protein from other sources, but I'm not going to list them all. These include things like beef protein isolate and pea protein isolate.

Whey protein: What you need to know about whey is that it's the fastest acting of all the proteins and the best absorbed by your body. By taking in whey immediately after your workout, you are beginning the process of rebuilding your muscles as soon as possible.

Casein protein: Casein is another popular form of protein that is often overlooked by those not serious about building or maintaining strength. It's a slow-digesting protein that should be taken at night. The slow digestion of casein in your stomach will provide building blocks for your muscles while you sleep. Since sleep is essential for recovery and so is nutrition, this should be toward the top of your supplement list.

Soy protein: Men typically don't take soy due to fear of it causing an estrogenic effect in the body. There is little research to support any estrogenic effect from taking soy protein; however, I still don't recommend using it as your primary source of protein. Better to play it safe and just go with whey. Soy is digested slightly slower than whey but not nearly as slowly as casein. Occasional use is okay, but I don't recommend purchasing a container of soy protein.

I recommend a protein supplement for all athletes for convenience. OCR athletes are breaking down large amounts of tissue through the stress of running and strength training. Without proper protein intake, you are not optimizing your ability to recover. This can be accomplished through regular food intake, but often protein is the macronutrient most likely to be too low among endurance athletes.

Pre-Workout Drink

> Strength: ++
>
> Speed: -
>
> Strength & Speed: ++

If you plan on training hard twice a day, I definitely recommend a pre-workout drink. If you are only strength training once a day, then you may still want a pre-workout drink. The important thing is to do research regarding what you are putting into your body prior to using a product. When Ephedra, and later DMAA (aka geranium root, methylhexa-namine, and 1,3 dimethylamylamine), arrived on the scene, people were amazed at the level of alertness they provided. Ephedra was later banned, however, and DMAA is in the process of being banned by many companies and organizations. Pre-workout drinks are among the supplements most likely to contain substances banned by the World Anti-Doping Agency (WADA). You can manually check supplements by comparing labels with the yearly published WADA prohibited substance list or enlist the help of a company like Aegis Shield, which does the research for you for a small annual fee.

I personally only take items with caffeine as the main stimulant. Some of these products contain other substances that are supposed to enhance the effect of caffeine, but they are primarily caffeine-based. If you took caffeine out of these products, their "secret pre-workout" formula would probably have a minimal energy-enhancing effect. I primarily use caffeine-based products because I plan to use the products for a long time. I generally understand there are very few to no side effects associated with long-term caffeine use. Indeed, people have been drinking coffee for hundreds of years.

As a rule, you want to avoid pre-workouts for speed training. A small amount of caffeine—the amount contained in a cup of coffee: 100mg for most coffee, or 200mg for some of the popular chain coffee shops—can be helpful to dull pain and improve cardio performance. However, the caffeine levels in pre-workouts (often 200 to 500mg depending on the brand and dosing) will often elevate the heart rate to an unnaturally high level. I know people who have taken pre-workout powder designed for strength improvement and tried to run a 5K. Their performance suffers, and many report feeling very uncomfortable and concerned for their health due to elevated heart rates.

An alternative to taking a designated pre-workout product is using caffeinated gels. These typically contain fewer chemicals; it's very easy to understand their contents. The best are the caffeinated gels that provide complex carbs for energy, caffeine as a stimulant, and amino acids to prevent muscle catabolism. Most companies do not put in amino acids, so if you're going to use gels as a pre-workout, pay attention to their ingredients. Companies like Hammer Nutrition offer gels like this.

Multivitamin

> Strength: ++

> Speed: ++

> Strength & Speed: ++

A multivitamin is always a good idea. You should not rely on multivitamins to get all your vitamins and minerals, but you can use them to support your already healthy diet. There is a reason they are called supplements. Multivitamins will help fill any gaps to optimize strength and speed gains.

BCAAs

> Strength: ++

> Speed: ++

> Strength & Speed: ++

Branched chain amino acids (BCAAs) are the building blocks of protein. They are essentially protein broken down into an already digestible form. If you're looking to ensure that your body has adequate protein but want to limit weight gain, BCAAs are a good choice instead of protein, especially if you're trying to cut fat. Their minimal caloric load will ensure that you are not overloading you body with whatever fillers protein companies use. They can also be used pre-workout or intra-workout to support muscle building and fat burning. For especially taxing training periods, BCAAs can be consumed in the middle of the night to ensure your body has the required building blocks to repair muscle while you sleep.

Creatine

> Strength: ++
>
> Speed: -
>
> Strength & Speed: 0

Creatine-containing products are very popular—and for good reason: They are effective at building strength, and they work. Creatine pulls water into muscle cells, causing them to expand. This expansion leads to further muscle growth and strength gains. It also adds fuel to the adenosine triphosphate (ATP) cycle, enhancing energy available for short-term bursts of strength.

While creatine is highly recommended for strength athletes, it isn't recommended for speed athletes. The positive effects of creatine for speed training only apply to very short track sprints; it won't have a positive effect even in the shortest of obstacle races. The majority of times I have had a cramp that would not loosen, it was because I was taking creatine for my lifting but still doing some endurance training. Be sure to drink plenty of water while using creatine to avoid this. I was sure I was hydrated, but the muscle cramps said otherwise and most likely could have be avoided with the proper hydration level and electrolyte supplementation. Previously most creatine products had a "loading" phase and then a maintenance phase. This is generally viewed as obsolete; everyone now just follows the instructions on the bottle, which typically lists a uniform dosing from day one.

Another common problem with creatine intake is gastrointestinal (GI) issues. I have found that if I take half to three-quarters of the recommended dose, I get the positive effects of creatine without the GI issues. The problem with taking the recommended dose is often there is no adjustment for body weight. A 150-pound athlete should not be taking the same amount of creatine as a 200-pound athlete.

Fat Burners

> Strength: —
>
> Speed: —
>
> Strength & Speed: —

As I previously stated, a lean athlete is more efficient than an athlete carrying excess fat. While I stand by this statement, I do not promote the use of fat burners. Fat burners often contain unhealthy large amounts of caffeine that can affect your sleep cycle, which will in turn hurt your ability to recover. Many overweight people will use fat burners to try to shed pounds, but without understanding that they need to change their diet to make a difference. The fat burning is getting rid of ounces of fat and not pounds, which is what most people need.

I do think fat burners have a purpose if you're trying to peak for a specific event such as a bodybuilding competition, or you want to look good for your wedding photos. However, I don't think they have a valid place in obstacle racing. The bottom line is that the majority of your fat loss needs to come from a healthy diet and exercise; fat burners can then help you burn off that little extra bit of fat to enhance your definition. This can be especially useful if you are on a low-carbohydrate diet. The constant feeling of being tired will be minimized from the caffeine included in the fat burner. As with all products, the individual substances in a fat burner should be monitored. Therefore, if you normally drink a lot of coffee during the day, you should not be taking a fat burner; that would elevate your caffeine intake to ridiculous levels.

Final Thoughts

A lot of research has been done on supplements, and there's a lot of literature discussing the details of each. In fact, you could write an entire book just on supplements. Understand this, though: Often the experiments referenced in supplement studies really were conducted, but by untrained groups. Someone who has been lifting for five years is not going to see 100 percent increases in strength like the ad states. Often these ads also tout experiments done with very small sample sizes, which can lead to overstated conclusions if researchers choose who goes into which group. Whatever supplements you decide to take to enhance your training, do your research, and remember that these are *supplements*, not your major source of nutrition.

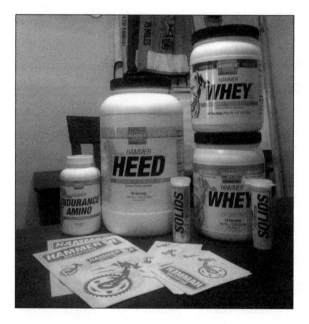

The right supplements can help you achieve a goal such as qualifying for the OCR World Championships or earning one of the colored bibs from World's Toughest Mudder.

Chapter 3

REST AND RECOVERY

The second-most-overlooked portion of a complete exercise program (after diet) is rest and recovery. People assume that just because they work hard, they will grow and improve regardless of what they do the other twenty-three hours of the day. If you do not rest and recover properly, though, you won't develop as fast or to your maximum potential. After all, your body actually improves during the rest periods while you are sleeping and resting. The stress you add to your body while exercising is the stimulus that makes your body adapt.

Rest

Rest is a simple concept, but it's easy to overlook it if you don't schedule properly. Rest can be broken down further into two categories: sleep and rest days. Sleep is simple to explain but hard to apply in practice. In order for your body to recover to the best of its abilities and grow the strongest and fastest, you need to sleep close to eight hours a night. Everyone is different, so some people require a little more or a little less than this. Still, eight hours is generally a good starting point.

Occasionally I hear people make statements like "I only need to sleep four or five hours a night to function." Let me be clear: The eight-hour sleep requirement is to maximize growth and fitness gains. You can sleep significantly less than that and still improve or still be functional. I have done multiday events where I was only sleeping an hour or two each night for day after day. I was still able to function but my ability to perform tasks properly was severely degraded, and I definitely was not improving in physical performance.

Sleep is important for several reasons. First, when you sleep your growth hormone levels spike, helping you recover and improve. Without adequate sleep, you will not get as productive a spike in growth hormone. Another reason is that sleep consolidates skills you have learned over the day in your brain, allowing you to perform what you learned that day much easier the next time. As you sleep, your brain essentially organizes and stores the information learned throughout the day. Without adequate sleep, you will not "learn/store" the correct actions to improve. Remember, many of your initial fitness gains come from neurological improvement. This is when that neurological improvement takes place. As you sleep, the muscle movements that enabled you to complete those monkey bars or vault over that wall are reinforced.

Rest days are also important. Don't be a typical gym rat and insist, "I'm going to work out Monday through Friday and then take two rest days on the weekend." Your body will perform better if you space out the rest days. I often like to use the Wednesday and Sunday rest-day split. This allows me to catch up on sleep on Wednesday if I start getting behind and then hit the workout harder on Thursday. The Sunday rest day allows for more family time and/or church attendance.

Strength & Speed athlete and MAOCR member Cody Peyton climbing over the Destroyer.

I like to do absolutely no physical activity on my rest days. Some people will still go for a short jog. I generally discourage this because I think complete rest is not only important physically but also important mentally. Having a day with no physical activity can help reset your brain so you can train harder the rest of the week.

Recovery

Recovery can take place in many ways, including active and passive recovery. I generally like passive recovery, because after I exercise I am tired and just want to lie down. However, both can enhance your ability to recover and exercise again in the future. If you don't think recovery is important, just look at steroids. Steroids allow your body to heal faster than the normal person can. This means you can train hard again in shorter period, resulting in greater strength gain. People who take steroids may be training harder or easier than a natural athlete, but they are recovering at a much faster rate. This gives them an edge that is hard to overcome as a drug-free athlete. Performance-enhancing drugs will be covered later in the book, but let me make it clear that I do not support or encourage their use.

Also, look at the differences between men and women. A major difference is testosterone levels. It takes a woman a lot of time to be able to lift more than a man. Most women, except for serious lifters, will never be able to lift more than a man. This is due to the levels of testosterone in their respective bodies. This analogy is comparable to a drug-free athlete and an athlete who takes steroids. The drug-free athlete may never reach the same level as the steroid-taking athlete regardless of training. The one advantage the drug-free athlete has is that some of the people who take steroids are just looking for a shortcut; they may not be dedicated to improving over the long term. This will allow a drug-free lifter to outperform a steroid user in certain instances.

The techniques described below are primarily for cardiovascular exercise recovery. However, the rolling, stretching, and massage also provide numerous benefits for recovery from strength-based workouts, including lifting and obstacles. The other techniques may improve recovery slightly when it comes to strength movements, but I have not seen enough studies to state that as a fact.

Passive Recovery: The Cheap Way

Most people have heard about taking ice baths after a hard practice or a hard workout. However, I don't plan on filling up my bathtub with ice every weekend after my long run. A cheaper and easier solution is almost as effective: alternating hot and cold in the shower.

After getting in the shower and warming up, follow these directions: 1 minute of cold water (as cold as your shower will go), followed by 2 minutes of warm water. Repeat this cycle three times. Simple, effective, and requires zero preparation time. I typically just put the target body part(s) in the cold water; after a run, for instance, just the lower half of my body will be in the water, which makes the process more bearable. If it's an obstacle day, then my whole body will have to deal with the alternating temperatures.

The alternating cold and hot water cause your blood vessels to constrict and dilate, which increases circulation. The increase in circulation helps get rid of waste products and speeds recovery. While the cold is somewhat painful, it makes your legs feel great after the shower. This isn't something I do after every run or every hard run, but I do practice it regularly. It's especially useful when I know I have another hard workout or race coming soon and I am worried about recovering in time. If you're the type of person who is doing a race on Saturday followed by a race on Sunday, definitely use this technique. During the height of obstacle racing season, this is a normal activity for me.

Passive Recovery: The More Expensive Way

Several big-name companies offer compression clothing to help speed recovery. I am also a big fan of this. Applying compression in varying degrees over different parts of your muscles helps speed recovery by returning the blood to the heart. As you lie on the couch, the pressure squeezes your muscles, which helps circulate blood. The only bad part is that compression clothing is typically not cheap. Several big-name companies, including Under Armour, offer everything from pants to just calf sleeves, and from full shirts to just sleeves. If you are going to be serious about obstacle racing, I highly recommend the leggings or pants. If you have some extra money to spend, then invest in the compression sleeves designed for recovery.

Strength & Speed owner Evan Perperis putting on recovery compression sleeves and recovery compression socks immediately after race day 1 to prepare for day 2 of the Obstacle Course Racing World Championships.

The pants are better for recovery but are more difficult to put on. Having a pair of recovery socks allows you to put on your socks immediately post-race versus waiting an hour or more until you get home, where you can put on your pants. If you want a challenge, try putting on recovery pants after crushing yourself in an obstacle race while inside a Port-a-Potty. It is not going to go well.

Team Strength & Speed at the Obstacle Course Racing World Championships. Left to right: Rusty Palmer, Kevin Righi in recovery compression pants, Rimas Radzius, and Evan Perperis. After racing in the individual event the day before, Kevin is taking advantage of compression to prepare for the team competition.

Compression clothing is typically sold as either active/performance compression or recovery compression. There is a difference between the two, so make sure you know which one you want before making a purchase. Active compression is slightly looser than recovery compression and is designed to be worn while racing or training. Recovery compression is typically tighter and designed to be worn after the race.

CTG Pro Team member Nathan Palmer wearing active compression during the OCRWC.

Passive Recovery: The Really Expensive Way

Do you have $1,500 burn? Then buy the fanciest pair of pressurized recovery pants you can afford. NormaTec pants plug into the wall and inflate and deflate to provide varying degree of pressure on different parts of your muscles in order to speed recovery. Only the very serious athletes with money to spend own their own pair. Sports clubs or larger organizations with multiple personal trainers are more likely to own these. Why would people spend so much money on a pair of pants? It is because they work. I have personally used them and found their benefits to be amazing. This is the reason you will see pictures and videos of Grand Tour pro cyclists wearing these to recover during their three-week races. As far as recovery compression goes, you won't get better than this.

Active Recovery: Stretching

Stretching can also help with recovery and improve flexibility. For stretching post-exercise, perform static stretching: Assume a stretched position and hold it. You should never bounce while stretching. The stretching action will cause increased blood flow in that muscle, which will help speed recovery and increase flexibility.

Never do static stretching prior to exercise. Research has shown that such stretching will stretch the muscle but also make it weaker during activity. Pre-exercise, all stretches should be dynamic. This means doing warm up movements, rotations, light jogging, and any other activity that requires low effort but allows the body to heat up. The more similar these dynamic movements are to the actual activity you will be conducting, the better they prepare you to exercise.

Active Recovery: Massage

My personal favorite form of recovery is massage. Some professional athletes recommend getting a massage once a week. If you willing to spend $80 to $120 a week, depending on the place and length of the massage, then right on. I would love to get weekly massages. However, most of us can't afford or don't want to commit that much money to massages each year.

A variety of massage types are offered. As an athlete, you want deep-tissue sports massage or myofascial release. These massages are hard enough to provide the positive benefits listed below. Swedish massages or the delicate versions designed to relax you do not provide the same athletic benefits. Most likely, you will have to go to a sports-specific masseuse to get the proper pressure and intensity. Before purchasing any massage, be sure to check what types are on offer so you aren't wasting your money.

Typically, I try to get a couple of massages each year, with each one falling sometime during a hard training period or right before or after a big race. The benefits of massage are numerous and include speeding recovery, breaking up scar tissue, and mental relaxation. Massages speed recovery the same way a lot of these other recovery techniques do. The constant changes in pressure cause blood to circulate, thus taking out waste products and bringing in fresh blood, which speeds healing.

Furthermore, as you continue to train, your body will create scar tissue in some places where muscles are healing. This scar tissue isn't as flexible as muscle and can limit your range of motion along with power production. Massaging the scar tissue or knots can help unbind the muscle, allowing it to function the way it was designed. It does require a lot of pressure to effectively loosen and break up scarred muscle tissue. This is why you want to stick with the harder forms of massage.

The final benefit of massages is mental. Who does not enjoy lying on a table and being groped for an hour? It's relaxing and benefits performance. What's not to like, besides the price? If you don't want to spend all that money on massages, a good alternative can be to purchase a massage chair or cushion for your back. Full massage chairs are expensive, usually close to $2,000, but the cushions can be significantly cheaper. I recommend a full back massage cushion ($200), a massage pillow ($50), and a foot/calf massager ($200). These products can be purchased at a store like Bed Bath & Beyond. This provides all the benefits of a full chair at a fraction of the cost. The pillow can used to apply pressure to the front of your body: quads, chest, and arms. The back cushion and calf massager will cover massaging the muscles on your back, resulting in full body massage.

Active Recovery: Rolling

Rolling is very similar to massage but all you pay for is the roller. This is typically a large foam cylinder, sometimes with studs or teeth. If you leave the roller on the floor and use your body weight to press your muscles into it, it acts like the hands of a masseuse. Spending thirty seconds to a minute on each body part will cause an increase in blood flow and breakdown of scar tissue, which in the future will allow for a more efficiently functioning muscle. Rolling is often slightly painful, but it's an important part of recovery. Perform a couple of minutes after a hard workout; this allows you to do your next workout at a higher intensity level. To be safe, be sure to roll over muscles only and never over joints.

In addition to the foam cylinder, rollers come in other forms that include a stick-like wand that you press into your muscles with both hands, a tennis-ball-type item, and a hand paddle covered in studs or ball bearings. All of these basically do the same thing, just with a different technique. I personally recommend the foam roller over all of them, though. I find that it provides the most pressure with the least effort. The other versions are especially useful for traveling to races or competitions, since a foam roller typically takes up the majority of your bag while the variations can easily fit inside it.

Alter Ego gets ready to take on World's Toughest Mudder 2013.

Chapter 4

GETTING STARTED AND THE COMPETITIVE DRIVE

Eric Woody practicing the Weaver.

This chapter isn't just for people who haven't trained before; it can also serve as a good reminder for anyone updating their exercise program. Often athletes forget some of the most important aspects that led them to grow in the first place. Even experienced athletes need reminders about the path to improvement. Otherwise, many fall into complacency and forget to adjust their plans for consistent improvements. This is often why people get such positive results from trainers. The trainer is changing up the routine of the clients from whatever they normally do, and then continuing to change it from week to week or month to month. These constant changes lead to improvement often not seen when people control their own exercise regime.

The Competitive Drive

The competitive drive is a term I apply to everyone who has that desire to improve, set a new personal record (PR), and/or push themselves. While almost all of us probably view ourselves like this, I don't think many people actually apply the competitive drive in their daily lives, whether that's in sport improvement, personal relationships, or their job. The first step in ensuring you have the drive is to set goals. These need to be a combination of short-term and long-term goals.

Short-term goals should be set with the intentions of meeting long-term goals. For example, a short-term goal might be completing X number of races this year or reaching a new distance PR in a race. Your short-term goal should be attainable within a couple of months or a year. A medium-term goal might be qualifying for the Obstacle Course Racing World Championships. Your medium goal should be attainable in a year or two. A long-term goal might be placing in the top fifty at the world championships. Such a goal should be something you focus on for the next three to five years. This will ensure that you are maintaining progress.

Due to obstacle course racing's variety in terrain, number of obstacles, and race length, I often use road races to monitor my performance. For example, if you are a 3:20 marathon runner and your ultimate goal is to run a sub-3-hour marathon, you could set a short-term goal of a new PR of 3:15. Your medium-term goal could be running a 3:10 in two years and a 3:05 in three years—which is also a Boston Marathon qualifying time, for under-thirty-five males (another medium-term goal). By improving five minutes a year, you should be able to run sub-3:00 within five years. This allows for some flexibility due to changes in personal life and the challenge of continuing to run faster. When you add in successive years of marathon training, your body develops the system to make

Demetrios "Sty" Karellas jumping to reach the top of a wall.

Strength & Speed–ERA—Erin Brooks, Barbara Bass, and Ashley Jeanne Samples—running up the warped wall.

the next year's goal attainable.

A quick review of goal setting: Your goals should be attainable with a realistic time line for improvement, assuming you put in the required work to improve. You should always have short-term goals and a long-term goal that looks outward three to five years. This will help keep you on track and provide continuous improvement. Having intermediate goals will also keep you motivated and provide positive success-reinforcing milestones.

To stoke the competitive drive, try signing up for something on the edge of your limits. This is a technique I used when I first started racing. I would sign up for stuff on the edge of or sometimes far beyond my current physical limits. I did a moderate amount of exercise and then suffered horribly on race day.

Here is a little recap of that race history. Prior to October 2003, my longest run was 12 miles. Here's what I did in 2003/2004:

> October 2003: First marathon
>
> March 2004: 40-mile run from Baltimore to DC
>
> May 2004: First triathlon, half Iron distance
>
> August 2004: Third triathlon, full Iron distance

While I do not recommend this technique of signing up for events beyond your physical limits without proper training, the principle of reaching still applies. Sign up for something at the edge or just beyond your current limits. Just give yourself adequate time and training to prepare. Four months is more than adequate to prepare for something just beyond your capacity. The competitive drive to finish will help guide you through training and the race.

You don't have to sign up for an ultra to take advantage of this. Just sign up for something on the edge of your limits. *Your limits* are the key words in this sentence. For some people it may be World's Toughest Mudder or a Spartan Ultra Beast. For others it may be a Warrior Dash or Savage Race. Just sign up for a race and push yourself. By having the external stimulus to perform in the future, you will increase the likelihood of exercising hard every day.

Maybe you don't want to sign up for a longer or more challenging race but still want to improve. You're wondering, *Why am I still stagnating?* There are a variety of reasons, but most can be covered with the simple statement that most people are unwilling to go into their uncomfortable zone. What does going into the uncomfortable zone mean? It means pushing harder than you normally push in either volume or intensity.

Perhaps you're thinking, *I go to my uncomfortable zone all the time. It hurts on every set or every run.* That's true because exercise hurts, but are you really in your uncomfortable zone? If you lay out a training plan for the next couple of months and there are no workouts on your schedule that make you cringe slightly, or a lot, then no, you are not going into your uncomfortable zone.

When I recommend training plans to people, I tell them the first couple of weeks should seem doable, but after that there should be at least one workout a week that you dread and maybe even wonder whether you can finish. This challenge can be due to distance or pace. This is how you know you're going into your uncomfortable zone.

Now that we've covered some general information regarding the three pillars of fitness—exercise, diet, and rest/recovery—let's get into the details. Specifically, let's start improving your cardiovascular fitness and your ability to complete obstacles.

The start of Mud Run Guide's Summer Splash event at the permanent obstacle course site The Battlegrounds.

Chapter 5

OBSTACLE RACE TRAINING: THE OBSTACLES

Even though the sport is called obstacle course racing (OCR), the majority of participants' time is spent running and not completing obstacles. However, this doesn't mean that a pure runner will be successful in OCR. To be successful, you need to have the upper-body strength to complete each obstacle.

Many races have obstacles that seem straightforward. If there's a wall you go over it; a set of barbed wire, you go under it. Nothing groundbreaking here. However, if you're looking to be competitive, there are tricks to navigating these obstacles as fast as possible. Here are some of the secrets used by elite obstacle racers to shave seconds and minutes off their times.

Monkey Bars

Monkey bars can be challenging if you don't have the required grip strength. I have identified three levels of competence for monkey bars: beginner, intermediate, and advanced.

Beginner: Beginner level involves using the two-hands-per-bar method all the way across. If your grip strength is low, you may have to resort to this method, but be advised that this can actually make the obstacle *more* challenging. The beginner method is also useful for monkey bars that have unusually wide grips or may be wet/muddy from other racers.

Intermediate: This is the one-hand-per-bar method. Each bar is only

OCR Gear—Icebug athlete and OCR Warrior champion Nikki Call crossing the monkey bars right before the finish line at Conquer the Gauntlet.

touched by one hand, and you use your body's natural swing as you move across the bars. Find that flow and use that momentum to your advantage; this will make the movement across the bars easier.

Advanced: This is also a one-hand-per-bar method, but your arms are kept flexed. This allows you to touch each bar very briefly as you speed your way across. To improve, think of each bar as a hot piece of metal, and work on keeping your hand on it as briefly as possible. In this method, you are actually pulling yourself across the bars instead of just using your natural momentum.

Regardless of your method, the secret to monkey bars and any other obstacle that requires hanging from your hands is that you want to go across as smoothly and quickly as possible. The two-hands-per-bar method actually requires more grip endurance than the one-hand method, because you are often moving slower. Find a playground with monkey bars to practice on and do them until you reach the point where you can do one-hand-per-bar all the way across.

Completing inverted monkey bars can be more challenging. The easiest way will be whatever works best for you. Going straight forward is often too challenging if the monkey bars have a steep angle. Personally, I like going sideways using the beginner method, two hands per bar. Other techniques include going backward or climbing the monkey bars like an inverted ladder.

Rusty Palmer and Kevin Righi use two different techniques to complete inverted monkey bars.

BattleFrog Pro Team member Corinna Coffin climbing the monkey bar like a ladder.

Conquer The Gauntlet Pro Team member Lucas Pfannen-stiel crossing rings at a Rugged Maniac race using the inter-mediate method.

Rings

Most people's initial reaction to rings is to swing across with one hand on each ring, similar to the intermediate monkey-bar method described above. In this case, however, the additional torque created when swinging with one arm can make this technique harder. The beginner method actually is faster and decreases the likelihood of falling. When crossing rings, use a beginner method but move sideways, leading with whatever side makes you feel comfortable. This method provides maximum control and maximum speed.

Hammer Nutrition sponsored athlete Evan Perperis crossing an obstacle that consists of circular pieces of hoses much like sets of rings.

Small Horizontal Pipe / Horizontal Board

As long as the obstacle has decent grip traction, I recommend the sideways method. Hanging all your weight on one side and then taking long reaches with your arms to move sideways provides a controlled method of crossing. I found the straightforward method to be slower and less efficient. It causes many of the same control issues you face when trying to cross rings straight forward. In extreme cases, where the obstacle is very muddy, you may want to cross it like a Tyrolean Traverse (see Tyrolean Traverse section).

Conquer The Gauntlet Pro Team member Evan Perperis using a Tyrolean Traverse method on the horizontal pipe due to excessive mud.

Horizontal I-Beam

The horizontal I-beam has grips on both sides of the obstacle. Ideally, you can cross this obstacle much as you might use the advanced method to navigate monkey bars: by pulling yourself across with a hand on each side. If the beam is very muddy and wet, you may want to use a sliding technique. By holding on to both sides, you use your body's momentum to scoot forward without ever removing your hands from the beam. The sliding method is slower but may prevent you from falling off the obstacle.

Crossing a "floating I-beam" obstacle at The Battlegrounds race site.

Vertical Cargo Nets Requiring Ascent/Descent

When you approach the cargo net, you want to take a running start and then leap as high as possible. This allows you to cover the greatest possible amount of net without actually climbing, providing a gain of a couple of seconds. Climbing up a cargo net can be annoying due to the net flexing and swaying. To minimize net slackness, stick to the edges. Typically, it'll be tightest where it's secured to the support posts. Avoid the tendency of most racers to shoot straight up the middle. The only exception is when there's a support beam in the middle of the net. Such a beam can sometimes be used as a stable platform for climbing in addition to the net. Just be sure that there is no rule against using the support beam before trying this.

As you climb, grip the vertical sections of the rope instead of the horizontal sections. The vertical sections will be tighter, allowing for a more stable climbing grip. Take large steps with your legs, allowing you to cover the most ground possible. Many people make the mistake of stepping on every horizontal piece of rope, which is often not necessary.

At the top, many athletes do a flip to begin their descent. By holding on to the net and flipping their legs over, they cover the first 5 feet of the net almost instantly. I do not recommend this unless you've practiced it first, since it is very easy to fall and get hurt. If you fall, your race time is going to suffer more than if you'd just climbed down normally. Still, it's a fairly easy technique to learn and just requires you to commit to the movement.

Once you get near the bottom of the net, leap off, skipping the last couple of feet of netting. This will also save a second or two. All these techniques combined can dramatically reduce your time per cargo net obstacle, allowing you to pass other racers.

Cargo net technique including the flip at the top and the jump off the bottom.

Using a running leap to cover the first several feet of the cargo net in one quick movement.

Horizontal Cargo Nets

The net setup will determine how you approach this obstacle. If there's a support beam running down the middle, you can often complete horizontal cargo nets by simply walking across that beam, avoiding the saggy part of the net altogether. If the net is sagging, the fastest and easiest method is usually to roll across it just as you would roll under barbed wire.

Vertical Cargo Nets Crossed Horizontally

Many of the principles used to traverse the regular cargo net can be applied here. As you approach the obstacle, take a running leap to cover as much net as possible. As you move across, continue take large reaches with both your legs and arms to cover the net as fast as possible. Staying near the point of attachment and using the vertical sections can provide a more stable surface.

Tires / Taut Cargo Net Requiring High Knees

The mistake people often make with these obstacles is stepping in every hole or every tire. If the holes are close enough together you can often step in every other one, allowing you to traverse the obstacle faster. With tires it is usually possible just to step on the tire itself instead of in the hole, bounding from tire to tire until the obstacle is complete.

Vertical Chain-Link Fence

To cross a vertical chain-link fence, grab hold of the fence near the top with your hands while digging your toes or the bottoms of your feet into the mesh. There is no great way to complete this without some discomfort; a lot of this technique involves pushing through the pain. Just as with vertical cargo nets, use big reaches and big steps to cross the obstacle with as few moves as possible.

Digging both feet and hands into the fence to continue to make forward progress at The Battlegrounds permanent obstacle course.

Barbed Wire

Your technique should change depending on the height of the barbed wire. With wire that is around knee to hip height, you most likely want to use a bear-crawl technique. Aggressively bounding between hands and knees in a modified crouch will most likely be the fastest. If the race organizers are using wire without barbs and accidentally put the wire around hip height, you may just be able to crouch and run under it, allowing your back to brush against it.

If the barbed wire is below knee height, you may want to use a rolling technique. If the terrain allows for it, an aggressive roll is even better. In an aggressive roll, you are actually using small arm movements to push off the ground and propel your roll forward as fast as possible. If the wire is too low, try extending one arm over your head, which will drop your profile another couple of inches.

In cases where the terrain is very rocky, the wire is very high, or there is deep mud, the rolling technique is typically slower than crawling under the wire. When the wire obstacle is really long, an alternating-rolling-and-crawling method can be useful. This helps prevent dizziness after you stand up from a 30m roll. I have also found that focusing on a point in the distance during a roll can help reduce dizziness.

Inverted Wall / Slanted Wall / Wall / Quarter Pipe

Any obstacle that requires climbing above your height will get easier if you know the right technique. The trick to clearing these obstacles is speed. By attacking the walls with speed, you will be able to get higher and utilize momentum to pull yourself over. This begins as soon as you can see the obstacle approaching. Start with a jog and gradually pick up the pace until the last 5 to 10m, when you should be sprinting. Keep running until you cannot make any more forward progress, then leap at the wall, grab the top, and use your momentum to pull yourself over. Too often, I see racers approach a tall wall and stop to analyze it. They lose all momentum and make the climb twice as hard as it should be.

Rusty Palmer using the crawl technique due to the height of the wire.

Evan Perperis rolling under barbed wire to save time.

Podium finisher from 2015 OCR World Championships Claude Godbout accelerating toward a slanted wall and using her momentum to help bring her over it.

Evan Perperis showing the importance of a running start by easily conquering Everest at the 2014 World's Toughest Mudder.

Others make the mistake of starting their run at the wall too late or starting from a complete stop. Both of these will hurt your momentum, making the obstacle more difficult than it is.

Vertical Wall

Just as with the inverted wall, you want to attack this obstacle with speed. Run full speed toward the wall and then leap as you get close to reach the top. As with the inverted wall, pull yourself over by hooking an elbow or hooking a leg. As you clear the far side, push off the wall with your hands. This provides you with forward momentum as you continue your race. If you're involved in an ultra-distance obstacle race, this technique isn't always workable due to extreme fatigue. In those cases, using the support structures or getting assistance from other racers is usually an option. However, if you need assistance from another racer and it is allowed based off the rules, the polite thing to do is help at least one other person over the obstacle.

Hanging Chains

Some obstacles involve grabbing chains to support you. Just like the cargo net, grab the chain as close to the point of attachment as possible. The lower you grab the chain, the more flex it will have and thus the more unstable it will be as a handhold. This principle can be applied to traversing hanging ropes as well. If additional gripping power is required, you can wrap the chain around your hands. The downside to this technique is that it's slower due to the wrapping and unwrapping required to move across the obstacle. However, it may prevent you from losing your grip on the chain. As you move across the obstacle, you may not need to use every rope or chain. If possible, skip unnecessary chains to shave off a couple of seconds.

Balancing Obstacles

Some courses require you to balance either on a balance beam, across several balance beams, or by jumping from stump to stump. The trick for these is to maintain a combination of forward momentum and bal-

Kevin Righi starting BattleFrog's Tip of the Spear obstacle two chains in.

Evan Perperis grabbing close to the point of attachment.

Demonstrating the alternate grip, which can provide a more stable grip but is slower.

ance. Often you'll find it easier to keep your balance if you go at a moderate pace. Moving too slow will make it harder to keep your balance—and so will moving too fast. Keep your toes pointed in the direction of movement, which should make it easier to balance than trying to keep your feet sideways. Once you get toward the end of the obstacle, increase your speed and leap off so you can continue running.

For practice it is best to build your own balance beam using 2x4s on laid on their side and nailed together in a zig-zag or C configuration. This is very easy to build and will greatly improve you balance by walking back and forth. Another option for those serious about improving balance is purchasing a slackline and using that for practice. Slacklines are very difficult so when initially training on them you may just have to practice while holding a cane or PVC pipe for additional stability or you may have to start off with just standing still.

High Wire and Low Wire

These obstacles have a wire up high to grip with your hands and a wire down low for you to stand on. They vary in length from 10 to 50

Eric Woody taking his time mid-balance-beam and then accelerating as he reaches the end during a Strength & Speed training session.

feet and are usually elevated above the ground or above water. Grab the overheard wire with your hands and place your feet on the lower wire. Instead of using a foot-over-foot method, which is slow, just slide your hands and your feet—it's easier and faster. People who remove their feet from the wire will find it difficult to regain contact, thus slowing their forward movement.

Tyrolean Traverse / One-Rope Bridge / Thick Pipe Crossing

If you're wearing the appropriate attire you can go with a sliding method; if not, use a sloth climbing method. The sliding method just

Using a sliding-foot method for maximum speed and control on the hire wire / low wire obstacle.

involves hooking your legs and letting them drag while you pull yourself hand over hand. To use this method, you need to have made the right clothing choices before the race. If the rope or pipe is causing chafing as you slide, switch to a hand-over-hand and foot-over-foot method, aka the sloth climbing method. The best advice is to keep powering through until you hit the far side. Too often I see people stop to check progress, which just slows you down and means you will be hanging from the rope longer.

Water Crossing

As you approach the water obstacle, the first thing you should do is leap as far as possible. This allows you to cover the most amount of

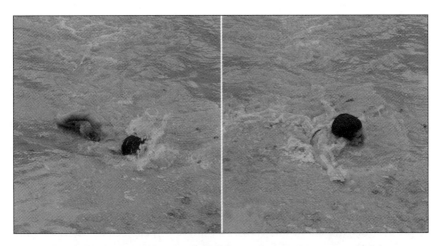

Evan Perperis swims through 3 feet of water to save seconds.

water in the shortest time possible. Just make sure you keep a slight bend in your knees, because the depth of the water is often unclear. This allows you to absorb the landing if the water ends up being very shallow. If the water is deep enough to swim through, then that will be your fastest option. The bottom of most water obstacles is thick mud, which is extremely slow to walk through. When possible swim, using the crawl or freestyle stroke to get the fastest time.

Mud Mounds with Water Pits in Between

If the pits are small enough, you may be able to leap from one mud mound to the next without ever having to go in the water. This is rarely the case, though; usually you will have to get into the water. As with other water obstacles, leap across as much as you can. When pulling yourself out of the mud, look for foot or hand indentations from other racers. These will often provide a shelf to step on or help you pull yourself up with your hands. If the mud is especially wet, you may have to dig your hands into the mound to get traction. Try to get your hands into a position where you can push off, similar to doing the upward motion of a dip. If there are grip obstacles like a rig or monkey bars later

Kevin Righi leaping over the majority of an over/under obstacle, so he doesn't have to wade through muddy soil.

Evan Perperis uses the alternate grip on two different obstacles to save his grip strength. (above, and next page top)

Kevin Righi shifting the focus of effort to his legs in order to save upper-body strength for later obstacles.

in the course, make a fist when pushing off the ground. This will keep your palms free of mud and make future obstacles easier.

Alternate Grip for Giant's Ladder / Confidence Climb / Ladder to Heaven

If your race is very grip-strength-heavy, you can use this technique to save some energy. Your forearms can be used in lieu of your hands to grip bars on some obstacles. This will transfer the stress from your grip strength to your biceps, which are larger muscles. Although this technique is slower, it can help preserve some energy for future obstacles. In extreme cases, you can also use it to traverse extra-wide monkey bars or rings. Hopefully, you possess grip strength such that this technique isn't necessary at all. For all climbing activities, consciously shift the load to your legs. Instead of muscling your way up obstacles using your arms, step with your legs and use your arms just to hold you to the obstacle.

Climbing Ropes

While you can use an all-arms method while climbing, this generally isn't recommended due to the effort required. However, it may be faster to use the technique near the end of a race if it is one of the final obstacles. A better way is to use your legs to lock into the rope. The two techniques primarily used are the J hook and the S wrap. I personally prefer the S wrap, but experiment on your own to find out what works best for you. The techniques are best explained via video or in person.

As you approach the rope, jump high and grab it, then pull your legs as high as you can and lock into the rope. Continue to pull your legs up high on the rope, lock in, and then stand up. This shifts the majority of the effort to your legs and not your arms. Typically, courses with rope climbs also have many other heavy upper-body obstacles. Occasionally you will see elite athletes invert themselves near the top to kick the bell instead of hitting it with their hands to finish the climb. I encourage you to test both techniques, but I have found that for me, the transition time required to invert and kick the bell takes just as long if not longer. The

J-hook technique.

S-wrap technique.

inversion also increases the possibility of missing the bell or slipping and falling. (Note: In 2016, Spartan Race made the upside down bell kick on the vertical rope climb against the rules due to the danger of falling.)

Sandbags / Bucket Carry / Tire / Other Weighted Movement

The higher you carry the load on a weighted carry, the easier it will be. The important thing is having the requisite strength to explosively lift the sandbag, bucket, or tire to your shoulders initially. Once the weight is on your shoulders, move forward at a quick pace. Try to keep your feet as low to the ground as possible, without tripping, to save energy. This low, fast shuffle will be faster if the terrain is flat. Finally, as you approach the end of the obstacle, plan the dismount of your weight. As you cross the finish line for that obstacle, just let the object fall off your shoulders without breaking stride. There is no use losing seconds when transitioning the bag from your shoulders to the ground.

For especially long versions, you may want to alternate how you carry the load. Switching from shoulder to shoulder and occasionally to a front carry can help distribute the stress on your body. Just be careful not to drop the bucket and spill your sand or gravel. For a bucket carry in front, dig the part of the weight closest to your body into your stomach, resting the edge on the front of your shorts if possible. This will transfer some of the weight to your hips and shorts. When possible always carry the weight on your shoulder instead of using your hands. This will keep your forearms fresh for future obstacles.

For events like a very long double Jerry Can carry, the limiting factor is forearm strength not cardiovascular ability. In this instance, you want to move as fast as possible taking frequent short rests to give your hands a break. I recommend developing a pattern that works for you such as walk as fast as possible for 10-20 steps, put the cans down for four deep breaths and repeat.

American Ninja Warrior competitor and Spartan Pro Team member Rose Wetzel not wasting time by tossing the 50-pound Wreck Bag off her shoulders so she can continue running.

Rope Descent on Inclined Terrain or an Almost Vertical Wall

This technique requires gloves or hand protection and should be approached with caution. I have used this in the past wearing only arm sleeves by pulling them down slightly to cover my palms. To descend as fast as possible safely, approach the rope from the side and step over it with both feet. Reach down and grab the rope with both hands. Assuming you are descending to your right, the rope should be running through your left hand, behind your back, and through your right hand. Next, turn, face the downhill, and jog forward. The friction of the rope between your hands and your back creates bights that will slow you down enough that you can safely reach the bottom.

Evan Perperis setting up his vertical descent technique; notice he is passing other athletes.

Spear Toss

Throwing the spear is a matter of practice. If you never practice it, you will probably be standing in the penalty area doing burpees. The spears used at Spartan Races are easy to make; instructions are provided in chapter 9. Find a method that works best for you, whether it be throwing it like a football with some spin or a straight toss at the target. Most people find it comfortable to grab the spear's center of balance prior to the toss. Wherever you decide to grab it, you should be able to quickly identify that point when approaching the spear. This can be by doing a quick balance test or using your forearm to measure out a distance from the end of the metal tip. Grabbing the spear at the same place every time will ensure your throws are consistent. Also, make sure you aren't standing on the spear's tether; that will cause a guaranteed miss.

Rig Obstacles

These are often the hardest obstacles on a course. Their ability to change, add, or remove hand- and footholds makes for an infinite num-

Platinum Rig sponsored Marco Bédard locking in his feet as he continues to breeze through the Platinum Rig.

ber of variations. The first thing you need to do is look at the obstacle and determine your plan of action. If possible, do this prior to the race. This allows you to attack the obstacle when reaching it and not sit there figuring out the best technique.

When it comes to the first section: Feel free to jump to the second or even third hold before continuing. Most rules only specify that you must not touch the ground, not use the support structure, and touch the last hold in a controlled manner.

A common mistake is trying to use every hold, which is often not necessary. Often one or two grips or footholds can be skipped altogether, especially the more difficult ones like the vertical nunchakus. If the grips are easy, like a bar or a ring, then feel free to use every one for maximum control. As with most obstacles, the faster you move, in a controlled manner, the less grip strength this obstacle will require. Most rigs will end with a bell to mark completion. If allowed you often can kick the bell from two or even three holds out signifying you finished without ever having to make it to the last hold.

Overall, I strongly recommend watching other elite techniques online via Facebook and YouTube prior to trying this obstacle. Then practice it if you can. Even if the race is over and the course is empty, go back and run through the rig a couple of times to get your technique down.

General Rules for All Obstacles

If possible, conduct a recon: This isn't always an option, but having an understanding of what obstacle is coming next will help you understand when and where to conserve energy along with when to empty the tank. Often race websites post details about the course, videos, and pictures of the obstacles online prior to the race. Look at the obstacles, look at the course elevation, and figure out your game plan in your mind. By visualizing how you will conquer each obstacle, you are creating a positive mental image in your brain that can be accessed when you actually reach the obstacles.

"Staring at obstacles will not make them any easier": Use this slogan when determining your plan for conquering obstacles. Very few obstacles require intense analysis to complete. Most of them just require you to attack ferociously and maintain forward movement. Before going into your next race, keep this saying in mind. This will prevent hesitation and continue forward progress. It also helps prevent fear from setting in. Obstacles like World's Toughest Mudder's King of Swingers and The Cliff require jumping from heights above most people's comfort zone. Hesitating just gives your brain time to realize it's a bad decision to jump. Trust me, don't think, just go. It will be mentally easier and allow you to save your mental energy for the race. Also use this technique for conquering obstacles with live electricity, ice-cold water, or tear gas.

Evan Perperis and other World's Toughest Mudder competitors not hesitating by jumping off The Cliff.

"Smooth is fast": If you try to rush through the obstacle above a pace that is comfortable, you will end up burning energy and making mistakes. Moving through the obstacles smoothly, on the other hand, will help you keep that fast pace without even realizing it. Watch videos of elites like Ryan Atkins and Jonathan Albon going through the Platinum Rig. They appear to move through obstacles effortlessly and smoothly, resulting in a fast pace.

Accelerate out of obstacles: Racers often slow down without realizing it as the course continues. As you reach an obstacle, you usually have to slow down to some degree to complete the obstacle. This slowdown is

BattleFrog Pro Team members Corinna Coffin and Lindsay Webster flowing through the Platinum Rig using the smooth-is-fast principle.

often translates to the far side of the obstacle, causing an overall slower pace. (You can often see the same concept in action when road racers navigate turns.) To avoid slowing, make a conscious effort to accelerate back to your normal pace after completing an obstacle. It will save seconds or possibly minutes over the course of a race. The only exception is if you know there is a very difficult obstacle coming up like a rig and want to try to keep a lower heart rate before attacking this extremely challenging obstacle.

Dress for success: Your clothes matter more for obstacle racing than regular racing. Races often see you bear crawling, low crawling, or in other uncomfortable positions. This leaves your knees and elbows sus-

BattleFrog Pro Team member Marco Bédard accelerating out
of an obstacle to attain the fastest time possible.

ceptible to cuts, bruises, and scrapes. If you protect them with clothing,
you'll be able to attack the obstacles with more vigor. At the end of the
next chapter you'll find a detailed explanation of good clothing choices.

Most obstacles are variations on preexisting obstacles: The list of obstacles above does not cover every obstacle you will encounter in your racing. However, it does provide techniques and principles that you can
apply to new obstacles. Finding a obstacle similar to the one you're facing
and applying the established method for success will allow you to complete this new challenge with greater ease.

Work on your weaknesses: If during any of your races you fail an obstacle, then it's time to focus your next round of training. Ideally, you

can find a similar obstacle at either a gym, a local climbing wall, or if necessary one of the permanent obstacle courses that are being built across the country. Practice that obstacle or movement until it becomes second nature. For example, if your weakness is monkey bars and upper-body grip strength, I recommend doing one run a week where you are running 0.25- to 0.5-mile sections and then completing a set of monkey bars. Continue to do this for your entire run, even if it's 8 miles. This will give you the strength and confidence required to know that even when you're exhausted, you can still complete what used to be your weakest obstacle.

Believe in yourself: Nothing will cause you to fail an obstacle like approaching it and thinking, *I can't do this.* Negative thinking like that will cause your grip strength to give out faster and provide an excuse to give up. Always approach the obstacle with the opinion, *I am going to breeze through this obstacles because I am strong and capable.*

Chapter 6

OBSTACLE RACE
SPEED TRAING

Strength & Speed–Ignite—Jordan Smith, Kevin Righi, and Adam Baylor—cross the finish at 2015 OCRWC.

Included in this chapter are several training programs. To determine which one to follow, you need to look at your long-term goals. Obstacle races vary in distance and types of obstacles. To keep things simpler, I chose common distances for races that also align with the four established world championships as of 2015: distances of 5K, 8 miles, 13 miles, and 26-plus miles.

Success in obstacle racing comes from being a fast runner with the ability to complete obstacles. Therefore, these training plans place a heavy emphasis on running. Each day of the week has a specific focus. You should never be running just to run; rather, you should understand what the goal is for that run. The majority of the runs are long slow distance or aerobic runs. Aerobic runs build your aerobic system through many of the methods previously mentioned, including improving your body's ability to process oxygen, nervous system function, strength of heart, quantity of mitochondria, and quantity of capillaries. I firmly believe that most people do not get better at running because they simply don't put in the necessary mileage. That's why most of these plans are higher volume than you would typically find in running magazines. These plans are designed for serious improvement and not just participation. However, if your goal is just participation, completing one of these plans will allow you to coast through your next race with greater ease.

Through personal experimentation and by observing my friends who are athletes, I have found that the body responds best to volume. Every time I PR a 5K time, it's right after I finished marathon season. I still improve my PR despite doing very little speed work. This is because my aerobic system is so large at this point that my body can run at those faster speeds while producing the majority of the energy aerobically. This is especially true for people who are not naturally gifted athletes. If you were one of the people in the middle to bottom of the pack in gym class back in high school, don't worry; there is still hope. I know several people who turned their fitness completely around by using a high-volume approach; they're now getting on the podium at races.

I have many fit co-workers and friends who do not understand how I can keep getting faster year after year. The answer is simple: I increase either quantity of running or intensity of running every year. Constant stress to the system causes adaptation. When the system is not stressed,

BattleFrog Pro Team member Claude Godbout knows the importance of running speed for OCR.

it will not adapt. If you are trying to improve your 5K time, but have never run more than 15 or 20 miles in a week, your body is not developing the required systems to improve. People often follow 5K training plans found in magazines and do not see the improvement they are looking for. If you look at professional 5K runners, though, they are adding mileage at a level comparable to an intermediate or advanced amateur marathon runner—often even higher, with mileage peaks above 100 miles a week.

If you are looking at starting a plan and your goal is to PR, then you need to choose a plan on the outer edges of your capability. When choosing the appropriate fitness plan, the first two or three weeks should look easy and maybe similar to what you're already doing. Afterward the workouts should start to look difficult. After about three weeks there should be one or maybe two workouts a week that make you cringe slightly (you are entering your uncomfortable zone). This is what you want and what your body needs. It means that the workout is difficult enough that your body will be forced to adapt to the stress.

These plans are not meant for someone to go from a couch to an obstacle race. If you're looking for plans that go from couch to completion, you'll have to look into beginner running books or beginner obstacle racing books. I firmly believe that with a moderate amount of fitness and a lot of willpower, you can complete almost any distance race. My first marathon was my longest run at a time when my second-longest run was 12 miles. I do not recommend that, but it shows what's possible with willpower and very little training. I also did my first 40-mile run with my second-longest run being a marathon. The general rule my friends and I would apply is that if I am capable of running distance X, then I am capable of covering distance 2X with a lot of suffering but still making it to the finish line. I may not be able to run all of 2X, but I can complete the distance. I personally have found that this holds true, but be prepared to suffer horribly on race day without proper training.

Due to variations in obstacle races, the average-minutes-per-mile pace can vary widely. I have run 5K obstacle races with 8:30 min/mile splits and others with a 13:30 min/mile splits. This is due to different terrain, difficulty of obstacles, and quantity of obstacles. In order to monitor progress, we need a more controlled method of measuring performance. Therefore, a lot of the information regarding pacing below references road race paces. I encourage using road races as hard workouts to help monitor performance progression.

As with any exercise program, consult a doctor to be sure you are healthy enough to complete the required program. Any changes in your personal exercise regime are at your own risk.

Strength & Speed–ERA crossing Skull Valley at the OCRWC.

Training Chart Terminology

For all paces, I recommend you use the McMillan Running Calculator, which is available online via a simple search. The McMillan Running Calculator is a great resource for determining training paces and race paces; it can help predict performance based on your current level of fitness. If you choose not to use the running calculator, the explanations below will provide a suggested starting point for paces, as well as definitions of the terms you'll find in the training plan charts.

WU: Warm-up. A very comfortable pace; you can easily talk during the run. I encourage you not to even record your pace on warm-ups. Just run a known distance of 1 or 2 miles without looking at your watch. Speed up toward the end of the warm-up, getting closer to your target workout pace. These are required before VO_2max or LT workouts, but they should be done anytime you feel like you want to get the blood moving prior to starting a workout, especially for any race pace, obstacle interval, or race simulation workout.

CD: Cool-down. Cool-down pace is similar to your warm-up pace, but getting slower as you reach the end of your cool-down. It's a very comfortable pace; you can easily talk during the run. I encourage you not to even record your pace on cool-downs. Just run a known distance of 1 or 2 miles without looking at your watch. Cooling down will help move the blood around so you can train hard again sooner.

Easy: Easy pace means running at what feels comfortable for you. If you're running with a group, you should be able to engage in some light conversation. Your easy pace should be consistent each week. For example, if you were running 8:30 miles on Monday for an easy run, you should be running at about the same pace on Friday for an easy run. As the program progresses, it's okay to improve your easy run pace as long as it improves uniformly from week to week. You should not run a 7:15 pace for an easy run on Monday and run at 8:45 min/mile pace on Friday. That means your easy run pace is probably somewhere between these two paces. People are often surprised at how slow their easy run pace is. The point of the easy run is to develop your aerobic system but not destroy your body so you can continue to train the following day. Easy run paces are often between one and two minutes slower than your road marathon pace.

LT: Lactate threshold pace. For simplicity's sake, since most of us do not have access to equipment to determine our actual LT, you can use your 10K road race pace as your LT pace. Another option is to use a recent race result on the McMillan Running Calculator to determine your LT pace.

VO$_2$max: VO$_2$max pace. Again for simplicity, since most of us do not have access to equipment to determine true VO$_2$max, use slightly faster than your 5K road race pace as your VO$_2$max pace. The actual pace is a little closer to your 2-mile pace, but there are very few 2-mile races available to truly test this. All intervals from 400m to 1200m should be at this pace. You should strive for even pacing across all intervals. Therefore, if your intervals start slowing toward the end of the workout, slow down your early intervals on the next workout so they are even splits.

RI: Rest interval. Rest intervals are listed either as a time or as a distance. For example, if it says "½ RI," that means your rest interval is half of your work interval. So, if you ran a 6-minute mile and it listed ½ RI, your rest interval would be 3 minutes. This can be done at a complete standstill, a walk, or a very slow jog; just don't lie down. Rest intervals may also be listed by distance: for example, "400m RI." This means covering that prescribed distance at a very slow jog. The idea is to keep your blood pumping and body in running mode while maintaining a running-like motion. This helps teach the body to jog slowly instead of walking, even when you're tired. If RI is not listed in the plans below, use half of your work interval time or half of your work interval distance for recovery.

RP: Goal road race pace. Race pace is the pace you could run for the distance of your obstacle race if there were no obstacles and it was run on a road. So if you were doing a 5K obstacle race, run RP runs at your 5K road race pace. This is your *goal* race pace, not your current pace. However, when setting a goal race pace, do not be too ambitious. I like to use the general rule that if I can sustain my goal race pace for half the desired race at the beginning of the season, then I believe after a thorough training cycle I can extend that pace over the full distance. For example, if I can run a 1:30 half marathon in my current shape, then in four months I believe I can run a full marathon in 3:00 assuming I put in the required training. This is sometimes a little too ambitious, but it at least gives me a starting point.

X miles + obstacles: This is primarily an obstacle-focused workout but is designed to also improve your aerobic conditioning. The pace should be easy, allowing you to talk to someone without gasping. The emphasis is on completing obstacles with good form and as fast as possible. To do this, find a playground with a stretch of road or track nearby. After a warm-up, run 0.25 mile and complete an obstacle. If you are weak at obstacles, you can increase the frequency of obstacles—say, every 0.1 mile—so you complete more per mile. Repeat until you hit your mileage goal. Once you hit your mileage goal, complete every obstacle in succession one more time. This helps simulate the common setup in obstacle races where you find fewer obstacles in the beginning and an abundance of them right before the finish line.

Strength train: There is a difference between "X miles + Strength Train" and "AM: X miles PM: Strength Train." When the workout is listed as X miles + Strength Train, the run workout and strength training workout are designed to be conducted back-to-back. You choose which to do first based on your weakness: Complete the one you are weakest at first since you will be able to put more effort into that workout. When the workout is listed as AM then PM, it is designed as two separate workouts. Breaking a workout into two separate ones is preferable but sometimes hard due to personal life. Two separate workouts, separated by at least five hours, will allow you to give maximum intensity to both workouts. If you are training for one of the ultra-distance plans, then doing both in one workout may be more beneficial than the AM/PM split. What to train at each strength training routine is listed in a separate chart.

OI: Obstacle intervals. These are repeats designed to spike your heart rate yet still require you to complete obstacles. They are run at a VO_2max pace. For OI, run 400m then complete an obstacle until you hit your target distance. For example, 800m OI has two obstacles, and 1200m OI has three. Obstacles are the ones listed above under "X miles + obstacles."

RS: Race simulation. This is a workout designed to mimic your race. You should be running at race pace (or LT if indicated) for the distance of your race. You should also wear the same clothes you plan to use on race day. Race day hydration, nutrition, and warm-up procedures should also be practiced. This will help you identify any problems ahead of time. If you know what obstacles you will be facing, arrange obstacles in that manner. For example, if you know you are going to have a mile of running and then the first obstacle is three mud pits, followed by 0.25 mile of running and then monkey bars, the beginning of your workout would be 1 mile of running, three standing long jumps at max effort, 0.25 mile of running, and then a set of monkey bars. This prepares you for the race not only physically but also mentally. Setting up your race simulation forces you to study the course, allowing you to crush it on race day.

To help you figure out how to train obstacles, take a look at the list below. Actual obstacles from races are on the left; a suggested equivalent is on the right. Most of us don't have access to a permanent obstacle course, but these replacements can simulate the same motions.

Mud pits = repeated standing long jump: To simulate jumping mud pits, perform the number of standing long jumps that align with the number of mud pits you will be required to clear. It simulates the explosive movement of jumping alternated with the requirement to transition back to running. Options include standing long jump for 5 to 10 yards, then jogging 10 yards, repeated for the length of a football field.

Walls = fence climb: Find a fence similar to the height of a wall you will be required to clear.

Low walls = short fence: Find a fence around chest height and vault over it, placing your hands on top of the fence as you clear it. Repeat two to ten times.

Spear throw + burpees = spear throw + burpees: See the section on building your own training spear in chapter 9. If your environment isn't conducive to spear training, train by doing burpees instead.

Barbed wire = low crawl or roll on the grass or bear crawl: To simulate this obstacle, just crawl or roll on the ground based on your desired completion technique. If you choose to crawl, be sure your pelvis is touching or almost touching the ground to simulate the low height of the wire.

Monkey bars = monkey bars: Traverse the monkey bars until you reach the far side. Since most playground monkey bars are short, turn around and come back. For increased difficulty, add more laps on your monkey bars.

Other hanging-type obstacles = swing set: Traverse the pipe on top of the swing set by hanging from the crossbeam. Move by sliding your hands until you reach the far side. Once you are at the far side, return to the beginning.

Angled Pegboard (like Tough Mudder's The Liberator) or climbing = children's climbing wall: Pull yourself up the wall using only your upper body. Let your legs hang limp so the stress is completely on your upper body.

Peg Board (like Conquer The Gauntlet's Pegatron) = Peg Board. If you have a course that has an actual peg board, the only way to truly get better is to build or buy a pegboard for practice. The technique requires repetition, which is very hard to simulate without actually practicing the obstacle. Sandbag carry = sandbag carry: Pick up the sandbag and run around a designated point on the ground. For added difficulty, go up a nearby hill.

Bucket carry = bucket carry: Pick up the bucket using a shoulder carry or by carrying it in front of your body. Most buckets at events are missing the handles, so stay away from the handle carry. Carry the bucket around a designated point or up a hill. Try to mimic the length of the obstacle at the race you'll be attending by either doing one long carry or breaking it up into different sets.

Platinum Rig = "Aluminum Rig": To practice a version of this obstacle in training, you can set up what I refer to as the Aluminum Rig. Since most of us cannot afford a Platinum Rig in our house, I buy attachments I can carry to the gym, such as rings, rock rings (the hanging climbing holds), and various-sized ropes. These can be hung up on a playground set of monkey bars or the crossbeam of a pulley machine in the gym. By traversing back and forth, you get used to changing grips and changing holds while moving side-to-side.

Other Notes

Using Trails

Any easy run or LT run can be replaced with trail running if so desired. It is recommended that you do at least one trail run a week to help you get used to the awkward footing and uneven terrain associated with trail running. I did not specifically put any trail runs in the training plans, because athletes having varying degrees of access to trails. For trail runs, take the time it would take you to finish the equivalent road run and run along the trail for that amount of time. For example, if an 8-mile run takes you 64 minutes, you could replace it with a trail run of 64 minutes. Often trails have spotty GPS coverage, so using a time-based approach may work better.

Hill Work

If you know you're going to be doing a race with lots of hills, then definitely add in specific hill work. If you're a fan of Spartan Races, which take place at a ski mountain, or racing in Cincinnati at the site of Mud Guts & Glory, this is crucial. Use hill work to replace one of your easy days using one of these options: Find a very hilly route, find one big hill and continue to run up and down it, or run on a treadmill with an elevated surface.

Adding in Cross-Training Machines

If you'd like more variety in training, want more volume, or just don't feel like training in inclement weather, you can always add in cardio machines or other types of cross-training. With the exception of the Stair-Master and inclined treadmill, it's better to add these to your weekly mileage rather than replacing your runs with cross-training. If you climb for twenty-four minutes, for example, that doesn't provide the same physiological benefits twenty-four minutes of running provides for obstacle racing. Overall, the more closely the movement mimics the actions performed in obstacle racing, the better. If available, try adding these cross-training options:

Upper-Body Cross-Training

These options are great to add to your routine during the off-season, after running during race season, or after lifting for additional cardiovascular benefit. They're also good when you're recovering from lower-body injuries without losing all your cardiovascular gains.

Climbing: Climbing will enhance grip strength and mimic many of the motions required for obstacles. If upper-body strength is your weakness, climbing can be a great tool to increasing grip strength.

VersaClimber: The VersaClimber is great for adding endurance to your upper body.

Jacob's Ladder: Also great for adding endurance to your upper body.

Erg (rowing machine): The erg is another great option that provides a total body workout. By working your forearms, arms, back, and legs, this machine should be a go-to option for total body cross-training.

Lower-Body Cross-Training

These cross-training options for the lower body can replace running. For most, work out for the same amount of time you were planning on running.

StairMaster: This machine is great for preparing for courses with large elevation gains. Preferably, use one of the machines with actual rotating stairs and not just the pedals that move up and down. Holding on to the sides is okay for stability, but you should not be supporting your weight with the bars. I recommend just resting your wrists on the bars for stability instead of actually placing your hands there to avoid the desire to lean.

Treadmill with incline up to 10 percent: This machine is also great for preparing for courses with large elevation gains. It will require you slow considerably from your normal running pace.

Cycling: Indoor and outdoor cycling is great exercise when done with the proper intensity. Typically substitute 10 minutes of cycling for 1 mile of running. While cycling, maintain high revolutions per minute (RPMs) to stress the aerobic system. Your RPMs should be between 80 and 95, in order to stress your cardiovascular system. If you cycle at lower RPMs, you will be stressing muscle strength over your aerobic system.

The elliptical is not an equivalent replacement for running. It's only good for a couple of uses. The first is if you are recovering from an injury. The machine is low-impact, which will help you out while providing some cardiovascular benefit. The second use is if you're hitting all your mileage goals but still want to add cardiovascular activity without putting more stress on your joints. In general, though, do not use the elliptical as a replacement for running. Many people like it because it's easy—and the reason it's easy is that it doesn't require the same intensity level. If you are using the elliptical to replace running, try to maintain close to your normal running heart rate while on the machine, or a similar rate of perceived exertion.

Strength Training for the Workout Plans

The programs listed below are designed for a two-times-a-week strength routine (three if you count the obstacles + miles workouts). If you are a great runner but have trouble with the obstacles, you can add in more strength training days using the three-times-a-week or four-times-a-week program. For the three- or four-times-a-week strength routines, either add the strength training days on top of the schedule or replace the lowest-mileage day with another strength training session. Do not add strength routines on your rest days. The rest days are there to ensure you adapt from the stress of exercise.

Your strength sessions need to have the following three aspects: specificity, progressive and enjoyable. Specificity means it should mimic movements of OCR or develop muscles used for OCR. Progressive means it should get harder as you get better so you continue to improve. Finally, having a strength routine that is enjoyable is important because people tend to perform the best when they have a routine they enjoy, so you are encouraged to add to or modify these strength training routines. However, this provides a strong starting point to ensure you work the important muscles for obstacle racing without neglecting entire body parts.

Additional strength days can be added or replace the ones in your training schedule by attending things like an indoor rock climbing gym, a obstacle course training center or a ninja warrior training gym. These are the most specific type of training available and are best for improvement but I hesitate to prescribe them as the workout for each week because most people do not have access to these awesome facilities. MudRunGuide.com often has the latest and greatest information on the availability of OCR and ninja specific gyms in your area.

Notes for the workouts:

Recommend using Fat Gripz for all sets.

Add in intensity-boosting methods as needed, as explained in chapter 7.

2-Day:

• *Add a fourth set of each exercise as needed and as your body progresses along the program.*

•*If training at an OCR/Ninja Warrior Gym, replace Strength Session 1 or add it as your Friday PM workout*

3-Day:

• *Add a fourth set of each exercise as needed and as your body progresses along the program.*

• *If using this strength-training regime, train on Tuesday, Thursday and Friday. If training at an OCR/Ninja Warrior Gym, replace Strength Session 1 or 3 or add it in the evening of your Saturday workout.*

4-Day: -

• *If using this training split have your strength sessions occur on Tuesday, Thursday, Friday and Saturday. If training at a OCR/Ninja gym replace Strength Session 1,2 or 3 with the OCR specific work.*

Two-Day-a-Week Strength Training Regimen

Strength Train 1: Legs, Forearms, and Chest	Strength Train 2: Back and Arms
3 sets of squats	5 sets of rig work (using the cross-beam of a pulley station to build your own rig)
3 sets of walking weighted lunges (to maximize stress on legs use a barbell, or to emphasize grip strength use dumbbells)	3 sets of muscle ups max reps (if can't do muscle ups, do 3 sets of pull-ups immediately followed by dips)
3 sets of standing shoulder press	3 sets of towel pull-ups max reps (if can't hold on with both hands on towel, use one hand on bar and one hand on towel)
3 sets of bench press	3 sets of wide-arm pull-ups max reps (palms facing away, the more awkward the grip, the better, e.g., door-frame pull-ups, pull-ups on the square support of Smith machine)
3 sets of drop set farmer's walk (1st set is one walk, 2nd set is two walks, 3rd set is three walks. Use decreasing weight for the sets with multiple walks.)	3 sets of 1 min extended arm hang (increase time as you become more proficient)
3 sets of forearm curls	3 sets of weighted dips max reps (increase weight once you can do more than 10)
3 sets of reverse forearm curls	3 sets of alternating dumbbell curls
3 sets of crunches	3 sets of standing rope triceps extension (hold on to rope, not plastic balls at end of rope or bring your own rope/chain to use as a handle)
• *May need to go light on legs if your running volume is high.*	3 sets of leg raises
	• *Max reps means most amount of reps you can do across all three sets. E.g., your sets of pull-ups should look like 10, 10, 10 and not 17, 10, 6. Once you get even reps on all sets, add an additional rep to each set.*

Three-Day-a-Week Strength Training Regimen

Day 1: Push and Quads	Day 2: Pull	Day 3: Shoulders, Forearms, and Hamstrings
3 sets of squats	3 sets of deadlifts	3 sets of walking weighted lunges (use a barbell with weight to emphasize leg muscles, or dumbbells to emphasize grip strength)
3 sets of bench press	5 sets of rig work (using the crossbeam of the pulley station build your own rig)	3 sets of standing shoulder press
3 sets of weighted dips max reps (increase weight once you can do more than 10)	3 sets of muscle ups max reps (if can't do muscle ups, do 3 sets of pull-ups immediately followed by dips) or 3 sets of one arm counter-weighted pull-ups	3 sets of lateral raises
3 sets of overhead triceps extension (preferably use single rope or single bar handle)	3 sets of towel pull-ups max reps (if can't hold on with both hands on towel, use one hand on bar and one hand on towel)	3 sets of ab wheel
3 sets of farmer's walk	3 sets of wide-arm pull-ups max reps (the more awkward the grip, the better, e.g., doorframe pull-ups, pull-ups on the square support of Smith machine)	3 sets of leg raises
3 sets of forearm curls (can be replaced if your gym has forearm-specific machines)	3 sets of 1 min extended arm hang (increase time as you become more proficient)	3 sets of drop set farmer's walk (1st set is one walk, 2nd set is two walks, 3rd set is three walks; use less weight for sets with multiple walks)
3 sets of reverse forearm curls	3 sets of standing barbell curls	3 sets of forearm curls (can be replaced if your gym has forearm-specific machines)
3 sets of crunches	3 sets of alternating dumbbell curls	3 sets of reverse forearm curls
• May need to go light on legs if your running volume is high.	• May need to go light on deadlifts if it causes excessive soreness in your lower back and hamstrings, resulting in poor running performance.	• May need to go light on legs if your running volume is high.

Four-Day-a-Week Strength Training Regimen

Day 1: Chest, Abs, and Forearms	Day 2: Arms and Forearms	Day 3: Shoulders and Abs	Day 4: Back and Forearms
3 sets of squats	3 sets of one arm counter-weighted pull-ups	3 sets of walking weighted lunges (use barbell with weight to emphasize legs, or dumbbells to emphasize grip strength)	3 sets of deadlifts
3 sets of bench press	3 sets of weighted dips max reps (increase weight once you can do more than 10)	3 sets of standing shoulder press	5 sets of rig work (using the crossbeam of the pulley station to build your own rig)
3 sets of inclined dumbbell press	3 sets of cable overhead triceps extension (preferably use single rope or single bar handle)	3 sets of lateral raises	3 sets of muscle ups max reps (if can't do muscle ups, do 3 sets of pull-ups immediately followed by dips)
3 sets of cable fly	3 sets of standing rope triceps extension (grab rope, not plastic ball at end)	3 sets of single-arm front plate raise (use bumper plate if available to make grip more awkward)	3 sets of towel pull-ups max reps (if can't hold on with both hands on towel, use one hand on bar and one hand on towel)
3 sets of crunches	3 sets of standing barbell curls	3 sets of ab wheel	3 sets of wide-arm pull-ups max reps (the more awkward the grip, the better, ex. doorframe pull-ups, pull-ups on the square support of Smith machine)
3 sets of fitness ball crunches	3 sets of alternating dumbbell curls	3 sets of leg raises	3 sets of bent-over row
3 sets of farmer's walk	3 sets of 1 min extended arm hang (increase time as you become more proficient)	3 sets of drop set farmer's walk (1st set is one walk, 2nd set is two walks, 3rd set is three walks; use less weight for sets with multiple walks)	3 sets of 1 min extended arm hang (increase time as you become more proficient)
3 sets of forearm curls (can be replaced if your gym has forearm-specific machines)		*• May need to go light on legs if your running volume is high.*	3 sets of forearm curls (can be replaced if your gym has forearm-specific machines)
3 sets of reverse forearm curls			3 sets of reverse forearm curls
• May need to go light on legs if your running volume is high.			*• May need to go light on deadlifts if it causes excessive soreness in your lower back and hamstrings, resulting in poor running performance.*

8-Week Easy 5K Training Plan for a PR (Peaking at 21 Miles a Week)

Week	Sunday	Monday	Tuesday	Weds.	Thursday	Friday	Saturday	Total Mileage
1	REST	2 mi easy + obstacles	am: 1 mi WU 4x400m VO$_2$max (2 min RI) 1 mi CD pm: Strength Train 1	REST	2 mi easy + Strength Train 2	REST	3 mi easy	10
2	REST	3 mi easy + obstacles	am: 1 mi WU 4x800m VO$_2$max (2 min RI) 1 mi CD pm: Strength Train 1	REST	3 mi easy + Strength Train 2	REST	3 mi easy	13
3	REST	3 mi easy + obstacles	am: 1 mi WU 2x1mi RP (2 min RI) 1 mi CD pm: Strength Train 1	REST	2 mi easy + Strength Train 2	1 mi WU 4x800m VO$_2$max (2 min RI) 1 mi CD	3 mi easy	16
4	REST	3 mi easy + obstacles	am: 1 mi WU 2x400m, 2x800m, 1x1200m VO$_2$max (400m RI) 1 mi CD pm: Strength Train 1	REST	3 mi easy + Strength Train 2	4 mi easy	3 mi RS	18

(continued from previous page)

Week	Sunday	Monday	Tuesday	Weds.	Thursday	Friday	Saturday	Total Mileage
5	REST	3 mi easy + obstacles	am: 1 mi WU 6x800m OI (2 min RI) 1 mi CD pm: Strength Train 1	REST	3 mi easy + Strength Train 2	5 mi easy	0.5 mi WU 2 mi LT 0.5 mi CD	19
6	REST	3 mi easy + obstacles	1 mi WU 4x200m w/ 200m RI, 4x400m w/ 400m RI VO$_2$max 1 mi CD pm: Strength Train 1	REST	3 mi easy + Strength Train 2	1 mi WU 3 mi RS 1 mi CD	5 mi easy	21
7	REST	3 mi easy + obstacles	am: 1 mi WU 2x1200m VO$_2$max (2 min RI) 1 mi CD pm: Strength Train 1	REST	3 mi easy + Strength Train 2	1 mi WU 4x400m RP (2 min RI) 1 mi CD	4 mi easy	17
8	REST	1 mi WU 2x800 OI (3 min RI) 1 mi CD	Rest	3 mi easy	REST	REST	OCR	6 + Race

8-Week Medium 5K Training Plan for a PR (Peaking at 30 Miles a Week)

Week	Sunday	Monday	Tuesday	Weds.	Thursday	Friday	Saturday	Total Mileage
1	REST	3 mi easy + obstacles	am: 1 mi WU 4x800m VO_2max (2 min RI) 1 mi CD pm: Strength Train 1	REST	3 mi easy + Strength Train 2	3 mi easy	1 mi WU 2 mi LT Pace 1 mi CD	17
2	REST	3 mi easy + obstacles	am: 1 mi WU 4x800m VO_2max (1.5 min RI) 1 mi CD pm: Strength Train 1	REST	3 mi easy + Strength Train 2	4 mi easy	5 mi easy	19
3	REST	4 mi easy + obstacles	am: 1 mi WU 3x1200m VO_2max (1.5 min RI) 1 mi CD pm: Strength Train 1	REST	4 mi easy + Strength Train 2	5 mi easy	1 mi WU 3 mi RS 1 mi CD	22
4	REST	6 mi easy + obstacles	am: 1 mi WU 3x1mi RP (1.5 min RI) 1 mi CD pm: Strength Train 1	REST	5 mi easy + Strength Train 2	4 mi easy	1 mi WU 3 mi LT Pace 1 mi CD	25

(continued from previous page)

Week	Sunday	Monday	Tuesday	Weds.	Thursday	Friday	Saturday	Total Mileage
5	REST	6 mi easy + obstacles	am: 1 mi WU 8x800m OI (1.5 min RI) 1 mi CD pm: Strength Train 1	REST	am: 6 mi easy pm: Strength Train 2	3 mi easy	1 mi WU 3 mi RS 1 mi CD	26
6	REST	6 mi easy + obstacles	am: 1 mi WU 3x1mi RP (1 min RI) 1 mi CD pm: Strength Train 1	REST	am: 6 mi easy pm: Strength Train 2	5 mi easy	1 mi WU 3x2 mi LT Pace (4 min RI) 1 mi CD	30
7	REST	6 mi easy + obstacles	am: 1 mi WU 3x1200m VO_2max (2 min RI) 1 mi CD pm: Strength Train 1	REST	5 mi easy	3 mi easy	2 mi LT + Strength Train 2	20
8	REST	1 mi WU 4x800 VO_2max (3 min RI) 1 mi CD	REST	4 mi easy + obstacles	very easy 2 mi	REST	OCR	10 + Race

8-Week Hard 5K Training Plan for a PR (Peaking at 40 Miles a Week)

Week	Sunday	Monday	Tuesday	Weds.	Thursday	Friday	Saturday	Total Mileage
1	REST	6 mi easy + obstacles	am: 1 mi WU 4x800m VO$_2$max (2 min RI) 1 mi CD pm: Strength Train 1	REST	am: 6 mi easy pm: Strength Train 2	4 mi easy	1 mi WU 2 mi LT Pace 1 mi CD	24
2	REST	6 mi easy + obstacles	am: 1 mi WU 6x800m VO$_2$max (1.5 min RI) 1 mi CD pm: Strength Train 1	REST	am: 6 mi easy pm: Strength Train 2	6 mi easy	1 mi WU 3 mi LT Pace 1 mi CD	28
3	REST	7 mi easy + obstacles	am: 1 mi WU 4x200m w/ 200m RI, 4x400m w/ 400m RI, 4x200m w/ 200m RI 1 mi CD pm: Strength Train 1	REST	am: 7 mi easy pm: Strength Train 2	6 mi easy	1 mi WU 3 mi RS 1 mi CD	31
4	REST	8 mi easy + obstacles	am: 1 mi WU 6x800m OI (1 min RI) 1 mi CD pm: Strength Train 1	REST	am: 8 mi easy pm: Strength Train 2	5 mi easy	1 mi WU 2x2 mi LT Pace (3 min RI) 1 mi CD	32

(continued from previous page)

Week	Sunday	Monday	Tuesday	Weds.	Thursday	Friday	Saturday	Total Mileage
5	REST	8 mi easy + obsta-cles	am: 1 mi WU 4x800m VO$_2$max (1 min RI) then 4x800m OI (1 min RI) 1 mi CD pm: Strength Train 1	REST	am: 8 mi easy pm: Strength Train 2	5 mi easy	1 mi WU 3x2 mi LT Pace (3 min RI) 1 mi CD	35
6	REST	8 mi easy + obsta-cles	am: 1.5 mi WU 3 mile RS 1.5 mi CD pm: Strength Train 1	REST	am: 10 mi easy pm: Strength Train 2	8 mi easy	1 mi WU 3x2 mi LT pace (2 min RI) 1 mi CD	40
7	REST	8 mi easy + obsta-cles	am: 1 mi WU 4x1200m RP (2 min RI) 1 mi CD pm: Strength Train 1	REST	am: 8 mi easy pm: Strength Train 2	4 mi easy	1 mi WU 3 mi LT 1 mi CD	30
8	REST	1 mi WU 4x800 RP (3 min RI) 1 mi CD	6 mi easy + obstacles	4 mi easy	REST	REST	OCR	14 + Race

8-Week Easy 8-Mile Training Plan for a PR (Peaking at 25 Miles a Week)

Week	Sunday	Monday	Tuesday	Weds	Thursday	Friday	Saturday	Total Mileage
1	REST	2 mi easy + obstacles	3 mi easy + Strength Train 1	REST	2 mi easy+ Strength Train 2	2 mi easy	1 mi WU 4x400m VO$_2$max (2 min RI) 1 mi CD	12
2	REST	3 mi easy + obstacles	1 mi WU 4x800m VO$_2$max (2 min RI) 1 mi CD	REST	3 mi easy+ Strength Train 2	2 mi easy	4 mi easy + Strength Train 1	16
3	REST	3 mi easy + obstacles	1 mi WU 2x400, 2x800, 1x1200 w/ 400m RI 1 mi CD	REST	3 mi easy+ Strength Train 2	4 mi easy	1 mi WU 2x1mi at LT Pace (½ time RI) 1 mi CD + Strength Train 1	19
4	REST	4 mi easy + obstacles	1 mi WU 6x800m OI (2 min RI) 1 mi CD	REST	3 mi easy + Strength Train 2	4 mi easy	2 mi RS + Strength Train 1	18
5	REST	4 mi easy + obstacles	1 mi WU 3x1200m VO$_2$max w/ 400m RI 1 mi CD	REST	3 mi easy + Strength Train 2	5 mi easy	1 mi WU 2x1.5mi LT Pace (2 min RI) 1 mi CD + Strength Train 1	22
6	REST	4 mi easy + obstacles	1 mi WU 6x800m OI (2 min RI) 1 mi CD	REST	3 mi easy+ Strength Train 2	7 mi easy	1 mi WU 2x2mi LT Pace (3 min RI) 1 mi CD + Strength Train 1	25
7	REST	3 mi easy + obstacles	1 mi WU 4x800m VO$_2$max (2 min RI) 1 mi CD	REST	3 mi easy + Strength Train 2	4 mi easy	1 mi WU 2x1mi LT (2 min RI) 1 mi CD + Strength Train 1	18
8	REST	1 mi WU 2x800 RP (3 min RI) 1 mi CD	4 mi easy	3 mi easy	REST	REST	OCR	10 + Race

8-Week Medium 8-Mile Training Plan for a PR (Peaking at 33 Miles a Week)

Week	Sunday	Monday	Tuesday	Weds	Thursday	Friday	Saturday	Total Mileage
Week 1	REST	3 mi easy + obstacles	am: 1 mi WU 4x800m VO$_2$max (2 min RI) 1 mi CD pm: Strength Train 1	REST	4 mi easy + Strength Train 2	3 mi easy	1 mi WU 2x1mi LT Pace (2 min RI) 1 mi CD	18
Week 2	REST	4 mi easy + obstacles	am: 1 mi WU 4x800m OI (2 min RI) 1 mi CD pm: Strength Train 1	REST	4 mi easy + Strength Train 2	4 mi easy	1.5 mi WU 2x1mi LT Pace (2 min RI) 1.5 mi CD	21
Week 3	REST	4 mi easy	am: 1 mi WU 4x1200m VO$_2$max (1.5 min RI) 1 mi CD pm: Strength Train 1	REST	4 mi easy + Strength Train 2	5 mi easy	1 mi WU 3x1mi LT Pace (2 min RI) 1 mi CD	23
Week 4	rest	6 mi easy + obstacles	am: 1 mi WU 4x1200m OI (1.5 min RI) 1 mi CD pm: Strength Train 1	REST	5 mi easy + Strength Train 2	4 mi easy	1 mi WU 2x1.5mi LT Pace (2 min RI) 1 mi CD	25

(continued on next page)

(continued from previous page)

Week	Sunday	Monday	Tuesday	Weds	Thursday	Friday	Saturday	Total Mileage
Week 5	rest	7 mi easy + obstacles	am: 1 mi WU 4x1200m RP (1.5 min RI) 1 mi CD pm: Strength Train 1	REST	6 mi easy + Strength Train 2	3 mi easy	1 mi WU 2x2mi LT Pace RS (3 min RI) 1 mi CD	27
Week 6	rest	7 mi easy + obstacles	am: 1 mi WU 2x400, 2x800, 1x1200, 1x800, 1x400 (400m RI) 1 mi CD pm: Strength Train 1	REST	8 mi easy + Strength Train 2	4 mi easy	2 mi WU 1.5 mi, 1.25 mi, 1 mi, 0.75mi, 0.5 mi LT (RI = ½ work interval) 1 mi CD	33
Week 7	rest	6 mi easy + obstacles	am: 1 mi WU 4x1200m OI (2 min RI) 1 mi CD pm: Strength Train 1	REST	6 mi easy + Strength Train 2	3 mi easy	2 mi LT	22
Week 8	REST	1 mi WU 3x1200 VO$_2$max (3 min RI) 1 mi CD	Rest	4 mi easy	very easy jog 2 miles	Rest	OCR	11 + Race

8-Week Hard 8-Mile Training Plan for a PR (Peaking at 40 Miles a Week)

Week	Sunday	Monday	Tuesday	Weds	Thursday	Friday	Saturday	Total Mileage
1	REST	6 mi easy + obstacles	am: 1 mi WU 4x800m VO$_2$max (2 min RI) 1 mi CD pm: Strength Train 1	REST	6 mi easy	4 mi easy + Strength Train 2	1 mi WU 2 mi LT Pace 1 mi CD	24
2	REST	6 mi easy + obstacles	am: 1 mi WU 3x1200m VO$_2$max (1 min RI) 1 mi CD pm: Strength Train 1	REST	6 mi easy	am: 6 mi easy pm: Strength Train 2	1 mi WU 3x1mi LT (3 min RI) 1 mi CD	28
3	REST	7 mi easy + obstacles	am: 1 mi WU 4x1200m OI (1.5 min RI) 1 mi CD pm: Strength Train 1	REST	7 mi easy	am: 6 mi easy pm: Strength Train 2	1 mi WU 3 mi RS 1 mi CD	28
4	REST	8 mi easy + obstacles	am: 1 mi WU 2x400, 2x800, 2x1200 VO$_2$max w/ 400m RI 1 mi CD pm: Strength Train 1	REST	8 mi easy	5 mi easy+ Strength Train 2	1 mi WU 2x2mi LT pace (2.5 min RI) 1 mi CD	33

(continued on next page)

(continued from previous page)

Week	Sunday	Monday	Tuesday	Weds	Thursday	Friday	Saturday	Total Mileage
5	REST	6 mi easy + obstacles	am: 1 mi WU 3x1200m VO$_2$max (1 min RI), 3x1200 OI (2 min RI) 1 mi CD pm: Strength Train 1	REST	10 mi easy	5 mi easy+ Strength Train 2	1 mi WU 2 mi, 1.5 mi, 1 mi, 0.5 mi LT pace (½ RI) 1 mi CD	35
6	REST	8 mi easy + obstacles	am: 1 mi WU 2x400, 2x800, 2x1200, 1x800, 1x400 VO$_2$max w/ 400m RI 1 mi CD pm: Strength Train 1	REST	12 mi easy	6 mi easy pm: Strength Train 2	1 mi WU 2x2mi LT (2 min RI) 1 mi CD	40
7	REST	8 mi easy + obstacles	am: 1 mi WU 4x1200m OI (1.5 min RI) 1 mi CD pm: Strength Train 1	REST	8 mi easy	4 mi easy+ Strength Train 2	1 mi WU 3 mi LT 1 mi CD	28
8	REST	1 mi WU 4x800 VO$_2$max (3 min RI) 1 mi CD	3 mi easy + obstacles	5 mi easy	REST	REST	OCR	12 + Race

12-Week Easy 13-Mile Training Plan for a PR (Peaking at 28 Miles a Week)

Week	Sunday	Monday	Tuesday	Weds	Thursday	Friday	Saturday	Total Mileage
1	REST	3 mi easy + obstacles	4 mi easy + Strength Train 1	REST	4 mi easy + Strength Train 2	REST	5 mi easy	16
2	REST	4 mi easy + obstacles	4 mi easy + Strength Train	REST	5 mi easy + Strength Train 2	REST	6 mi easy	19
3	REST	5 mi easy + obstacles	3 mi RP + Strength Train	REST	4 mi easy+ Strength Train 2	3 mi easy	8 mi easy	23
4	REST	5 mi easy + obstacles	am: 4 mi RP pm: Strength Train	REST	3 mi easy+ Strength Train 2	3 mi easy	5 mi easy	20
5	REST	5 mi easy + obstacles	am: 1 mi WU 2x1mi LT (2 min RI) 1 mi CD pm: Strength Train 1	REST	5 mi easy+ Strength Train 2	REST	9 mi easy	23
6	REST	3 mi easy + obstacles	am: 1 mi WU 2x1mi LT (1.5 min RI) 1 mi CD pm: Strength Train 1	REST	am: 1 mi WU 2x400, 2x800, 1x1200 VO$_2$max (½ RI time) 1mi CD pm:Strength Train 2	3 mi easy	11 mi easy	25

(continued on next page)

(continued from previous page)

Week	Sunday	Monday	Tuesday	Weds	Thursday	Friday	Saturday	Total Mileage
7	REST	3 mi easy + obstacles	am: 1 mi WU 3x1mi LT (2 min RI) 1 mi CD pm: Strength Train 1	REST	5 mi easy+ Strength Train 2	REST	8 mi easy	21
8	REST	3 mi easy + obstacles	am: 1 mi WU 1.5 mi, 1 mi, 0.5 mi (½ time RI) 1 mi CD pm: Strength Train 1	REST	3 mi easy+ Strength Train 2	3 mi easy	11 mi easy	25
9	REST	3 mi easy + obstacles	am: 6 mi RP pm: Strength Train 1	REST	3 mi easy+ Strength Train 2	3 mi easy	13 mi easy	28
10	REST	3 mi easy + obstacles	am: 1 mi WU 2x2mi LT pace (4 min RI) 1 mi CD pm: Strength Train 1	REST	1 mi WU 6x800 OI (½ RI) 1 m CD Strength Train 2	4 mi easy	10 mi easy	28
11	REST	5 mi easy + obstacles	3 mi easy	REST	3 mi easy	REST	7 mi easy	18
12	REST	4 mi easy	4 mi easy + Obstacles	3 mi easy	REST	REST	OCR	11 + Race

12-Week Medium 13-Mile Training Plan for a PR (Peaking at 35 Miles a Week)

Week	Sunday	Monday	Tuesday	Weds	Thursday	Friday	Saturday	Total Mileage
1	REST	4 mi easy+ obstacles	1 mi WU 2 mi RP 1 mi CD + Strength Train 1	REST	5 mi easy + Strength Train 2	REST	6 mi easy	19
2	REST	4 mi easy+ obstacles	am: 1 mi WU 4 mi RS 1 mi CD pm: Strength Train 1	REST	3 mi easy + Strength Train 2	3 mi easy	7 mi easy	23
3	REST	5 mi easy+ obstacles	am: 2 mi WU 3x1mi LT (2 min RI) 1 mi CD pm: Strength Train 1	REST	4 mi easy+ Strength Train 2	3 mi easy	8 mi easy	26
4	REST	6 mi easy+ obstacles	am: 4 mi RP pm: Strength Train 1	REST	am: 1 mi WU 6x800 of OI (2 min RI) 1 mi CD pm: Strength Train 2	4 mi easy	9 mi easy	28
5	REST	6 mi easy+ obstacles	am: 1 mi WU 4x1mi LT (2 min RI) 1 mi CD pm: Strength Train 1	REST	4 mi easy+ Strength Train 2	4 mi easy	10 mi easy	30
6	REST	4 mi easy+ obstacles	am: 1 mi WU 5 mi RP 1 mi CD pm: Strength Train 1	REST	6 mi easy+ Strength Train 2	4 mi easy	11 mi easy	32

(continued on next page)

139

(continued from previous page)

Week	Sunday	Monday	Tuesday	Weds	Thursday	Friday	Saturday	Total Mileage
7	REST	6 mi easy+ obstacles	6 mi easy + Strength Train 1	REST	am: 1 mi WU 2x400, 2x800, 2x1200 VO_2max 1 mi CD (1 min RI) pm: Strength Train 2	6 mi easy	12 mi easy	35
8	REST	5 mi easy+ obstacles	am: 1 mi WU 6 mi RS 1 mi CD pm: Strength Train 1	REST	4 mi easy+ Strength Train 2	3 mi easy	10 mi easy	30
9	REST	6 mi easy+ obstacles	am: 1 mi WU 7 mi RP 1 mi CD pm: Strength Train 1	REST	1 mi WU 6x800 VO_2max 1 mi CD (1 min RI) + Strength Train 2	4 mi easy	12 mi easy	36
10	REST	5 mi easy+ obstacles	am: 1 mi WU 6 mi RP 1 mi CD pm: Strength Train 1	REST	4 mi easy + Strength Train 2	3 mi easy	11 mi easy	32
11	REST	6 mi easy+ obstacles	6 mi easy	REST	1 mi WU 2x400, 2x800, 2x1200 (RI = ½ work interval time) VO_2max 1mi CD	REST	8 mi easy	25
12	REST	5 mi easy+ obstacles	4 mi easy	3 mi easy	REST	REST	OCR	12 + Race

12-Week Hard 13-Mile Training Plan for a PR (Peaking at 45 Miles a Week)

Week	Sunday	Monday	Tuesday	Weds	Thursday	Friday	Saturday	Total Mileage
1	REST	5 mi easy + obstacles	5 mi easy + Strength Train 1	REST	5 mi easy + Strength Train 2	4 mi easy	6 mi easy	25
2	REST	6 mi easy+ obstacles	am: 1 mi WU 4x1mi LT (2 min RI) 1 mi CD pm: Strength Train 2	REST	6 mi easy	4 mi easy + Strength Train 2	8 mi easy	30
3	REST	7 mi easy+ obstacles	am: 1 mi WU 5x1mi LT (2 min RI) 1 mi CD pm: Strength Train 1	REST	1 mi WU 8x800 VO$_2$max (1 min RI) 1 mi CD	5 mi easy+ Strength Train 2	8 mi easy	33
4	REST	7 mi easy+ obstacles	am: 1 mi WU 5 mi RS 1 mi CD pm: Strength Train 1	REST	8 mi easy	6 mi easy +Strength Train 2	9 mi easy	37
5	REST	8 mi easy+ obstacles	am: 2 mi WU 6x1mi LT (2 min RI) 1 mi CD pm: Strength Train 1	REST	am: 1.5 mi WU 2x400, 2x800, 2x1200 VO$_2$max 1 mi CD (400m RI) pm: Strength Train 2	8 mi easy	10 mi easy	42
6	REST	9 mi easy+ obstacles	am: 2 mi WU 8x800 OI (1.5 min) 2 mi CD pm: Strength Train 1	REST	am: 10 mi easy pm: Strength Train 2	7 mi easy	11 mi easy	45

(continued on nexrt page)

(continued from previous page)

Week	Sunday	Monday	Tuesday	Weds	Thursday	Friday	Saturday	Total Mileage
7	REST	6 mi easy+ obstacles	am: 1 mi WU 5 mi RP 1 mi CD pm: Strength Train 1	REST	am: 1 mi WU 2x400, 2x800, 2x1200, 1x800, 1x400 VO_2max 1 mi CD (400m RI) pm: Strength Train 2	6 mi easy	12 mi easy	39
8	REST	10 mi easy+ obstacles	6 mi easy + Strength Train 1	REST	am: 9 mi easy pm: Strength Train 2	7 mi easy	10 mi easy	42
9	REST	6 mi easy+ obstacles	am: 1 mi WU 7 mi RS 1 mi CD pm: Strength Train 1	REST	am: 10 mi easy pm: Strength Train 2	8 mi easy	12 mi easy	45
10	REST	6 mi easy+ obstacles	1 mi WU 4x 1mi LT (1 min RI) 1 mi CD	REST	am: 2 mi WU 8x800 OI (1 min RI) 2 mi CD pm: Strength Train 2	7 mi easy	11 mi easy	38
11	REST	5 mi easy+ obstacles	am: 1 mi WU 4 mi RP 1 mi CD pm: Strength Train 1	REST	am: 2 mi WU 6x800m VO_2max (1 min RI) 2 mi CD pm: Strength Train 2	5 mi easy	8 mi easy	31
12	REST	6 mi easy+ obstacles	5 mi easy	4 mi easy	REST	REST	OCR	15 + Race

16-Week Easy 26-Plus-Mile / Ultra Plan
(Peaking at 38 Miles a Week)

Good for training for 25 to 40 miles at World's Toughest Mudder or finishing an Ultra Beast.

Week	Sunday	Monday	Tuesday	Weds	Thursday	Friday	Saturday	Total Mileage
1	REST	4 mi easy + obstacles	3 mi easy + Strength Train 1	REST	3 mi easy + Strength Train 2	REST	8 mi easy	18
2	REST	4 mi easy + obstacles	3 mi easy + Strength Train 1	REST	4 mi easy + Strength Train 2	REST	9 mi easy	20
3	REST	5 mi easy + obstacles	3 mi easy + Strength Train 1	REST	4 mi easy + Strength Train 2	REST	10 mi easy	22
4	REST	5 mi easy + obstacles	3 mi easy + Strength Train 1	REST	4 mi easy + Strength Train 2	3 mi easy	11 mi easy	26
5	REST	6 mi easy + obstacles	3 mi easy+ Strength Train 1	REST	4 mi easy + Strength Train 2	3 mi easy	12 mi easy	28
6	REST	7 mi easy + obstacles	4 mi easy+ Strength Train 1	REST	5 mi easy + Strength Train 2	3 mi easy	13 mi easy	32
7	REST	7 mi easy + obstacles	4 mi RP+ Strength Train 1	REST	am: 7 mi easy pm: Strength Train 2	4 mi easy	14 mi easy	36
8	REST	4 mi easy + obstacles	4 mi RP+ Strength Train 1	REST	am: 6 mi easy pm: Strength Train 2	3 mi easy	15 mi easy	32

(continued on next page)

(continued from previous page)

Week	Sunday	Monday	Tuesday	Weds	Thursday	Friday	Saturday	Total Mileage
9	REST	6 mi easy + obstacles	1 mi WU 2x1mi LT (½ RI) 1 mi CD + Strength Train 1	REST	am: 6 mi easy pm: Strength Train 2	4 mi easy	12 mi easy	32
10	REST	4 mi easy + obstacles	am: 6 mi RP pm: Strength Train 1	REST	am: 6 mi easy pm: Strength Train 2	4 mi easy	14 mi easy	34
11	REST	6 mi easy + obstacles	am: 1 mi WU 3x1mi LT (½ RI) 1 mi CD pm: Strength Train 1	REST	5 mi easy + Strength Train 2	4 mi easy	16 mi easy	36
12	REST	5 mi easy + obstacles	4 mi easy + Strength Train 1	REST	5 mi easy + Strength Train 2	3 mi easy	17 mi easy	34
13	REST	6 mi easy + obstacles	4 mi easy+ Strength Train 1	REST	6 mi easy + Strength Train 2	4 mi easy	18 mi easy	38
14	REST	4 mi easy + obstacles	3 mi easy + Strength Train 1	REST	5 mi easy + Strength Train 2	3 mi easy	13 mi easy	28
15	REST	5 mi easy + obstacles	3 mi easy + Strength Train 1	REST	4 mi easy + Strength Train 2	REST	10 mi easy	22
16	REST	5 mi easy	5 mi easy	4 mi easy	REST	REST	OCR	14 + Race

16-Week Medium 26-Plus-Mile / Ultra Plan (Peaking at 50 Miles a Week)

Good for training for 45 to 65 miles at World's Toughest Mudder or performing at an Ultra Beast.

Week	Sunday	Monday	Tuesday	Weds	Thursday	Friday	Saturday	Total Mileage
1	REST	5 mi easy + obstacles	1 mi WU 2 mi RP (all RP refer to road marathon RP) 1 mi CD + Strength Train 1	REST	3 mi easy + Strength Train 2	3 mi easy	10 mi easy	25
2	REST	6 mi easy+ obstacles	1 mi WU 2 mi RP 1 mi CD + Strength Train 1	REST	4 mi easy + Strength Train 2	4 mi easy	10 mi easy	28
3	REST	6 mi easy + obstacles	1 mi WU 3 mi RS LT Pace 1 mi CD + Strength Train 1	REST	5 mi easy + Strength Train 2	4 mi easy	12 mi easy	32
4	REST	6 mi easy + obstacles	1 mi WU 3 mi RP 1 mi CD + Strength Train 1	REST	5 mi easy + Strength Train 2	4 mi easy	14 mi easy	34
5	REST	6 mi easy + obstacles	1 mi WU 2x1.5mi LT Pace (2 min RI) 1 mi CD + Strength Train 1	REST	6 mi easy + Strength Train 2	4 mi easy	16 mi easy	37
6	REST	6 mi easy + obstacles	1 mi WU 4 mi RP 1 mi CD + Strength Train 1	REST	am: 7 mi easy pm: Strength Train 2	5 mi easy	16 mi easy	40

(continued on next page)

(continued from previous page)

Week	Sunday	Monday	Tuesday	Weds	Thursday	Friday	Saturday	Total Mileage
7	REST	5 mi easy + obstacles	am: 2 mi WU 3x1mi LT (2 min RI) 1 mi CD pm: Strength Train 1	REST	am: 1 mi WU 2x400, 2x800, 2x1200 (2 min RI) 1 mi CD pm: Strength Train 2	3 mi easy	16 mi easy	36
8	6 mi easy + obstacles	REST	am: 6 mi RP pm: Strength Train 1	am: 6 mi easy pm: Strength Train 2	REST	4 mi easy	18 mi easy	40
9	REST	10 mi easy + obstacles	am: 1 mi WU 4x1mi LT pace (2 min RI) 1 mi CD pm: Strength Train 1	REST	1 mi WU 6x800 (2 min RI) VO$_2$max 1 mi CD + Strength Train 2	3 mi easy	18 mi easy	42
10	8 mi easy + obstacles	REST	am: 8 mi RS pm: Strength Train 1	am: 6 mi easy pm: Strength Train 2	REST	4 mi easy	20 mi easy	46
11	REST	10 mi easy + obstacles	4 mi easy + Strength Train 1	REST	5 mi easy + Strength Train 2	5 mi easy	16 mi easy	40
12	REST	12 mi easy + obstacles	am: 1 mi WU 8x800 OI 1 mi CD pm: Strength Train 1	REST	am: 2 mi WU 2x400, 2x800, 2x1200, 1x800, 1x400 VO$_2$max (2 min RI) 1 mi CD pm: Strength Train 2	5 mi easy	16 mi easy	46

(continued from previous page)

Week	Sunday	Monday	Tuesday	Weds	Thursday	Friday	Saturday	Total Mileage
13	am: 6 mi easy pm: Strength Train 2	REST	am: 1 mi WU 6 mi RP 1 mi CD pm: Strength Train 1	12 mi easy + obstacles	REST	4 mi easy	20 mi easy	50
14	REST	8 mi easy + obstacles	am: 4 mi RS pm: Strength Train 1	REST	1 mi WU 6x800 VO$_2$max 1 mi CD (1 min RI) + Strength Train 2	4 mi easy	14 mi easy	35
15	REST	6 mi easy + obstacles	4 mi easy	REST	4 mi easy + Strength Train 2	REST	12 mi easy	26
16	REST	6 mi easy	6 mi easy	4 mi easy	REST	REST	OCR	16 + Race

16-Week Hard 26-Plus-Mile / Ultra Plan (Peaking at 75 Miles a Week)

Good for training for 70-plus miles at World's Toughest Mudder or attaining a PR at an Ultra Beast.

Week	Sunday	Monday	Tuesday	Weds	Thursday	Friday	Saturday	Total Mileage
1	REST	7 mi easy + obstacles	am: 2 mi WU / 3 mi RP (road marathon RP for all RP runs) / 1 mi CD / pm: Strength Train 1	REST	6 mi easy + Strength Train 2	6 mi easy	10 mi easy	35
2	REST	8 mi easy + obstacles	am: 2 mi WU / 2x2mi RS LT / 1 mi CD / pm: Strength Train 1	REST	7 mi easy + Strength Train 2	6 mi easy	12 mi easy	40
3	REST	10 mi easy + obstacles	am: 2 mi WU / 5 mi RP / 1 mi CD / pm: Strength Train 1	REST	7 mi easy + Strength Train 2	6 mi easy	14 mi easy	45
4	REST	10 mi easy + obstacles	am: 2 mi WU / 4x200 w/ 200 RI, 8x800 OI w/ 2 min RI, 4x200 w/ 200 RI / 1 mi CD / pm: Strength Train 1	REST	am: 9 mi easy / pm: Strength Train 2	6 mi easy	16 mi easy	50
5	REST	10 mi easy + obstacles	am: 2 mi WU / 7 mi RP / 1 mi CD / pm: Strength Train 1	REST	am: 11 mi easy / pm: Strength Train 2	6 mi easy	18 mi easy	55
6	REST	12 mi easy + obstacles	am: 2 mi WU / 6x1mi LT / 2 mi CD / pm: Strength Train 1	REST	am: 12 mi easy / pm: Strength Train 2	6 mi easy	20 mi easy	60

(continued from previous page)

Week	Sunday	Monday	Tuesday	Weds	Thursday	Friday	Saturday	Total Mileage
7	REST	10 mi easy + obstacles	am: 3 mi WU 8x800 OI (1 min RI) 2 mi CD pm: Strength Train 1	REST	am: 2 mi WU 2 mi, 1.5 mi, 1 mi, 1200m 800m, 400m LT (½ RI) 2 mi CD pm: Strength Train 2	7 mi easy	14 mi easy	50
8	REST	6 mi easy + obsta-cles	am: 2 mi WU 2x2 mi LT, 2x1 mi LT (2 min RI) 2 mi CD pm: Strength Train 1	REST	6 mi easy + Strength Train 2	4 mi easy	16 mi easy	42
9	10 mi easy + obstacles	REST	am: 2 mi WU 3x2mi LT (1 min RI) 2 mi CD pm: Strength Train 1	6 mi easy	am: 1 mi WU 2x400, 2x800, 2x1200 (400m RI) 1 mi CD pm: Strength Train 2	REST	18 mi easy	50
10	12 mi easy + obstacles	REST	2 mi WU 9 mi RP 1 mi CD RP	am: 10 mi easy pm: Strength Train 1	REST	am: 6 mi easy pm: Strength Train 2	20 mi easy	60
11	REST	12 mi easy + obstacles	am: 2 mi WU 2x2.5mi LT (2 min RI) 2 mi CD pm: Strength Train 1	5 mi easy	am: 12 mi easy pm: Strength Train 2	8 mi easy	17 mi easy	63
12	REST	12 mi easy + obstacles	am: 2 mi WU, 2x3mi LT (2 min RI) 1 mi CD pm: 6 mi easy	4 mi very easy	10 mi easy	8 mi easy	18 mi easy	67

(continued on next page)

(continued from previous page)

Week	Sunday	Monday	Tuesday	Weds	Thursday	Friday	Saturday	Total Mileage
12	REST	12 mi easy + obstacles	am: 2 mi WU, 2x3mi LT (2 min RI) 1 mi CD pm: 6 mi easy	4 mi very easy	10 mi easy	8 mi easy	18 mi easy	67
13	15 mi easy	REST	am: 10 mi easy + ob-stacles pm: 6 mi easy	am: 2 mi WU 10x800 OI (1 min RI) 2 mi CD pm: 3 mi easy	REST	10 mi easy	22 mi easy	75
14	12 mi easy + obstacles	REST	am: 2 mi WU 2mi, 1.75mi, 1.25mi, 1 mi LT (1 min RI) 2 mi CD pm: Strength Train 1	am: 8 mi easy pm: Strength Train 2	REST	6 mi easy	16 mi easy	52
15	REST	10 mi easy + obstacles	2 mi WU 2x2mi, 1 mi LT 1 mi CD	REST	5 mi easy	REST	12 mi easy	35
16	REST	8 mi easy	6 mi easy	4 mi easy	REST	REST	OCR	18 + Race

Common Questions, Complaints, and Statements

What if my race distance isn't in the book?

I encourage you to choose one level up from your race distance. For example, if you're going to be competing in a 6-mile obstacle race, I recommend following the training plan for an 8-mile obstacle race. The longer running distance develops the aerobic running systems more, allowing for greater speed. The majority of my speed in running came from high-mileage periods when I was training for marathons. After I sprinkled in the occasional speed workout, my speed would improve by leaps and bounds. This concept of building a strong endurance base from months of training before moving into speed work and shorter races is an effective race pace improvement technique.

Can I start these training plans after not running for weeks or months?

Not running at all and then jumping into a training plan is not recommended. Ideally, you should spend time building an endurance base through easy running. When you start any of these plans, you should already be at the equivalent mileage of week 1. The difference between your week 0 and week 1 should be the addition of speed work.

I feel slow on a lot of the days.

That's a common feeling or complaint. The important thing to realize is that your body is improving. Often intense training plans can take you to the edge of overtraining. Overtraining can be difficult to identify. However, you will start to notice it when you lose a desire to work out, your heart rate is above its normal resting rate in the mornings, or you feel sluggish all the time. It's natural to feel sluggish on some days—especially some of the long, slow distance days. When I was training for my first sub-3-hour marathon (6:52 pace), I would often do my easy runs, including my long slow distance runs, at around 8 min/mile or slower. Sometimes that was because it's what felt comfortable, but often it was because the intense training was beating up my body hard and it honestly felt like it was the fastest I could run at that moment. The important thing is that I continued to monitor my body and provided it with a proper taper, allowing me to perform on race day.

What do I do if I miss a day?

As a general rule if you miss a day, just let it go. Do not try to make up the mileage on a different day. I would like to say I follow this principle, but let's be realistic: There is something satisfying about hitting your weekly goal mileage every week for an entire training cycle. My real guidance, then, is: Don't try to make it up if it's going to screw up your other training days. For example, if I missed a 5-mile easy run on Monday, I might add 1 mile to each of my runs for the rest of the week, making up the mileage. The wrong answer is just adding 5 miles on top of one of your runs. Adding a second run to one of your training days is doable, but it should be approached with caution. For example, if I had missed a 5-mile run but I had another short to moderate-length run (like a 6-mile) on a different day, I might do the 6-mile in the morning and the 5-mile at night, *only* if I planned on resting the day after. I discourage doubling your runs one day unless you are taking a rest day immediately after. If you have already trained your body to do two runs a day it's no big deal, but if your body is used to once-a-day training and you suddenly double the workload, it can overload your system.

What if I can't do my long run on [say] Saturday, but I can do it on Thursday?

Understand how the schedule is designed and make adjustments based on your own life. No one's schedule is set in stone and can be planned out every day for four months. Adjust as necessary. The important thing is to understand that you should take rest days after your stressful days to allow your body to recover. If you move your long run to Thursday, then, take Friday off to allow your body to recover.

What do I do if I'm an obstacle course racing addict and feel the need to race year-round almost nonstop?

This is a common problem with OCR. Many athletes want to race multiple times a month. The problem with racing too often is it does not allow for that build-plus-taper that creates a peak performance. I recommend taking the first two to four months of the year to follow one or multiple high-volume training plans to build your fitness base. After those initial months of no racing, you can start your race season.

Try to schedule races three to four weeks apart. This allows for you to race. Do a two- or three-week building phase, then follow it up with a one-to-two-week taper phase. For shorter races, a small taper, such as one week, is acceptable, but for the longer races (13-plus miles) you want a two- or three-week taper. Just understand that when you race too often, you will sacrifice some performance because you are constantly recovering from or tapering for a race. Ideally, pick your goal race for the year and conduct a proper taper peaking for that specific event, while using the other races as intermediary goals or checks on fitness. When I'm racing multiple times during a training cycle, I use the race to replace the speed workout for that week. This allows me to train through the race, but still perform at a high level and avoid overtraining.

Some of these plans seem like the mileage is high. Why am I running 30 to 40 miles a week if my race is only 3 or 5 miles long?

Throughout my lifetime of interacting with hundreds of athletes and clients, I have found two types of people whom I would consider fast. The first is those who are born fast, also known as the genetically gifted. Because of their athletic gifts, they were drawn into sports and have most likely been great athletes their entire lives. Often they have trouble understanding why others cannot keep up with them even after the genetically gifted have been inactive for a long period. The second group of fast athletes are those who run high volume. If you are not genetically gifted, running high volume will produce the benefits needed to run fast.

Furthermore, the higher mileage in these training plans is closer to what professional runners do to train. Often professional road racers cover mileage totals that look like intermediate or sometimes advanced marathon training plans. The training plans are modeled along this concept, albeit at a lower volume, to allow for athletes who do not have all day to train time to complete the plans.

Finally, even on the shortest obstacle races, the primary system used is the aerobic system. Running higher volumes at slower paces develops that system to a higher level. Then when you add in one or two quality workouts a week where you really focus on speed, it helps bring everything together, creating a faster runner.

Do I need to do speed training if I'm running an Ultra Beast or World's Toughest Mudder?

While many of these plans have speed training mixed into them, you do not have to do speed training for these events. I usually recommend some speed training because it helps break up the monotony of just logging miles every day. Furthermore, most athletes racing at these big events are also doing some short races in the month prior. Having some speed-specific work will help with the results in those short races. Finally, having the feeling of running fast occasionally makes your aerobic pace seem even easier. So while it's not 100 percent necessary for success, I recommend speed training usually once per week, which allows for some variation without beating you down so you cannot reach the rest of your weekly mileage goals

Why do a lot of the workouts separate speed work and strength work into two separate workouts? Especially when obstacle racing is strength and speed work occurring simultaneously.

Why separate workouts? is a common question from obstacle racers who are used to training similar to CrossFit workouts. The argument here is that combining the two better mimics race conditions. While I agree this does better mimic race conditions, it's not the ideal way to train.

Obstacle racing at its core is a running sport. Improving running speed will lead to an overall improvement in time significantly more than completing obstacles faster. To maximize performance, the best technique is to improve each individual component before putting everything together.

We can see this principle already at work in other sports. Triathletes train swim, bike, and run separately on most days. This allows them to maximize the effort they are putting into each section of their race. Occasionally they put everything together and do brick workouts, which I have included in the form of running + obstacle workouts. Additionally, I have put in some race simulation workouts and obstacle interval workouts to mimic the higher level of intensity of obstacle racing. However, the majority of your running power comes from improving aerobic conditioning, hence the emphasis on volume of running at an easy pace.

Sports like baseball or football show this in application also. Baseball players practice batting by repeatedly swinging at pitches. They also improve running speed by running at a separate time. Occasionally they put it all together, but practicing skills separately allows faster adaptation. The same amount of batting experience a baseball player receives in multiple games can be compressed into one session of batting practice. This principle can be applied by repeating an obstacle multiple times during your obstacle training days.

Finally, as someone who strength trains and runs almost every day, I have found this to be most effective. If you do both in the same workout, whichever occurs second will get less attention and thus less results despite your best effort.

Remember to shock the body occasionally.

Here is where things can get confusing. These plans work great—but as with any exercise program, the body will eventually adapt. I have used these programs or variations on them for years and showed continued improvement. Occasionally you need to throw all the rules out the window, though, and really shock the body. What I mean is that usually I take the day after a long run day off to allow for recovery and improvement from the previous day's stresses. Then occasionally, about every two months on average, I will do something that my body is not used to, like two long runs on back-to-back days, or back-to-back interval days.

This additional stress will help the body adapt and continue to improve. Doing stuff like this all the time is too much stress for most people. If you are training for ultra-OCR, however, the double long run is a good technique to simulate the fatigue of ultra-distances while causing less damage to the body than just slugging out a 30-mile training run.

Should I do depletion runs?

Depletion runs are long runs where you skip breakfast beforehand, and you don't eat during the run. This forces your body to use fat instead of carbohydrates for fuel. The theory is that your body will become better at using fat for fuel if you force this to occur through the lack of adequate carbohydrate sources. These runs are typically miserable because your body is running on fumes; they're typically run at a slow pace, whether you want to or not.

If you're following a 5K or 8-mile training plan, these aren't necessary. If you plan on following one of the 13-mile or 26-plus-mile training plans, you can incorporate these into your training if you'd like. Doing one depletion run a month will help you develop this adaption of fat burning without making you dread every long run. However, if you are always doing depletion runs, all your long runs will be at a very slow pace and you won't get the same aerobic benefit.

Sometimes I don't feel motivated for my long runs or obstacle workouts.

Having a training partner or group for especially hard workouts can definitely make them more bearable. It also makes it easier to get out of bed in the morning. Most cities have a local running group that does

Saturday or Sunday long runs. Some even offer water stations and gel for those who show up to train. Use these groups to help keep you on track. Other cities have obstacle-specific training groups, like the Mid-America Obstacle Course Racers (MAOCR) located in Wichita. These training groups can help keep you motivated and even reduce cost by carpooling and hotel sharing at races.

What if I am doing a 5K-type obstacle race but the advanced difficulty plan is still too easy?

Continue to follow the advanced 5K plan but add in more mileage. For short distance races, you want one day a week working on VO$_2$max (1200m intervals and less), and one day working on lactate threshold (longer intervals of 1 to 3 miles run at your 10K pace); the rest is general easy aerobic work. I encourage you to continue with the plan as shown but increase the length of the longer runs. Having a rest day after your two hardest days of the week is a good idea to allow for recovery in preparation for the volume increase the following week. You can also remove one of the rest days if you feel that is necessary—but I caution against this unless you have a weekly total above 50 miles.

Expanding Beyond This Book and Developing Your Own Plan

If you work through these plans and need a routine that is more challenging, I encourage you to redo the plans but increasing the intensity as described above. If that still does not achieve your desired result, add a mile or two to each of the long run days. The increase in weekly mileage will improve results. Additionally, once you understand the basics of a plan—mine or anyone else's—you can modify it as opposed to blindly following along. The point is to understand the technique and adjust it to your body or your schedule.

If you want to make your own plans, here are a few simple rules you can follow to ensure you utilize your time effectively:

• Run three to six times a week. Preferably five, which keeps most people engaged without leading to mental and physical burnout.

• Be sure to do a VO_2max, LT, and long run each week. If you can only run three times a week, these are the three most important types of workouts. Doing one of these each week will keep those systems strong. If you have to skip a run, make it an easy day that's not your longest run of the week.

• "Build 3, Rest 1." Train for three weeks with building intensity, then reduce your volume for a week to allow your body to adapt from the stress.

• During build weeks, add no more than 10 percent to your weekly total. This rule of 10 percent will help prevent injury but still provide adequate change to create adaptation in your body.

• Taper before your race: For shorter races, a 1- to 2-week taper is adequate. For longer races, 2 to 3 weeks is preferable.

• Strength train weekly. Do some form of strength training to be sure you maintain enough muscle to complete your obstacles. Strength training has dozens of correct solutions, but pick something that follows the criteria of being enjoyable, progressive and specific. The number of times per week will be based on your current fitness level and daily schedule.

• Take one to two rest days a week. Rest means rest, not a light gym session or a 5-mile run. Resting allows your body to consolidate fitness gains and recover for the next hard effort.

Accessories for Speed Training: Shoes, Electronics, Masks, and Vests

As a runner and obstacle racer, I'm often asked how many shoes I own. The answer is a lot. However, if you're serious about OCR, I recommend a few different types of shoes. You can survive with less, but this is what I recommend to maximize performance. What's most important for all shoes is fit. If the shoe doesn't fit you well, you need to get a different shoe or switch brands. Shoe companies typically use a standard foot mold when developing their line of shoes. This is why some people say "I only buy brand X; they just fit my feet better." It's important to try a few different brands and a few different shoes before you make your final choice. If you are having issues with your current shoes, try switching brands. Another company's model foot may be a closer match to your own. When I have running shoes that fit well, I never get blisters regardless of the distance covered.

Using Minimalist Shoes to Improve Form and Performance at Road Races

The big trend over the last couple of years has been switching from a cushioned shoe to something with little to no cushioning. While a cold-turkey switch is not ideal, it is possible if you're willing to accept risk.

I do think minimalist shoes have their purpose and are effective at teaching good running form—but let's clear some things up first. Most people say they are switching to a minimalist shoe because humans were running without shoes for thousands of years. This is true, but humans thousands of years ago did not weigh as much as they do now, and the ground was not made of concrete. Just look at many of the African cultures that are not inundated by fast food, advertisements for big muscles, and gym franchises. You will see what the barefoot running humans looked like. They were skinny and lean. All these factors and more make runners in America weigh more. Because of this, Americans and members of other Western cultures should make the transition a little slower.

If you don't feel like spending $100-plus for a set of shoes that is less material than a normal cushioned running shoe, then there are a couple of easy solutions. The first is to do some running actually barefoot. I would not recommend this over long distances due to man-made hazards like broken glass and sharp pieces of concrete. However, I have run around the block in front of my house barefoot on concrete before. I also enjoy running barefoot on tracks and football fields. These fields are generally free from hazards and allow for safe barefoot running. Running on grass or sand is also an easier transition to barefoot running than moving directly to concrete.

The second cheap way to get the benefit of barefoot running without buying shoes is to run in your socks on a treadmill. This one works really well. However, at distances over a mile the rubber matt of the treadmill can cause irritation on the bottoms of the feet. Repeating this process once a week or more can gradually toughen your feet so you can run on the treadmill barefoot for a greater distance. I really enjoy doing this at the end of a workout because it helps break up the monotony of running on a treadmill.

If you want to run in minimalist shoes, they have many benefits, including improved form (thanks to a greater tendency to forefoot strike) and lighter weight. The lighter the shoe, the less energy is required to move your foot forward. Multiply this by the length of 8-plus-mile obstacle race and every ounce makes a big difference. One of the negative aspects of minimalist shoes is that transitioning to them too fast can sometimes lead to injury. A contributing factor is that people will still try to use their cushioned-shoe form of heel striking with a shoe that has no cushioning.

Whether you run in a fully cushioned shoe or usually race in a set of racing shoes, I recommend some barefoot running each week. It is a good way to improve your form, which will result in an overall better runner.

Using Training Shoes to Minimize Joint Stress During High-Mileage Periods

Training shoes can be whatever you're comfortable in for day-to-day running. I like to have a pair of moderately cushioned shoes that are on the heavier side. This extra cushioning will limit the joint stress that a high mileage-training program might provide. The theory is that if I train with slightly heavier shoes, then my race shoes will feel even lighter. The shoes need to be light enough to allow running with proper form.

For example, running with ankle weights would be an even bigger stress, but adding all that weight would change your form and not provide some of the benefits that normal running would provide. All easy runs are done in these shoes along with some occasional lactate threshold runs to provide added difficulty.

Using Trail Shoes to Prevent Injury During Trail Training

Trail shoes typically provide a little more support than road shoes over uneven terrain. This means your trail shoes will typically weigh more than your road shoes. When you're picking a trail shoe, look for one that offers good traction, drains water, and fits your feet well. I don't recommend trail shoes for road running, only because it will wear down your treads faster, causing you to go through trail shoes at a quicker rate.

Using Race Shoes to Improve Game Day Performance

If you are serious about racing, definitely buy a pair of race shoes. Your race shoes might just be an additional set of your trail shoes, your minimalist shoes, or something nicer. These are typically shoes with lower cushioning and lighter in weight; they should also provide drainage for water as well as good traction. They offer many of the same benefits as minimalist shoes, with the low rotating weight allowing for less energy expenditure.

If you do buy race shoes, don't wear them for the first time on the day of the race. It's important to do some training in them to make sure they don't cause hot spots, blisters, or chafing, or put new stress on your body. My race shoes are just another pair of my trail shoes but in a different color. I have worn them enough to ensure they are comfortable but not to the point that they have started to fall apart.

The benefit most people don't mention, though, is the mental edge racing shoes can provide. When I lace up my race shoes, I just feel faster. The only time I put those shoes on is if I plan on running fast by doing intervals or at a race. Every time I put on these shoes, my body knows it's about to go all-in.

GPS Watch

Besides shoes, this is the best piece of gear to purchase. A GPS watch allows you to analyze your pace in real time. Knowing your exact pace all the time can allow you to adjust in order to PR during a race or in training. Most of the time when people PR during road races, they run an even or a slightly negative split. Knowing your last time for a race will allow you to plan for this.

As an obstacle racer, you want a GPS watch that is waterproof, not just water-resistant. This may require purchasing a triathlon-specific watch, which may be more expensive. These are also crucial when traveling. I frequently run in other cities and states where I don't know where I am in the city. Having a GPS watch allows me to accurately record distance and pace.

Heart Rate Monitor

I personally go through cycles when I wear a heart rate monitor and others when I don't. Occasionally I like to know what my heart rate is and track its progress as I get ready for a race. Heart rate monitors let you train by heart rate zone and run at a pace that is optimal for your training type. I personally purchased a GPS watch that has a heart rate monitor included in the package. This allows me to wear the monitor when I feel like it and not wear it when I don't.

I generally believe that a stand-alone heart rate monitor is worthless. Buying a GPS watch with a heart rate feature is the way to go, because it's so much more functional. With the number of GPS watches on the market today, the price difference between GPS with heart rate function and just heart rate isn't large. Spend a little extra if you're serious about training. Your body will thank you for it later.

Calf Sleeves and Compression Socks

I talked about compression clothing in chapter 3; however, you should know that there is a difference between compression clothing designed for activity and that designed for recovery. The recovery compression clothing is typically more restrictive; running in it would cause discomfort. The compression clothing designed to be worn during activity is slightly looser, resulting in increased blood flow without restricting movement.

Calf sleeves and compression socks cover the entire calf with a moderate grade of compression. They do several things to enhance performance. The first is that they help return blood to the heart by pressing on the muscle. In addition, they stabilize the muscle every time your foot slams into the ground. This stabilizing effect is supposed to reduce the amount of damage done to your calves, theoretically allowing you to run harder and/or longer. Another benefit of compression is that it keeps the muscle aligned and in a good position. The calf sleeve or sock essentially acts like an additional fascia (which is what covers your muscle fibers) on your calf. This theoretically helps align the muscle fibers so they are in the optimal position for use.

I personally own a set of compression calf sleeves and several sets of socks that I wear on occasion. Their biggest benefit for OCR comes due to the protection they provide your lower legs while racing. (More on this later in the chapter.) As with all products, do not race in them if you haven't worn them for a similar length of time in training.

Training Mask

One of the newer items on the market is the training mask. This is a mask that restricts the amount of air you can pull in by providing resistance and causes an increased CO_2 buildup by not allowing complete exhalation. These masks typically come with adjustments to increase and decrease the amount of resistance against your lungs. I generally believe these are a waste of money. Until more research is completed highlighting their benefits, their science is questionable at best and dangerous at worst.

When elite runners are preparing for events, they go by the principle of "Train low, sleep high." This means that they train at a lower altitude that allows them to push their body to the limit but sleep in a hypobaric chamber at night, or at elevation. The chamber simulates elevation and results in an increased red blood cell count.

Now look at the training mask. Users are "training high and sleeping low." While there are benefits to training high—just look at the high-altitude running meccas found all over the country (Flagstaff, Arizona; Boulder, Colorado)—this is usually not the preferred technique. The mask itself does not actually simulate training high, but rather just makes it more difficult to breathe.

Research may eventually prove some value to training masks, but I have not seen any yet. If I had a client dead-set on one, I would recommend using it on a recovery or easy run. Theoretically, it may help you deal with a buildup of CO_2 and strengthen your exhalation/inhalation muscles. This is assuming that these muscles are the weak point in your cardiovascular system, which I don't think is the case for most people. If you're doing less than 20 miles a week or working out fewer than five times a week, you'd be better served just running without the mask and improving your cardiovascular system the regular way.

Weighted Vest or Weighted Backpack

Using a weighted vest or weighted backpack can make running significantly more difficult. However, by adding weight to your torso, you are also increasing the weight on your joints. As with most unique techniques for training, you can try this periodically if you like. Training with a weighted vest or backpack is essentially a strength workout similar to doing repeats or running a hilly course.

Weighted vests tend to distribute the weight slightly better for running and are available from a variety of retailers. They vary in weight from 8 to 40 pounds or more. The price runs anywhere from $50 to $250, depending on quality.

The weight will cause your muscles to work harder and your heart rate to be higher for a given speed. Because of this increased workload, you will have to reduce your pace. The added weight may also alter your running style and cause increased stress on your joints, especially weights of 35 pounds or more. For these reasons, weight training vests or backpacks should be used at most twice a week unless you are specifically training for an event that requires moving with backpacks, like an adventure race, GoRuck, or other Assessment and Selection Events (ASE). If you choose to use a backpack, pack the weight high and as close to your back as possible. This puts the majority of the weight over your center of gravity, making it easier to carry the load.

The biggest benefit to a weighted vest is for improving obstacle proficiency. Training on obstacles is very specific and enjoyable for most people, but it usually falls short on being progressive. Slowly adding weight to a vest can solve that problem, making you stronger at completing obstacles. Just be sure to add weight slowly and if you are using obstacles that require climbing do not jump off of them with a weighted vest. The extra weight plus the impact of your body weight could cause a joint injury.

Racing

Race Week

Race week can mean the difference between a PR and a mediocre performance. If you've been following one of the prescribed plans, just continue following it as you see it written. If you have missed a lot of the runs, make sure you adjust your taper. It's important to rest your body those last two to three weeks prior to the race, allowing it to overcompensate and recover. If you have missed many workouts, then adjust the last couple of weeks to taper based on your current weekly mileage. As a general rule, apply the one-third rule for tapering. This means that if you are tapering for three weeks, reduce your mileage by one-third each week. So if your weekly mileage was 30 three weeks out, it should be 20 two weeks out and 10 the week leading up to the race.

Strength & Speed–ERA members helping one another over a wall.

For nutrition, continue to eat as you normally would, but add carbohydrates such as whole wheat pasta or quinoa pasta to your evening meals. These additional carbohydrates will ensure that your glycogen levels are full. Carbohydrate loading can take anywhere from eight to forty-eight hours before a race; that amount of time allows carbs to actually store in your body as glycogen. Be sure to load up gradually throughout the week instead of cramming it all in on the last night. Last-minute carbohydrate cramming often leads to runners having stomach issues and feeling sluggish. If it's a short obstacle race, 6 miles or less, there's no need to eat additional carbohydrates unless you're on a low-carbohydrate diet. Races of that duration will not burn through all the glycogen normally stored in your muscles. If you're racing between 7 and 12 miles, I recommend a carbohydrate load just to be safe. However, a lack of loading probably will not affect your performance significantly. If you're racing 13-plus miles, or your race will last more than two and a half hours, then carbohydrate loading is highly recommended. This loading plus eating frequently during the race will help keep you from hitting the wall. *The wall* is a term used by runners to describe the moment when they have burned through all the easily available carbohydrates in their body. It usually occurs in runners who have been racing for more than three hours or about 20 miles of road running. Not eating or poor training may cause you to hit the wall even sooner. Your body does not have enough carbohydrates to fuel itself for 20 miles, so if you are competing in a long-distance obstacle race be sure to continue feeding the machine as you move along the course on race day.

Race Day

The day of your race can be a big event if you've been preparing for weeks or months. Preparing for a race is actually simple. The important thing to remember is not to do anything that isn't part of your normal routine. Many people make the mistake of changing things on the day of the race—new shoes, new shirt, new shorts, new food—because they want the day to be special. This is the worst thing you can do. Just remember: Prepare as if you are going for a normal run of similar distance.

You should eat breakfast before every race, but if you are running longer than a 5-mile OCR then breakfast is crucial. If you typically don't eat before running, I recommend adjusting your schedule so that becomes normal for you. By the time you get to the starting line it has been several hours since you woke up. If you add in the eight hours of sleep you got the night before, you probably haven't eaten in twelve hours. Be sure to eat over an hour before the start of your race, so your body starts with a full tank of energy before the run.

In-Race Nutrition

For short races, 5 miles and below, no food is required during the race. Your body has enough stores to fuel itself for the entire run. I typically eat a Hammer Gel in the last fifteen minutes before starting the race. This is a last-minute carbohydrate increase to ensure I ate enough that morning to fuel me for the race.

For races that are 6 miles and longer, I strongly recommend eating. If your race is longer than 13 miles or more than two hours, then eating while racing is mandatory. Without giving a specific diet plan for each race, here are some general rules that you can scale to your race distances. For all race distances, I eat a gel fifteen minutes before the start. Be sure to wash it down with water so you aren't thirsty when the race starts. For all race distances above 7 miles, I start eating at mile 5 and then continue to eat every 2 to 3 miles for the rest of the race. For Spartan Beast–length races, I typically just eat energy gels. For races that are around 20 miles or more, I typically eat half a sports bar at mile 5, the second half at mile 8, and then continue to eat energy gels every 2 to 3 miles for the rest of the race. It's important to eat only when you are in sight of a water station. This ensures you have water to wash down your food. Races that are twelve to twenty-four hours long require a different fueling plan. See the section specifically regarding ultra-distance race considerations later in this chapter for more details.

Carrying Food and Water

Carrying your own water typically isn't necessary if the race is less than 13 miles. This rule is flexible, though, depending on weather conditions and available water on the course. Most races provide plenty of water stops along the route. If you're racing 13 miles or above, be sure to drink water at every stop even if it's just a small splash in the mouth. The problem with not eating frequently or drinking water frequently is the debt you incur. By the time you realize that you should be drinking or eating more, it's often too late. This will result in you hitting the wall as your muscles empty of glycogen and your pace significantly slows.

If I choose to carry my own water, I like the CamelBak Marathoner vest. The vest carries your water high on your back, which is easier than using a handheld water bottle. Handheld water bottles put the weight of the water at the end of a limb, which is less efficient for movement. Just as in cycling, you want your rotating or moving weight as light as possible. Adding a heavy water bottle to the end of your hand simply adds to that weight. Moreover, in obstacle racing, you need your hands free.

Corinna Coffin choosing to carry her own food and water for a 16K (~10 mile) BattleFrog race due to rough terrain conditions, which meant athletes were on the course much longer than usual.

Most women have wider hips and narrower shoulders than most men, so many prefer a water carrier that shifts the weight to the hips, something similar to the CamelBak Delaney. Some men may also want this type of water carrier; it's a matter of personal preference and comfort.

If the race is 8 miles or longer, I typically carry my own food. For races that are less than 10 miles, the food will usually just consist of a couple of Hammer Gels. For ultra-distance obstacle races, I carry enough food for one lap plus. This adds a buffer in case I'm extra hungry on a lap and need more calories. The food for ultra-distance racing varies greatly and is the topic of another section altogether later in this chapter. However, Hammer Perpetuem and Sustained Energy are a good foundation. Both are fuels designed for two-plus hours of racing. They provide a constant stream of complex carbohydrates and small amounts of protein to prevent your body from eating its own muscles. I like to use these two products along with some other solid fuel to add variety to my diet during a race. When I'm carrying my own food I typically use built-in pockets in my shorts or pants. If I'm carrying water, I use the pockets on my water-carrying vest instead. Finally, if I have neither, I will add a SPIbelt. This expandable pouch is great for snugly carrying food during races or training. I personally like to position the pouch on my hip since I think it results in the least amount of bouncing.

Dressing for Success

If you're looking to perform at your best for the next obstacle race, you need to be dressed for success. As a runner, you typically want to stay as cool as possible, because your body performs better when it is operating a cooler temperature. That's why runners typically dress in a singlet and short shorts. However, if you've ever crawled around through the dirt and slid down walls, you understand the value of having your skin covered to prevent scrapes. The correct outfit for obstacle racing lies in between protecting your skin and allowing for cooling. We will start with your head and work our way down.

As a rule, avoid any headgear, including sunglasses. Although I always wear sunglasses while running, I never wear them when obstacle racing. Having water or mud splash on the lenses will obstruct your vision and result in loss of time as you try to clean the lenses with your muddy clothes. Furthermore, when jumping from large heights into water or going down a waterslide, this is just another item that you can lose. Most obstacle races wind through the woods, which makes the need for sunglasses low—the trees provide adequate shade. The same logic is applicable to hats. Unless the weather is very cold, I stay away from hats. They're more trouble than they're worth during a race.

What about your upper body? I think the best solution is to wear no shirt but still wear arm sleeves. The sleeves still provide some arm and

Evan Perperis using fingerless gloves to protect his hands from rope burn.

elbow protection as you move through the obstacles. They will allow you to crawl faster and be less concerned about scrapes. The reason you are not wearing a shirt is to vent heat from your upper body. Since your arms are covered and possibly your legs, you want some exposed skin to keep your core temperature down. You can use arm sleeves that provide active compression or the kind that just cover your arm.

For your hands, I recommend fingerless gloves or nothing. The determining factor for gloves or no gloves is if the race has a rope descent. Gloves allow for extremely fast abseiling down ropes without rope burn. I prefer the fingerless version so I can still open food packages and maintain a level of dexterity. The important part is to make sure you test out your gloves on monkey bars and other obstacles you might encounter. Depending on the glove and the traction on your hands, you may have to remove them for some obstacles.

Your choice for legwear is definitely weather-dependent. If it's cool enough, pants are recommended, because they give full protection to your legs. However, in hot conditions, this may be too much covered skin. If I think it's going to be hot or if I suspect there won't be a lot of crawling, I go with shorts. Typically spandex, compression, or tri shorts are preferable because they don't absorb water and lack extra material that will become uncomfortable while wet. If you wear shorts, I recommend high-compression socks to go along with them. These provide a similar amount of protection as the pants but allow for airflow around the knees and legs. Having your lower leg covered is especially important if there is a Tyrolean Traverse in the course. The protection allows you to just slide along the rope instead of crawling along it like a horizontal ladder.

Rusty Palmer and Kevin Righi exiting a drainage pipe. Kevin's sleeves and long pants protect his arms while he stays shirtless to vent heat.

Your shoe selection may vary slightly depending on the course. There are several things to consider when choosing an obstacle racing shoe. The ideal shoes are lightweight, provide protection from rocks, provide some ankle support, drain when filled with water, do not increase a lot in weight when wet, and offer traction on muddy terrain. Most of all it's important to find a brand that fits your foot well. Shoe companies typically use a standard mold for making their shoes. If your foot is similar to a company's mold, then its shoes will fit you well.

Companies like Salomon use a foot mold that has too large an arch and thus creates foot problems for me. If I wear their shoes for an extended period, I get blisters on my instep. Although I seem to have the same problem with most Under Armour shoes, their line of Speedform shoes fit me very well. These are my go-to race shoes for non-mountain courses because they have all the desirable characteristics listed above, although they do not have the best traction. Furthermore, the shoes have no insole and are made of a fabric that does not absorb water. Even when they're wet, they're lighter in weight than many competing shoes. I have even used the Speedform road race shoes for some obstacles races if I know there will be minimal mud. Icebug USA is an emerging company that specializes in obstacle racing shoes that include all the necessary characteristics. If I'm racing on mountain or very muddy course, Icebugs are my go-to shoes because their traction is insane even when I'm descending mountains at full speed.

The most important dress-for-success rule is: "Don't do anything on race day that you haven't done in training." This does not mean you have to train in the above clothing choices for every run, though. Clothing should vary accordingly based on weather condition and your exercise plan for the day.

Feel free to make your own modifications to your outfit when dressing for race success. However, here are five questions to ask yourself when picking your outfit on race day:

1. Have I trained in this before? If not, immediately adjust your outfit.

2. Does it provide protection from scraping my elbows, knees, and/or legs?

3. Does it adequately vent heat from my body, allowing me to maximize performance?

4. Do I need to carry my own food or water?

5. If yes, is there a place to carry my own food or water?

Using Caffeine to Maximize Race Performance

Caffeine is a legal performance-enhancing supplement with dozens of trials that have proven it effective. The Olympics and World Anti-Doping Agency (WADA) have imposed limits on the amount of caffeine that you can have in your system at the time of competition. Take advantage of this supplement in your daily training and racing. Caffeine has been shown to lower perceived exertion rate. This makes it easier to push your body to higher levels. However, it can also unnaturally elevate your heart rate—as you may know if you've ever had too many cups of coffee or too many energy drinks. So when should you take caffeine?

The answer depends on several factors, including race distance, caffeine tolerance, body weight, and estimated finish time. Without going into caffeine tolerance, which will vary per person, I will focus on race distance and finish time.

Short Races

For races that are 5K to 10K or less than forty minutes, I recommend taking nothing during the race. While it's true that caffeine can lower perceived exertion rate, making it easier to push yourself, having too much caffeine before or during cardio (say, the amount in a pre-workout drink, 200mg or more) will elevate heart rate unnaturally. When you're racing, you want a low steady heart rate to keep you in that aerobic zone as long as possible.

I don't believe short races are long enough for you to feel the effects of caffeine. You can compensate for this by having caffeine before the race. That way the caffeine is affecting your body while you race. Having a small amount (35 to 100 mg) can wake you up and make you feel more energetic.

This comes with a few warnings. Typically, caffeine is consumed via carbonated energy drink or coffee. Both can cause gastrointestinal issues either through burping or the need to find a bathroom. You don't want to be on the starting line worrying about finding a Port-a-Potty ten minutes before the gun goes off. Furthermore, just as having caffeine during a race should be kept below 1mg per pound of body weight, you don't want to consume too much prior to the start, causing an abnormally high heart rate.

Long Races

For races that are an hour or longer (or 7 miles and up), I recommend starting to take caffeine during the second half of the race. It gives that extra boost when your body starts fatiguing. I do not recommend taking it from the beginning—I think there's an added benefit to feeling the change when the caffeine hits my body. Pain at the beginning of races is easy to ignore given the excitement of being on the starting line, so caffeine is not necessary; in addition, most racers start too fast and caffeine will only worsen this. For mid-race, I recommend smaller amounts—say, what's contained in caffeinated gels (usually 35 to 50mg) versus the amount in an energy drink. I am willing to take up to 1mg per pound of body weight, but I usually keep it less than 100mg total for events under three hours.

Again, I recommend having no caffeine before long races. There are exceptions to this. If you normally have that cup of coffee when you wake up, you may want to keep it in your race day plan. Just as with your clothing and food choices, do not change your routine on race day. You want to leave as many known variables in the equation as possible. Let the conditions of the race be the variable, not the new drink or new pair of shorts you're using.

Ultra-Distance Racing Considerations
Fueling for Ultra-Distance

Fueling for ultra-distance races requires a different technique than fueling for shorter races. Not eating in an event that lasts multiple hours or a full day will cause a disaster in your race performance. On the other hand, it's not only impossible but also unfeasible to replace all the calories you lose in an event. If you try, you will most likely end up with stomach problems and generally feeling sluggish.

I recommend consuming between 200 and 300 calories an hour, because studies have shown that is about the maximum most people can consume and process without causing problems. This equates to three to four gels every hour, since gels are typically about 90 calories each. The big difference for ultra-distance racing is that it requires the consumption of protein and fats in addition to carbohydrates. If you don't consume any protein, your body will start pulling amino acids from your muscles to sustain your intensity. This essentially means your body is eating its engine to sustain your current rate of activity. If your body is consuming muscles for fuel, it will cause a decrease in performance.

To fuel ultra-distance events, I recommend a mix of supplements and whole foods. For supplements, Hammer Nutrition is a great company to go with. This is an endurance company that understands the holistic approach to training—as you can see from their product line. Hammer Nutrition is one of the few companies that provides products for improvement twenty-four hours a day. Additionally, they have products that are designed for ultra-distance racing. For races lasting two hours or more, they offer Perpetuem and Sustained Energy. Both provide complex carbohydrates mixed with some protein, ensuring you have a steady stream of energy. This provides a better fuel source than sugar, which causes spikes and drops in energy. While these products can be solely used for the duration of the event, I personally enjoy consuming whole foods to further supply me with energy. Depending how I feel on race day, there are times when the thought of eating more gel or another mixed drink sounds unappealing. Typically, for whole food, I bring things like peanut butter and jelly on wheat bread, turkey or chicken cold cut sandwiches on wheat bread, trail mix, and bananas. Additionally, I will have some junk food such as Oreos or Snickers because you never know what type of craving is going to hit you when you have been racing for over twelve hours.

Caffeine for Ultra-Distance

The principles for caffeine consumption on long-distance races apply here as well. I recommend no caffeine for as long as possible. That way when you start taking caffeine, you will be able to feel its effects. Overall, take caffeine as needed throughout the race but try to finish half to three-quarters of the race before you start. The big difference is I am willing to consume more caffeine than I normally would in a day to fuel my performance. I personally recommend no more than 100mg per hour for two reasons. One, it prevents any large unnatural spike in heart rate, and two, it limits the chances of caffeine causing a bowel movement in the middle of a race. Caffeine also has a diuretic effect, but that is usually not an issue unless it is hot and you haven't been drinking enough water. Everyone is different; just be aware of these possible negative effects of caffeine as you are racing.

Dressing for Ultra-Distance

Dressing for ultra-distance requires several outfits to be successful. Typically, I bring outfits for every type of temperature for twenty-four-hour-long races. You never know what the weather is going to be like on race day, and you never know how your body is going to react to temperature changes. Even in warm weather, I have been cold during ultra-races because of a change in temperature combined with switching from running to walking or slow jogging. When you slow down, you won't be generating as much body heat, which leaves you more susceptible to the cold.

Evan Perperis in daytime dress with minimal clothing due to unexpected warm weather at World's Toughest Mudder.

Just as with regular racing, do not try new things on race day that you haven't done in practice. The possibility for chafing or a small issue turning into a major one compounds when you're racing ultras. A shoe that does not fit perfectly and rubs your foot compounded over twelve hours can cause a dramatic issue. Unlike regular OCR, I recommend gloves or fingerless gloves for ultra-distance OCR. For courses like Shale Hill—which has an eight-hour and a twenty-four-hour ultra-OCR—with lots of obstacles that require you to grip objects, full-fingered gloves are preferred. Just one lap on the Shale Hill course will tear up your hands, let alone racing for multiple laps. Padded sleeves may also be a good idea instead of just regular sleeves. Small abrasions on your hands and arms add up over twenty-four hours; put some effort into minimizing their negative effect.

Twenty-four-hour races like the World's Toughest Mudder (WTM) held in cool or cold weather require a neoprene wet suit to survive. WTM—typically held in November in New Jersey—has freezing temperatures; only wearing a wet suit will prevent hypothermia. Even in

Evan Perperis transitioning into cool-weather clothing.

2014, when the race moved to Las Vegas where the weather was sup-posed to be warmer, the wet suit was necessary. With temperatures that dropped to the mid-30s and winds that averaged 22 mph, the conditions sucked the warmth right out of your body. Drastic conditions require drastic clothing choices including full wet suits, neoprene socks, neo-prene gloves, a face mask, and a wool hat or neoprene hood.

Your choice of neoprene accessories is up to you. The opinion of most experienced racers is to have a wet suit that is between 2mm and 5mm in thickness. As with most accessories, there is a trade-off. While a thicker wet suit provides greater warmth, it is also heavier and restricts movement more. A thinner wet suit will be lighter but not as warm.

Evan Perperis dressed in a wet suit and grabbing some food
on the go during World's Toughest Mudder.

However, the lighter wetsuit makes it easier to run, which means you
can naturally generate more heat. I personally recommend buying a
triathlon full-length wet suit. Triathlon wet suits are designed for movement and often have varying degrees of thickness to maximize ability
to move.

Other accessories such as a neoprene hood and neoprene gloves are
also a good idea. These are great because you can add or remove them
mid-lap as you heat up or cool down. Many racers choose to wear a
windbreaker-type jacket on top of their wet suit to try to avoid the wind
hitting directly on the wet suit.

Tactics for Ultra-Distance

Pacing tactics: There are a couple of famous phrases in the ultra-running community. I am not sure who originally said them or where they came from, but they are profound nuggets of wisdom. The first is: "If you think you're running slowly at the beginning of a race . . . slow down." The second: "The winner of an ultra-distance race is the person who slows down the least." The important element of both statements is that a steady, reasonable pace will provide you with your best result. Do not be fooled by other racers going out of the gate too fast; that will only hurt them in the end. If you're moving at a pace you can't sustain for the length of the race, slow down.

Easily identifiable pit crew location thanks to a giant Hammer Nutrition banner at the twenty-four hours of Shale Hell.

Pit tactics: Too many people view their pit as a place to relax between laps instead of as an aid station. If you're looking to maximize your mileage, treat your pit like a car racing pit. The idea is for you, the racer, to pick up what you need and keep moving. The only time you should actually go in and sit down is if you require a change of clothing or

Food and equipment laid out to allow for quick pit transitions.

shoes. For laps where you are just picking up food or refilling water, keep walking and have your pit crew pass you food and water as you walk through the corral. Ten minutes spent in a pit is ten minutes someone else is gaining ground on you.

WTM-specific tactics: The World's Toughest Mudder offers bibs for completing 50, 75, and 100 miles that are different from the standard white race bib. As a racer, you can pick up your bib at the completion of that specific distance or just wait until the end. I recommend waiting until the end. Stopping mid-race to pick up a bib is a waste of time, although granted it probably only takes about two minutes. The bigger problem is that you're making yourself a target. In a twenty-four-hour race, it's very hard to tell who is in front of you and who is a lap or laps

Evan Perperis and pit crew member Terry Perperis conducting a refill of food and water on the move.

behind you. When I am racing and I see someone with a colored bib in front, it gives me a boost of energy and I speed up so I can catch then pass him or her. I go by in my standard bib and my competitor has no idea he or she just dropped a place. If you're trying to place as high as possible, do yourself a favor and avoid the colored bibs.

Sample Packing and Clothing Lists

Below is my packing list for 2015 World's Toughest Mudder. I believe it is better to bring too much equipment and not use it than to risk not having what I need on race day. This list should provide you with a starting point to create your own packing list for ultra-distance obstacle races. This is a list for one person and provides a fair amount of buffer to prevent running out of supplies.

Sample Pit Packing List

Item	Quantity if More than One	Notes
10x10 canopy		
4-man tent		
550 cord or string (for clothesline)		
Bananas	12	
Blanket		
Sport gummy chews (cramp-buster type)	8	
Clorox Wipes		
Clothespins	1 package	
Cold cuts (turkey or chicken)	1 pound	Sandwich bags (½ sandwich per bag)
Container of Hammer Nutrition's Sustained Energy or Perpetuem		Add 1 scoop to water bottle (drink while walking through pit area)
Container of Hammer Nutrition's Heed		Add 1 scoop to water bottle (drink while walking through pit area)
Electrical tape		
Energy bars	6	
Gallon ziplock bags		
Hammer Gels, caffeinated	10	
Hammer Gels, noncaffeinated	30	
Hand warmers	2	
Huge family-sized bag of Skittles		Snack-sized
Jelly		
Loaves of bread	2	
Oreos		
Paper plates	4	
Paper towels		
PB		
Plastic silverware (sets)	4	
Red Bull	4–8	
Rolling luggage bag		To transport supplies to starting line
Sandwich-sized ziplock bags		
Sleeping bag		One per pit crew member
Sleeping mat		One per pit crew member
Snack-sized ziplock bags		
Snickers	Large package	
Sunscreen		Aerosol-spray type for quick application
Trail mix	Large container	
Vaseline or Body Glide		
Zip-ties	15	

Sample Clothing List

Item	Quantity	Notes
Beanie hat	3	Allows you to change into a dry or drier hat on each lap
Blinking strobe	3	1 required by race, 2 backups
Compression shirt	1	
Emergency space blanket	2	
Fingerless gloves	1	Protect hands during daytime laps
Full-fingered gloves	1	
GPS watch	1	
Headlamp	2	Extra one in the event one is lost during a lap
Heavyweight running gloves	1	
UA Infrared long-sleeved top	1	
Long compression pants (cold gear)	1	
Long compression pants (heat gear)	1	
Long-sleeved surf top	1	
CamelBak Marathoner vest	2	
Neck gaiter (thicker)	2	
Neck gaiter (thin as possible)	2	
Neoprene gloves	1	
Neoprene hood	1	
Neoprene socks	1	
Padded Arm sleeves	1	
Padded Knee sleeves	1	
Synthetic socks	4	
Regular watch or another GPS watch	1	GPS watch doesn't have 24 hours of battery life
Running shoes	2	
Running shorts	2	
Shoe gaiter	1	
Tri shorts	2	
Water bottle	1	
Wet suit (2–5mm)	1	Trade-off of warmth vs. weight depending on temperatures. Thicker suits are warmer but inhibit movement, resulting in generating less body heat. Thicker suits also weigh more, thus slowing you down.
Zip-ties	6	Secure watch and strobe so they do not fall off

Chapter 7

STRENGTH TRAINING: OFF SEASON CROSS-TRAINING AND IMPROVING YOUR WEAKNESSES

It's November, and most likely your obstacle course racing season is over for the year. You look at your wall of medals from the last year highlighting your accomplishments and maybe some races that didn't go so well. You are excited to race again but are mentally burned out from waking up early every day to run. Don't worry; it's now the off-season, and taking a break from running is not only good for you but also recommended.

Taking the time to have an off-season provides both physical and mental benefits. Physically, it will allow your body to heal from any nagging injuries, and it reduces the stress on your joints. The stress caused by the repetitive motion of high-volume running can sometimes wreak havoc on the body. When you take a couple of weeks, or a couple of months, to unwind and relax, those injuries have time to heal, you can actually perform better in the long run. If you don't have any injuries, then taking a break from running can still help prevent them in the future. Mentally, it helps rest your mind so you can hit the training hard again next year.

I recommend taking a week or two completely off from organized physical activity such as gym sessions or running for exercise. You should still remain active and not just sitting on the couch; just take a break from purposeful exercise. Afterward, switching to a strength training focus can help correct muscle imbalances and add overall strength to your body.

You have many different strength training options but it should meet the following three criteria: specificity, progressive and enjoyable. Specificity, as already discussed in the first chapter, involves mimicking movements required for OCR. Progressive means as you improve the training should become harder so it continuously challenges you. Finally, enjoyable is important because the more you enjoy it, the more likely you are to put in maximum effort. So feel free to use these training plans as a starting point and add or adjust exercises so they are designed to develop your weaknesses.

If you are following a CrossFit training plan, just be careful. CrossFit provides great strength benefits, but doing complex movements for speed while you're already fatigued increases the probability of injury. Kipping pull-ups, too, can add a lot of stress to your shoulder joint at the bottom of the movement. That being said, I have many friends who do CrossFit safely and successfully. If that's what you enjoy, then utilize CrossFit for your off-season strength building.

I don't recommend the strength programs found in most running magazines; I believe they are inadequate to build the strength required for elite obstacle racing. Those strength programs are designed for runners who are running while conducting strength training. Furthermore, the upper-body strength demanded in obstacle racing is significantly higher than what the typical runner needs.

When choosing your strength program, your goals should be as specific as possible. If you just state *I want to be stronger*, you probably won't be as successful as you could by adopting *I want to do X muscle ups* or *Y pull-ups* as your goal. The strength training routines in this book are designed to develop muscles and build overall strength.

Generally, strength training opinions fall into two camps. The first is convinced that since the majority of your competitions are endurance-focused, your strength training should be endurance-focused also. The other camp thinks that since you spend so much time endurance training, it's better to keep repetitions very low to balance the equation and focus on building maximum strength. I fall somewhere in the middle. If I am following a multi-week strength training plan, I start with around ten repetitions and continue to drop it down closer to five after a couple of weeks. If I'm not following a specific plan, I adopt a hybrid approach. I do my complex movements with lower reps, around five. As the workout progresses and I tire, I gradually increase my rep range until the last exercise has about twelve repetitions total. For instance, a back-focused day might include 3x3 muscle ups, 3x5 weighted pull-ups, 3x6–8 single-arm machine assisted pull-ups, 3x8–10 bent-over rows, 3x10–12 wide-arm lat pull-downs, and 3x12 straight-arm pull-downs.

Many OCR training programs do a great job being specific and presumably enjoyable, but fail on the progressive part of the three criteria I listed. If you are only doing bodyweight movements you eventually need to add additional stress through a weighted vest, more repetitions, longer workouts or shorter rest intervals.

Therefore, I decided to focus on strength training that primarily uses weights for the off-season for a couple of reasons. The first is that most people have access to weights. Many OCR athletes like to train using things like tire flips, box jumps, or battle ropes, but not every gym has access to those items. The routines here can be done in almost any gym—including many hotel gyms—with some modification. The second is efficiency. Training each of the muscles individually and then adding in race-specific movements later makes for overall stronger racers. For example, if you get really strong at deadlifts, the transition to being able to do tire flips is mostly a technique issue, not a strength issue. Finally, things like tires typically come in one weight, while barbells can be adjusted as you get stronger. The idea for off-season training is to build up your strength for the upcoming year. Barbells and dumbbells are the most efficient method for doing that.

I've separated strength training into two categories. The first is a bodybuilding split; the second is a bodybuilding split that also includes some light cardio in the off-season. If these routines do not interest you, feel free to find your own strength training routine. Just be sure to adhere to the criteria of being specific, progressive and enjoyable in addition to the principles laid out in this chapter.

8-Week Bodybuilding / Strength Gaining Split

	Sunday	Monday	Tuesday	Weds.	Thursday	Friday	Saturday
Weekly Routine	REST	Quads/ Calves	Chest/Bis	REST	Back	Shoulders/ Traps	Hams/ Calves /Tris

• *Recommend using Fat Gripz for all sets.*

• *Add in intensity-boosting methods as needed; these are explained later in this chapter.*

• *For all cable machines, use alternative grips (chains, ropes, purchased rig items like nunchukus from Sinery Sports, et cetera) to work on grip strength.*

Weeks 1–4

(see chart next two pages)

Weeks 1–4

Quads/Calves	Chest/Bis	Back	Shoulders/Traps	Hams/Calves/Tris
Bent-leg calf raise drop set: 3 sets total (1 set = 10 reps of a weight, drop half the amount of weight, 10 reps, then use body weight for 10 reps on last set)	Rope cable curl: 3x10–12	3 sets of wide-arm pull-ups max reps (palms facing away, the more awkward grip the better; e.g., doorframe pull-ups, pull-ups on the square support of the Smith machine)	Pinch plate upright row: 3x8–10	Skull crushers: 3x6–8
	Cable hammer curl: 3x10–12	3 sets of low cable row	Shrugs: 5x8–10	Triceps rope extension: 3x10–12
Farmer's walk: 3 sets		3 sets of 1 min extended arm hang (increase time as you become more proficient)		Cable kickback: 3x10–12
Static hang: 3 sets (equal time for each set; increase as you improve)	Wrist curl: 3x10–12		Farmer's walk drop sets: 3 sets	
	Reverse wrist curl: 3x10–12		Weighted static hang: 3 sets (equal time for each set; increase as you improve)	
Crunches: 3 sets				
Leg raise: 3 sets			Exercise ball crunches: 3 sets	
			Reverse crunches: 3 sets	

(continued next page)

(continued from previous page)

Quads/Calves	Chest/Bis	Back	Shoulders/Traps	Hams/Calves/Tris
Bent-leg calf raise drop set: 3 sets total (1 set = 10 reps of a weight, drop half the amount of weight, 10 reps, then use body weight for 10 reps on last set)	Rope cable curl: 3x10–12	3 sets of wide-arm pull-ups max reps (palms facing away, the more awkward grip the better; e.g., doorframe pull-ups, pull-ups on the square support of the Smith machine)	Pinch plate upright row: 3x8–10	Skull crushers: 3x6–8
	Cable hammer curl: 3x10–12	3 sets of low cable row	Shrugs: 5x8–10	Triceps rope extension: 3x10–12
Farmer's walk: 3 sets		3 sets of 1 min extended arm hang (increase time as you become more proficient)		Cable kickback: 3x10–12
Static hang: 3 sets (equal time for each set; increase as you improve)	Wrist curl: 3x10–12		Farmer's walk drop sets: 3 sets	
	Reverse wrist curl: 3x10–12		Weighted static hang: 3 sets (equal time for each set; increase as you improve)	
Crunches: 3 sets				
Leg raise: 3 sets			Exercise ball crunches: 3 sets	
			Reverse crunches: 3 sets	

Weeks 5–6

Quads/Calves	Chest/Bis	Back	Shoulders/Traps	Hams/Calves/Tris
Squats: Warm up then 4x6–8	Bench: Warm up then 4x6–8	Deadlift: Warm up then 4x6–8	Barbell shoulder press: 4x6–8	Stiff-legged deadlift: 4x8–10 (focus on squeezing hamstring and not quantity of weight)
Leg press: 3x6–8	Incline dumbbell press: 3x6–8		Lateral raise: 3x8–10	Walking lunge (use barbell to stress legs or dumbbells to stress fore-arms): 3x8–10
Leg extension: 3x8–10	Incline fly: 3x8–10	3 sets of muscle ups max reps (if can't do muscle ups, do 3 sets of pull-ups immedi-ately followed by dips)	Pinch front plate raise: 3x8–10	Lying hamstring curl: 3x6–8
Hack squat ma-chine / Smith machine hack squat: 4x10–12	Fly machine: 3x8–10	3x3 one-arm counterweighted pull-ups	Bent-over rear deltoid raise with dumbbells: 3x8–10	Single-leg ham-string curl: 3x8–10
		3 sets of towel pull-ups max reps (if can't hold on with both hands on towel, use one hand on bar and one hand on towel)	Face pulls (grab rope portion of handle): 3x8–10	
Smith machine calf raise: 3x10–12	EZ bar curl: 3x6–8	4 sets of rig work		

(continued on next page)

(continued from previous page)

Quads/Calves	Chest/Bis	Back	Shoulders/Traps	Hams/Calves/Tris
Bent-leg calf raise drop set: 3 sets total (1 set = 10 reps of a weight, drop half the amount of weight, 10 reps, then use body weight for 10 reps on last set)	Alternating dumbbell curl: 3x8–10	3 sets of wide-arm pull-ups max reps (palms facing away, the more awkward the grip, the better; e.g., doorframe pull-ups, pull-ups on the square support of Smith machine)	Pinch plate upright row: 3x6–8	Dips (weighted): 4x6–8
	Rope cable curl: 3x8–10	3 sets of 1 min extended arm hang (increase time as you become more proficient)	Shrugs: 5x8–10	Skull crushers: 3x6–8
Farmer's walk: 4 sets	Cable hammer curl: 3x10–12			Triceps rope extension: 3x8–10
Static hang: 3 sets (equal time for each set; increase as you improve)			Farmer's walk drop sets: 4 sets	Cable kickback: 3x10–12
	Wrist curl: 3x10–12		Weighted static hang: 3 sets (equal time for each set; increase as you improve)	
Crunches: 4 sets	Reverse wrist curl: 3x10–12			
Leg raise: 3 sets			Exercise ball crunches: 4 sets	
			Reverse crunches: 3 sets	

Weeks 7–8

Quads/Calves	Chest/Bis	Back	Shoulders/ Traps	Hams/Calves/ Tris
Squats: Warm up then 5x5	Bench: Warm up then 5x5	Deadlift: Warm up then 5x5	Barbell shoulder press: 5x5	Stiff-legged deadlift: 4x8–10 (focus on squeezing hamstring and not quantity of weight)
Leg press: 3x6–8	Incline dumbbell press: 3x6–8		Lateral raise: 3x8–10	Walking lunge (use barbell to stress legs or dumbbells to stress forearms): 3x8–10
Leg extension: 3x8–10	Incline fly: 3x8–10	3 sets of muscle ups max reps (if can't do muscle ups, do 3 sets of pull-ups immediately followed by dips)	Pinch front plate raise: 3x8–10	Lying hamstring curl: 3x6–8
Hack squat machine / Smith machine hack squat: 4x10–12	Fly machine: 3x8–10	2x2 one-arm counterweighted pull-ups	Bent-over rear deltoid raise with dumbbells: 3x8–10	Single-leg hamstring curl: 3x8–10
		3 sets of towel pull-ups max reps (if can't hold on with both hands on towel, use one hand on bar and one hand on towel)	Face pulls (grab rope portion of handle): 3x6–8	
Smith machine calf raise: 3x8–10	EZ bar curl: 3x6–8	5 sets of rig work		Dips (weighted): 4x6–8

(continued on next page)

(continued from previous page)

Quads/Calves	Chest/Bis	Back	Shoulders/Traps	Hams/Calves/Tris
Bent-leg calf raise drop set: 3 sets total (1 set = 10 reps of a weight, drop half the amount of weight, 10 reps, then use body weight for 10 reps on last set)	Alternating dumbbell curl: 3x6–8	3 sets of wide-arm pull-ups max reps (palms facing away, the more awkward the grip, the better; e.g., doorframe pull-ups, pull-ups on the square support of Smith ma-chine)	Pinch upright row: 3x6–8	Skull crushers: 3x6–8
	Rope cable curl: 3x8–10	4 sets of 1 min extended arm hang (increase time as you be-come more pro-ficient)	Shrugs: 5x8–10	Triceps rope ex-tension: 3x8–10
Farmer's walk: 4 sets	Cable ham-mer curl: 3x10–12			Cable kickback: 3x10–12
Static hang: 4 sets (equal time for each set; in-crease as you improve)			Farmer's walk drop sets: 4 sets	
	Wrist curl: 3x8–10		Weighted static hang: 4 sets (equal time for each set; increase as you im-prove)	
Crunches: 4 sets	Reverse wrist curl: 3x10–12			
Leg raise: 4 sets			Exercise ball crunches: 4 sets	
			Reverse crunches: 4 sets	

8-Week Bodybuilding / Strength Gaining Split with Leg Days Divided Up Because You're Still Doing Some Cardio

	Sunday	Monday	Tuesday	Weds.	Thursday	Friday	Saturday
Weekly Routine	REST	Chest + 1 Legs	Back+ 1 Legs	REST	Shoulders/T raps+ 1 Legs	Arms+ 1 Legs	REST

- *Recommend using Fat Gripz for all sets.*

- *Add in intensity-boosting methods as needed; these are explained later in this chapter.*

- *For all cable machines, use alternative grips (chains, ropes, et cetera) to work on grip strength.*

- *Pinch means you take two plates (could be two 5-pounders, 10-pounders, or 25-pounders) and pinch them together, then do the associated exercise; this helps work on grip strength. Pinch front plate raises, for example, involve squeezing two weights together while doing the front raise movement. This works best with Olympic-style bumper plates but can be done with standard weights.*

- *Triceps chain extensions are the same as Rope Extensions, only you bring your own chain and use that as a handle instead of the standard rope one found in the gym.*

Weeks 1–4

Chest	Back	Shoulders/Traps	Arms
Bench: Warm up then 4x8–10	Deadlift: Warm up then 4x8–10	Barbell shoulder press: 4x8–10	Dips (weighted): 4x8–10
Incline dumbbell press: 3x8–10	Muscle ups: 3 sets	Lateral raise: 3x8–10	Skull crushers: 3x8–10
Incline flys: 3x10–12	Single-arm counter-weighted pull-ups: 5x5	Pinch front plate raise: 3x10–12	Triceps rope (or chain) extension: 3x10–12
	Towel pull-ups: 3 sets	Bent-over rear deltoid raise with dumbbells: 3x10–12	Cable kickback: 3x10–12
Leg extension: 3x10–12	Rig work: 3 sets	Face pulls: 3x10–12	
	Pull-ups (palm away, add weight as necessary): 4x8–10		EZ bar curl: 3x8–10
Farmer's walk: 3 Sets	Single-arm row: 3x8–10	Pinch upright row: 3x8–10	Alternating dumbbell curl: 3x8–10
Forearm curls: 3 Sets	Face pulls: 3x10–12	Shrugs: 5x8–10	Rope cable curl: 3x10–12
Reverse forearm curls: 3 sets	Straight-arm pull-downs: 3x12–15	Farmer's walk drop sets: 3 sets	Cable hammer curl: 3x10–12
Crunches: 3 sets	Squats: 4x10–12	Leg press: 4x10–12	Lying hamstring curl: 3x8–10
Leg raise: 3 sets	Bent-leg calf raise: 4x10–15	Straight-leg calf raise: 4x10–12	
			Weighted static hang: 3 sets
	Static hang: 3 sets		
			Exercise ball crunches: 3 sets
			Reverse crunches: 3 sets

197

Weeks 5–6

Chest	Back	Shoulders/Traps	Arms
Bench: Warm up then 4x6–8	Deadlift: Warm up then 4x6–8	Barbell shoulder press: 4x6–8	Dips (weighted): 4x6–8
Incline dumbbell press: 3x6–8	Muscle ups: 3 sets	Lateral raise: 3x8–10	Skull crushers: 3x6–8
Incline fly: 3x10–12	Single-arm counter-weighted pull-ups: 3x3	Pinch front plate raise: 3x10–12	Triceps rope (or chain) extension: 3x10–12
Fly machine: 3x10–12	Towel pull-ups: 3 sets	Bent-over rear deltoid raise with dumbbells: 3x10–12	Cable kickback: 3x10–12
	Rig work: 4 sets	Face pulls: 3x10–12	
Leg extension: 3x10–12	Pull-ups (palm away, add weight as necessary): 4x6–8		EZ bar curl: 3x6–8
	Single-arm row: 3x8–10	Pinch upright row: 3x6–8	Alternating dumbbell curl: 3x8–10
Farmer's walk: 4 Sets	Face pulls: 3x10–12	Shrugs: 5x8–10	Rope cable curl: 3x10–12
Forearm curl: 4 Sets	Straight-arm pull-downs: 3x10–12	Farmer's walk drop sets: 3 sets	Cable hammer curl: 3x10–12
Reverse forearm curl: 3 sets			
	Squats: 3x8–10	Leg press: 4x10–12	Lying hamstring curl: 3x8–10
Crunches: 4 sets	Bent-leg calf raise: 4x10–12	Straight-leg calf raise: 4x10–12	
Leg raise: 3 sets			Weighted static hang: 3 sets
	Static Hang: 4 Sets		
			Exercise ball crunches: 4 sets
			Reverse crunches: 3 sets

Weeks 7–8

Chest	Back	Shoulders/Traps	Arms
Bench: Warm up then 5x5	Deadlift: Warm up then 5x5	Barbell shoulder press: 5x5	Dips (weighted): 5x5
Incline dumbbell press: 3x6–8	Muscle ups: 4 sets	Lateral raise: 3x8–10	Skull crushers: 3x6–8
Incline fly: 3x8–10	Single-arm counter-weighted pull-ups: 2x2	Pinch front plate raise: 3x8–10	Triceps rope (or chain) extension: 3x8–10
Fly machine: 3x8–10	Towel pull-ups: 4 sets	Bent-over rear deltoid raise with dumbbells: 3x10–12	Cable kickback: 3x10–12
	Rig Work: 5 sets	Face pulls: 3x10–12	
Leg extension: 4x8–10	Pull-ups (palm away, add weight as necessary): 4x6–8		EZ bar curl: 3x6–8
	Single-arm row: 3x8–10	Pinch upright row: 3x6–8	Alternating dumbbell curl: 3x8–10
Farmer's walk: 4 Sets	Face pulls: 3x10	Shrugs: 5x8–10	Rope cable curl: 3x8–10
Forearm curl: 4 Sets	Straight-arm pull-downs: 3x10–12	Farmer's walk drop sets: 4 sets	Cable hammer curl: 3x10–12
Reverse forearm curl: 4 sets			
	Squats: 4x8–10	Leg press: 4x8–10	Lying hamstring curl: 4x8–10
Crunches: 4 sets	Bent-leg calf raise: 4x10–12	Straight-leg calf raise: 4x10–12	
Leg raise: 4 sets			Weighted static hang: 4 sets
	Static hang: 4 Sets		
			Exercise ball crunches: 4 sets
			Reverse crunches: 4 sets

Strength Training Principles

Strength training can be a very broad topic. I am going to give you some general guidelines that will help guide your strength program. These principles are incorporated in the above plans but can also be applied to a program you design for yourself or one you pull from another source.

Prioritization

As with your overall plan, you need to prioritize your time in the gym. This means doing your most important exercises at the beginning of your workout routine. For OCR athletes, this means sticking to movements that mimic actions performed in races (such as muscle ups, pull-ups, dips, and weighted lunges). The larger muscle movements and/or compound movements start each day, which will help maximize strength gain. These larger muscles will also increase levels of growth hormone in your body. The larger muscle movements will strengthen not only your core and the targeted muscle but your entire body as well. The plans in this book are set up to build a blend of strength and endurance without causing muscle imbalances. However, if you are trying to hit specific goal such as doing weighted pull-ups with X amount of weight but are less concerned about your deadlift total, change these plans to put pull-ups first in the workout. That way they get maximum attention.

This method can also be used for your weak points. Most people will lose motivation and/or effort the longer a workout continues. Some of this can be avoided by focusing, but a lot of it has to do with your body using up energy in the gym. At the end of the workout, you will typically be more tired than you were at the beginning. If you have a lagging body part that needs special attention, feel free to move it earlier in the workout; just be careful not to tire it out if you're going to need it for a major muscle movement later. If you have weak biceps resulting in an inability to complete certain obstacles, for instance, move biceps to a different day rather than including them on back day or training them second.

Since grip strength is so important to OCR, try to turn every exercise into something that also stresses your forearms in addition to the targeted muscle through the use of intensity boosting techniques listed at the end of this chapter.

Follow a Set Plan

Many people go into the gym and just do whatever they want. This is not the best technique—if you're tired, you're likely to skip or exclude harder exercises. As you get more comfortable and experienced, you can operate with less of a plan. If you're new to lifting, though, definitely follow a set plan to ensure you stay on track.

Vary Your Routine

Often you see people in the gym doing the same thing day after day. They heard that the best way to build muscle is by staying around ten repetitions per set. While this is true, it's not the complete story. If you are a drug-enhanced athlete, which you should not be as an elite OCR athlete, this may work for you year-round. If you are natural, which you should be, you will find out very quickly that your body plateaus after a couple of months. To really see strength or endurance gains, you have to follow a different rep scheme. To gain strength, you need to use fewer repetitions with more weight. After decreasing the rep range for a couple of weeks, you can go back to eight to twelve repetitions. However, when you go back to the higher reps, you will be able to do significantly more weight than you could two months prior. The constant adjustment of rep schemes will ensure that you keep developing better strength.

Use Proper Form

Proper form is one of the most important aspects of weight lifting—and one that's commonly ignored. Be sure to use proper form on all exercises. If you are looking for detailed instructions on proper form, I advise you to view YouTube videos on proper exercise techniques. If you are looking for specific recommendations, feel free to contact me through the Strength & Speed website or Facebook page. This book assumes you already have a basic understanding of the different types of lifts. Online resources or beginner books will teach the basics of lifting if you need further instructions. This is especially important for compound movements such as squats, lunges, bench presses, and deadlifts. Using proper form will ensure longevity in lifting and racing by preventing injury, which is the key to improvement.

If you are new to lifting, proper form will keep you safe and also keep you from taking steps backward. New lifters are always upset if I correct their form and the weight on the bar suddenly drops 50 pounds. Or if someone has been "squatting" for years and I let him know he's nowhere close to parallel—that's demoralizing. When I have him squat to parallel and he can only lift half as much weight, it is devastating.

Furthermore, when you go to the gym and are throwing heavy weights around using bad form, others will identify you as having no idea what you're doing. Nothing is more painful than watching someone deadlift with a completely rounded back. It's an injury waiting to happen and it reveals your ignorance.

Occasionally Break All the Rules

There are certain principles almost every lifter follows. Some of these are listed above; others focus on volume. You will constantly hear people say things like "Be careful not to overtrain" or "That's too much volume." While they are sometimes right, it's important to throw out all the rules occasionally. This shock to the body can spur new growth. A couple of times a year, throw out all the rules for a week or two to see if it shocks your body into growth. Don't continue this for a month or more, though. The rules are there because they generally work well. The human body adapts to all stress eventually. Completely changing things up will force your body to adapt to the new stress.

Best Exercises for OCR

If you choose not to follow the routines listed above, I recommend you include some or all of the following exercises in whatever routine you develop. Many OCR athletes follow different strength training routines. Some do CrossFit, others metabolic conditioning; some have the benefit of obstacle courses near their house, and some follow bodybuilding splits. Whichever routine you follow, I recommend certain exercises to specifically target the muscles involved in racing. To be more specific, the best exercises for OCR are those that simulate racing movements. Below are several exercises that help simulate common OCR obstacles.

Barbell Lunges

The barbell lunge is a great exercise that builds strong legs and glutes. If you are looking to improve your running, the best exercises are those that mimic the motion of running. Lunges do this, thereby strengthening many of the same muscles. Lunges are especially useful if you're going to be racing on a mountainous route. As you lunge, I encourage you to take steps as large as you can. This will help ensure your knee does not move past your toes. When your knee extends past your toes, it can cause painful stress along the patella tendon, leading to injury.

If you want to really emphasize the legs, use a barbell. The barbell allows you to use more weight. Throwing a barbell across your back and lunging up and down the hallway of some gyms is frowned upon. To limit upsetting people and take up less room, use an EZ curl bar, which is smaller in length. If there isn't enough room, change directions to hit your desired rep range. If you want to emphasize your forearms simultaneously, you can use dumbbells—just understand that you typically won't be able to use as much weight, thus limiting strength gains in your legs.

Muscle Ups

Muscle ups simulate pulling your body weight over a wall. Many CrossFit competitors practice these on rings. As an OCR athlete, you should practice on a bar because that better simulates climbing over a wall. If you cannot do muscle ups, work on pull-ups and work your way up to pull-ups with weight. Additionally, work on dips, working your way up to dips with weight. Next, add in explosive pull-ups where you pull so hard that you almost come off the bar at the top. Eventually work on putting all of this together into a full muscle up.

Pull-Ups (Palms Facing Away)

Pull-ups are also a good exercise to strengthen back and forearm muscles. Both of these are crucial for obstacle racing success. Pull-ups done with your palms facing away simulate climbing over walls, hanging from monkey bars, and any other obstacle that requires upper-body muscle.

One-Armed Assisted Pull-Ups

Most gyms today have a counterweighted pull-up machine. Set the weight so you can perform between five and ten one-armed pull-ups. This will help simulate the stress required when you're transitioning on monkey bars, or at other times when you have only one hand on an obstacle. As you improve, continue to lower the counterweight, making each repetition harder.

Towel Pull-Ups

Towel pull-ups are another great back-focused exercises that also targets your grip strength. If towel pull-ups are too hard, try putting one hand on the towel and one hand on the bar. Eventually work your way up to both hands on the towel.

Intensity-Boosting Methods for Grip Strengthening

The gym is full of obstacles, but most racers don't take advantage of them. In between sets, feel free to add additional grip strength exercises. Indeed, your grip will play some role in completing almost every obstacle. A strong grip can mean the difference between finishing an obstacle easily and looking weak in front of your friends. It can also compensate for other mistakes while you move across an obstacle. If you aren't the fastest at monkey bars, having a strong grip can buy you more time, allowing you to finish the obstacle despite a slow pace.

With strong grip strength, Rusty Palmer and Kevin Righi conquer the Platinum Rig, an obstacle that eliminated over half the competitors at the Obstacle Course Racing World Championships.

To clarify what a difference strong grip strength can make in obstacle races, look at the inaugural Obstacle Course Racing World Championships. The addition of an obstacle called the Platinum Rig decimated the racing field. The Platinum Rig was a series of rings at different heights, rotating bars, extra-wide rectangular monkey bars, ropes, and vertical sections of swinging bars. Forty-six percent of men and 86 percent of women failed to complete the obstacle. In the elite wave, only nine women finished the Platinum Rig—a top ten finish was guaranteed for those with the required grip strength. Here are some minor adjustments you can make to your training schedule to ensure your grip is up to par.

Rig Work: More and more races seem to be adding rigs into their courses as a method to weed out pure runners. In order to get better at rigs, you need to practice crossing a rig. Whether that means building your own version in your garage or simply bringing some rig materials to the gym and constructing your own (the "Aluminum Rig"), you need to practice. Options are limited only by your imagination but good options are available for purchase from companies like Three Ball Climbing or Sinergy Sports. You can also bring your own items such as ropes, Olympic rings, chains or rock rings climbing holds.

• Use your environment: In between sets, you can add in movements along machines within the gym. The pulley machine that typically has a long crossbar with pull-up bar attached can be used as monkey bar training. Start at one end of the pulley machine and traverse the crossbeam to the other side before changing sides and coming back to where you started. Squat racks also usually have crossbeams that allow for practicing movements with your hands. Just make sure you clear the rack of bars, safety holds, and bar catches so you don't inadvertently hit your arm or legs on them.

• Thick handle training: Fat Gripz are rubber handles that go over the handles on dumbbells or barbells. Holding on to the thicker handle requires more grip strength. Incorporate these into your training and you will immediately notice a difference as your forearms get pumped to the max. The first couple of weeks using them, you will have to lower your normal weight for exercises, but you will eventually work your way back up in a couple of weeks. There's also an extreme version of the Gripz, which are even thicker, but I recommend using the regular ones for a while before moving up to the extreme.

• **Non-standard attachments for pulley machines:** If you're using a pulley machine, you should be using a non-standard attachment. Examples include using Fat Gripz on the D handle, holding on to the rope instead of resting your hands against the ball during triceps extensions, using a chain as a grip point instead of a normal handle, using a nunchaku handle, and grabbing the cable instead of the actual handle (be careful on that last one).

• **Turn every exercise into a grip improvement exercise:** Using the above three techniques, you can be sure to stress your grip strength on every exercise. Just be sure that your grip strength isn't what always gives out first; otherwise you risk seeing your other muscles stagnate.

• **Static holds:** Finish off your strength training routines with three sets of static hangs from the bar, shooting for the same amount of time per hang. As you reach your goal each week, increase the hang time by 1 second per set the following week. To facilitate a stable grip on the bar, you may want to throw some chalk into your lifting bag. I find that chalk balls are less messy than loose chalk.

• **Climbing, hangboards, and grips:** If you belong to a gym that has a climbing wall, replace one of your boring stationary bicycle cardio sessions with climbing. The best forearm pumps I have ever felt came when I was climbing. The amount of effort required will also elevate your heart rate into the lower end of the fat-burning zone. This type of cardio is typically more enjoyable than churning pedals on a stationary bike. I often like to use chalk to ensure my grip is not slippery after lifting. If you don't have a climbing wall in your gym or want additional grip training, purchase a hangboard. For between $50 and $150 you can get what looks like a piece of a

Evan Perperis practicing static holds and alternating static handholds while doing obstacle intervals.

rock wall for your house. This item screws into the wall and allows you to train grip strength by practicing static holds, doing pull-ups, or moving your hands along the various grips provided. Other versions can also be purchased like those attached to a rock wall or hanging grips like you might see on the show *Ninja Warrior*. Check out Three Ball Climbing for grips you can hang from beams in your garage. This is also the company that provides grips for *OCR Warrior*, the show of Mud Run Guide Brett Stewart.

• **Grippers:** Overall, I think people put too much emphasis on grippers and not enough on the other exercises listed above, but they can be used to improve grip strength. I am not talking about the cheap grip strength trainers available in most sports stores. The grippers by Captains of Crush are designed to build serious grip strength. The cheaper versions by Heavy Duty are also great if you're looking for grippers on a budget. Your forearms are like any other muscle and need attention. Just like other exercises, do three to four sets per forearm with rest periods. Avoid doing endless reps—twenty or more; instead use rep ranges that align with your goals. If you're looking to build strength, stay in the five- to eight-rep range. For more endurance, stay in the ten- to fifteen-rep range. For obstacle racing, you will want a mix of both. The endurance will help you tackle obstacle after obstacle on the course, and the strength will help you grip wide or oddly shaped handholds. I like to have two full-sized hand grippers to develop my overall grip strength; I then use two levels of the IMTUG by Captains of Crush to build individual finger strength. Ideally, you want to add these to the end of your workout and really focus, just as you would for any other body part. However, when pressed for time you can use them on the car ride home while your pre-workout is still coursing through your veins.

• **Lifting straps:** Leave the lifting straps at home, right? Wrong. Eventually, your forearms will give out completely, but you still have work to do. Keep the lifting straps with you but avoid using them until the last set or two of your four sets. This will ensure that you've adequately worked your forearms as well as your targeted muscle.

Common Questions, Complaints, and Statements
What if I miss a day?
Typically, if you miss a day at the gym, remove one of the smaller-body-part workouts. For example, always hit leg day and back day during

the week, because those are the main muscles used for OCR. Furthermore, these major muscle groups will cause a spike in growth hormone that will be more beneficial to the body than just blasting biceps. If you know you are going to miss a day, you can rearrange your schedule to ensure that every body part is still trained. This will probably involve doing less volume than normal, but it's better than not training that body part for the week.

The volume is making me tired all the time, and I feel weaker.

If you are following these lifting plans and feeling weaker from week to week, cut back on the volume. Every lifter has a different starting point and different history of lifting. These plans are a good starting point but can be scaled back if the volume is too high. That being said, be sure to cut out redundant exercises and not just the hard ones. You should always keep compound movements over isolation movements and exercises that simulate obstacle course movements over those that don't translate to OCR as well. Feel free to cut out some of the more supplemental exercises, such as variations on biceps training. Note if your body is using the exact same movement it just used for a previous exercise. That will give you a good idea if an exercise can be cut to reduce volume. I recommend four sets of each exercise once you're experienced, because the early sets are sometimes needed to fully warm up your muscles.

Should I use caffeine or a pre-workout supplement?

I highly recommend caffeine before strength training. It will give you that extra boost of energy to take your workouts to the next level. Having 150 to 250mg will give you a rush of energy (or 1 to 2mg per pound of body weight, depending on your caffeine tolerance). Typically, this is consumed ten to forty-five minutes prior to beginning exercise.

If, during strength training, you feel like your heart rate is too high, you probably took too much caffeine. I also recommend caffeine as the primary ingredient in any pre-workout drink. New ones come out all the time but lack long-term testing. In some cases, active ingredients such as Ephedra or DMAA (aka geranium root) were later identified as unsafe by the Food and Drug Administration and then banned. I like using caffeine because people have been drinking coffee for centuries, so we generally understand the long-term effects of caffeine consumption. Whether it is Ephedra, DMAA, or the next popular stimulant, I think it is safe to assume you should not take it long-term.

If you are following a two-a-day workout plan, then I feel caffeine is a necessary addition to your supplement list. Working out twice a day is physically exhausting and mentally taxing. Putting out large amounts of effort twice a day is significantly harder without a boost of caffeine.

I also use it as a point of no return. If I take a pre-workout drink or other caffeinated beverage, I feel obligated to exercise. On days when motivation is low, it's a lot easier to motivate myself to have a pre-workout drink than it is to motivate myself to go to the gym. However, once I finish the drink, I have no choice but to go work out because I don't want to waste my supplements (or money). Sometimes I also use caffeinated gels as a pre-workout supplement. Specifically I like Hammer Gel espresso-flavored gels because they have amino acids, complex carbohydrates, and caffeine—all the elements necessary for a strong workout.

Why am I doing exercises for my chest or other body parts if they are not heavily stressed during OCR?

The off-season training is designed to correct muscle imbalances and improve overall strength. Often body parts that are not directly stressed still provide stability during complex movements. The above routines provide total muscle improvement, ensuring that body parts are not neglected, creating a weak point in your body. And if you do Spartan Races, chest exercises will help with burpees in the event of a failed obstacle.

There is limited direct abdominal work because your core gets stressed heavily during running and heavy complex weighted movements (squat, bench, deadlift, shoulder press, and the like). In my opinion the stress provided by these movements creates stronger abs than endless series of crunches. If you're looking for more visible abs, the answer lies in losing fat, not in endless sit-ups.

Spartan Pro Team member and *American Ninja Warrior* competitor Rose Wetzel jumps over tires at BattleFrog Cincinnati.

Chapter 8

LEARNING FROM OTHER SPORTS

Corinna Coffin clears a low wall at BattleFrog Cincinnati.

Obstacle course racing is a relatively new sport, which means that other sports are decades and sometimes centuries ahead of us. Thus, the best place to look for advantages is often other sports with similar requirements. This chapter is filled with lessons pulled from other sports that you can use to achieve your maximum potential in obstacle racing.

A Lesson from Bodybuilding: Control Your Diet

Most runners and endurance-based athletes think that if they run enough or run hard enough, they can eat whatever they want. The theory is: "If the furnace is hot enough . . . it will burn anything." As a serious athlete you can get away with eating more crap than the average person—which doesn't mean that you should do so. When the furnace is hot enough it will burn most things, but what works better is putting good fuel in your body. Just as with bodybuilders, eating five or six small meals a day will supply your body with a consistent supply of energy as opposed to huge insulin spikes. The meals should generally be healthy, natural food consisting of a protein, slow-burning or complex carbohydrates, and healthy fats. Really, the only difference is that an OCR athlete will eat more carbohydrates and less protein than a bodybuilder. The constant stream of healthy food will allow your body to recover faster and more effectively repair muscle that has been damaged from training.

Once you are trying to reach a new personal best in racing, losing a few extra pounds might make the difference between a new personal record and a little bit too slow. Don't worry about losing too much body fat; even professional runners have enough body fat to fuel their bodies for ultra-distance races. If two runners are in the same shape and have the same amount of muscle but one is carrying around an extra 10 pounds of fat, who do you think will win in a race? Some people, not many, might be concerned that their body fat could get too low, but it won't get too low for you to run at your best effort. The only thing you should be concerned with is trying too hard to lose weight while training for a new personal best in a race. Your body needs fuel to recover and run hard again the next day. So make sure you aren't trying to cut weight on the last couple of months before an important race. You should be eating clean food, but calorie restriction is not okay.

Just like a bodybuilder rushes to get a protein shake after workout, the OCR athlete should rush to get a recovery drink post-run. The quicker those nutrients get into your body, the quicker your body can start repairing itself for the next day of training. Following exercise, the human body is in a heightened state in which it's better at absorbing nutrients. It's important to get the fuel into your body within this golden hour or anabolic window. I recommend a higher carb to protein ratio (3:1) for running and a lower ratio for strength workouts (closer to 1:1 or 2:1). Whole foods good for post-running include chocolate milk and Greek yogurt. If you choose to go with a supplement like Hammer Nutrition's Recoverite or a whey protein, be sure to have a meal of solid food within an hour or two.

Lindsay Webster knows the importance of a healthy diet to maintain a lean athletic physique, creating a champion OCR athlete.

A Lesson from Bodybuilding: Improvements Occur Twenty-Four Hours a Day, Not Just During Training

Bodybuilders understand this concept very well, because bodybuilding is an all-encompassing activity. If a bodybuilder is prepping for a competition, what he does the twenty-three hours a day when he's not lifting weights in the gym matters as much as his actual weight lifting.

I'm primarily referring to diet and rest. If you don't get the proper rest and nutrition to recover, allowing for harder training in the future, then you won't be able to perform to your full potential. Take a tip from people who live their sport twenty-four hours a day and take note of what you are doing the rest of the day when you're not running. It can be the difference between success and failure.

A Lesson from Elite Runners: Athletes Strength Train

Many recreational runners never lift weights ever. That is the wrong answer. As an OCR athlete, you hopefully don't have this problem, but if you primarily do the easier obstacle races, strength training may be low on your priority list. I'm not suggesting you go to the gym every day or do a lot of heavy lifting leading up to an important race. However, strength training is important, especially in the off-season. The quality muscle you put on in the off-season will make you a better runner by making all your muscles stronger. It helps prevent injury as well.

Some racers worry about bulking up. You needn't; it takes lots of lifting, time, and effort to build muscle. If it happened easily, every New Year's resolution gym rat would be jacked because they spent their three weeks at the gym each year. Sets of ten or more reps will help build overall muscle strength and endurance. Once you get into a race training block, you can reduce your strength training volume, as suggested by the plans contained within this book. Lifting will strengthen core muscles, provide a good change of pace from too much running, and help equalize muscle imbalances, which could prevent injury. Most OCR athletes use winter as their off-season, which is a perfect time to hit the gym to equalize those muscle imbalances. Running in the winter usually takes a backseat because of weather and the lack of OCR races between late November and February. Why not use that time more effectively by cross-training?

If you still have your doubts, what do you think hill repeats or short sprints are? Those are run-specific strength training. Have you ever worn a heart rate monitor while doing a heavy set of squats or deadlifts? Your heart rate profile will look very similar to a sprint lasting the same amount of time.

A Lesson from Power Lifters: Use Low Reps to Increase Maximum Strength

To improve strength rapidly, take a lesson from power lifters. Power lifters focus on very low repetitions to increase the weight they can lift. A sample power lifting training cycle is doing five sets of five repetitions for four weeks, three sets of three repetitions for two weeks, and two sets of two repetitions for two weeks. Performing lower reps with progressive heavier loads helps charge your nervous system to deal with the larger weights.

How does this apply to obstacle racing? If you are having trouble with your grip strength—say, you're struggling to hold on to a thick bar—follow a training split like this to increase your maximum grip strength. To do so, you will need a grip machine that allows for increasing weight. Follow a power-lifting-type routine for grip strength by doing four weeks of 5x5, two weeks of 3x3, and two weeks of 2x2. Be sure to try to raise your weight every week. By the end, you will have increased your maximum grip strength.

This concept can also be used to train for doing pull-ups. If you currently cannot do any pull-ups, how do you get better? Use a power lifting split for your pull-up workouts, preferably with one of the weight-assisted pull-up machines. Do four weeks of 5x5 with the minimum counterweight you can handle, two weeks of 3x3 with even less weight, and finally 2x2 with even less weight. At the end of the two-month cycle, test your pull-ups to see if you can do any.

Another technique is using this type of split to increase your ability to vault over walls or perform muscle ups. Do 5x5 of weighted pull-ups with sets of weighted dips in between for four weeks. Then perform 3x3 for two weeks, and finally 2x2 for two weeks. After a couple of days of rest, try a muscle up. Additionally, try working on pull-ups by exploding your effort as you approach the bar. This explosive movement will help with the transition between pull-up and dip, which is essentially the two parts of a muscle-up.

The final example I will give you is if you are trying to complete an obstacle you cannot cross like a peg board. If you can move a couple of spots over on a pegboard, use the 5 sets of practice at the beginning of your weekly back focused workout to improve. Just like in powerlifting, you will take long break (around 2-5 minutes with no other exercise) and repeat your attempt. This is going to help you build technique and strength needed for that type of obstacle.

A Lesson from Triathletes and Baseball Players: Practice Individual Sections Before Combining Them

I've discussed these concepts previously, but to drive the point home here is another, shorter explanation. Triathletes mostly practice swimming, biking, and running separately. This is because it allows better effort and focus for each sport before they're combined. Follow the same approach to your training, especially after you have identified your weaknesses. Practicing your weaknesses repeatedly prior to combining it into a holistic program will create better results.

A baseball player works on improving every muscle involved in his baseball swing separately for overall improvement. Take the same approach to obstacle training. If monkey bars are your weakness, work on improving grip, shoulder, biceps, and back strength separately before combining them. Finally, use the principle of specificity to improve at monkey bars. Practicing monkey bars repeatedly will result in greater improvement than just practicing them once during a training session or once during a race. Repeated sessions of high-volume monkey bar training takes months of racing experience and condenses it into one training session. This is the same concept at work when batting practice condenses the experience of a dozen games into one training session.

Alter Ego successfully completing the rings at World's Toughest Mudder 2013 thanks to supplemental strength training.

A Lesson from Cyclists: Ounces Make Pounds

Ounces make pounds and pounds means more weight to drag up the hill. I've mentioned this concept briefly, but additional emphasis is a good idea. This applies to both equipment and body composition. Adding fat to your body is useless weight that you have to carry around an obstacle course. Control your diet to prevent unwanted fat gain. And when it comes to equipment—again, ounces make pounds. Choose the lightest equipment, as long as it works well for you. This is more important the farther you get away from the center of your body. Weight at the distal end or at the end of your extremities (hands and feet) has a compounding negative effect. The conclusion is that an extra pound on your foot is more costly than an extra pound carried on your hips. When possible, trim away excess weight and fabric to reduce weight. This is why cyclists place such an emphasis on rotating weight. They start by trying to reduce the weight on their cranks, shoes, and wheels because of this. Although cyclists ultimately try to reduce the weight of everything, the rotational or moving weight takes priority.

A Lesson from Adventure Racers: The Drag Method for Team Competitions

If you are participating in a team competition that requires you stay as one group, you will want to keep this technique in mind. Due to the long distance of adventure races, there will always be at least one person who is falling behind. This is due not only to fitness level but also to the body's fluctuations in energy. To ensure that the team moves at the fastest pace possible, use the drag method.

The drag method involves tying a rope from your weakest person to your strongest person and having the strongest person pull slightly. This slight forward pull will allow the weakest person to reduce energy expenditure. This can also be used with two people pulling the weakest person, or the two strongest racers pulling the two weakest racers. This technique is primarily for multi-hour races. A bowline around each racer usually does the trick. Using a carabineer and clipping into another racer's backpack or water carrier is another good technique. The thickness of the rope is a matter of personal preference. Ounces make pounds, but if your rope is fishing-wire-thin, it probably isn't going to feel good digging into someone's back.

Alter Ego helping one another over obstacles.

A Lesson from Rock Climbers: Improve Grip Strength

Nothing in our sport is new, which means that our problems have already been solved by other sports. With grip strength, we look to the grip strength experts: rock climbers. Rock climbers have a dozen different portable devices for improving grip strength, including resistance putty, foam balls of varying resistance to squeeze, and rubber bands for expanding strength. While all these pocket-sized solutions are good for supplemental training, rock climbers have solved the grip strength problem with hangboards.

Hangboards are essentially grip tools that attach above a doorway or to a support beam in your house. Most look like a section of fake rock or consist of wood with different-sized holes for your fingers. They provide a variety of grips so you can practice hanging from your hands, shifting your weight and changing your grip. The large variety of holds offers endless training. They can also be used for exercises like pull-ups, leg lifts, offset pull-ups, and hanging for time. At a price that starts at around $50, they are a great tool for improving both endurance and the ability to grab awkward-shaped objects. Companies like Three Ball Climbing—which provides grips for *OCR Warrior*—also sell various grips that you can hang in your garage or on other support beams in your house. The bottom line is if you are looking to improve grip strength, look toward the climbing community.

The list of learning from other sports does not stop here. As you continue to identify weaknesses, you can continue to look at other sports for their solutions. Looking to the right sport just requires some creative thinking and a thorough analysis of the difficulty you are facing.

Strength & Speed (left to right: Rusty Palmer, Eric Woody, Paul Elliot, and Evan Perperis) take home a cash prize for their finish at Atlas Race Kansas City.

Chapter 9

OBSTACLE RACING ACCESSORIES AND EQUIPMENT

Like all sports, obstacle racing is fundamentally a business. Companies will always be trying to sell you new products to improve performance. Some of these will provide some benefit; others are just fads that will disappear in a couple of years. Often the cheapest method is to build your own versions of high-priced products. Here is a rundown of some of very easy-to-build training accessories that won't cost you much money.

Anytime you construct your own fitness equipment, remember that you are building and using it at your own risk. This is the recommended technique for building these objects, but the ultimate responsibility for safety and construction is upon the builder.

Building Your Own Obstacle Racing Equipment

The Spartan Spear

⅜-inch wood drill bit

Drill

Hand or electronic saw

5-foot handle (can be purchased from Home Depot)

⅜-inch by 12-inch railroad nail

Total Cost: $12 (assuming you own a drill already)

Building your own spear is surprisingly simple. I consider myself a poor craftsman and I still managed to make one with little effort. After buying all the required supplies, find an area such as your garage or outdoors to build your spear and follow these simple steps.

1. Insert the ⅜-inch drill bit into your electric drill.

2. Drill down as far as you can into the tip of the 5-foot handle. Try to keep the hole as straight as possible, for two reasons. The first is so your spear tip will be straight. The second is so that you don't drill through the side of the handle. This is unlikely but it is a possibility, so be careful and keep your hand below the length of the drill's maximum reach. Flip the handle over to shake out any remaining sawdust.

3. Take the ⅜-inch by 12-inch railroad nail and your saw. An electric saw is easier but also more dangerous. A cheap handsaw can be very economical but requires significantly more work. Saw off the head of the nail (where you would hit with a hammer).

4. Take the railroad nail—with its head missing—and jam it into the handle. A couple of slams into the ground can help secure it.

That's it; you're now ready to use your spear. For training targets, bales of hay purchased from a local home improvement store are preferable. Another option is just using bushes. Although the spear will not stick into a bush, as it will a hay bale, it will give you an idea whether your technique, angle, and aim are on target.

Bucket Carry

5-gallon bucket with lid (purchased from a home improvement store)

1–2 bags of sand or gravel (purchased from a home improvement store)

Not a lot of construction here; just purchase the bucket and purchase the quantity of sand you want to use to fill it. Sand, gravel, and water can give you different weights and different challenges for bucket carries. Other options include carrying the bucket with the top secured or with no top. Or you can put a sandbag in the bucket—you now have two training tools in one if you remove the sandbag and carry it on its own.

The Sandbag

Sandbag

2 heavy-duty garbage bags

Roll of duct tape

Pillowcase or other fabric casing

Sewing kit

Total Cost: $4–15, with a lot of extra duct tape and garbage bags

Athletic sandbags are sold on various websites and in stores with ridiculous markups. They typically cost between $1 and $2 per pound of weight. This can be quite an expensive training item for something that is deadweight. Going to a home improvement store or any other place that sells gravel, you can usually find sandbags for around $4. Ideally look for ones in a durable bag, not a cheap plastic bag like the kind typically sold at Walmart.

I've found that a $4 bag of sand that weighs 50 pounds lasts for months even with consistent use. I recommend purchasing two. Use one as a sandbag and keep the other as weight for your bucket. If the sandbag you use for carries gets a hole in it, pour it into the bucket and use the one that was in the bucket for a sandbag.

If you're looking for a more durable solution or a sandbag that is a lighter weight, you can build your own:

1. Pour the desired weight and quantity of sand into a heavy-duty garbage bag.

2. Apply duct tape to seal the bag and reinforce the seams—or the entire bag if you want to be extra secure.

3. Put that inside another heavy-duty garbage bag with another layer of tape.

4. Put that inside a pillowcase or fabric container and sew it closed. You will most likely have to trim off the excess pillow to completely encapsulate the sandbag.

Pegboard

2-inch x12-inch x 6-foot main wooden board (or multiples if you're making a more complex version)

1.25-inch drill bit (specialized for cutting holes, like a Lenox, which has a drill bit in the center and a circular attachment that cuts a clean hole)

Drill (plug-in version, not battery operated)

Tape measure

Stud finder

10 4-inch-long screws

1.25-inch-diameter wooden dowel at least 1 foot long

Sandpaper

Total cost: Under \$50 (as long as you do not have to buy the drill)

The pegboard can be customized to your personal preference. You can adjust most of the spacing and measurements to fit your needs. The items above make the simple variant on the pegboard. To make more complex versions, multiply the number of main wooden boards and screws by the number of pegboards you want.

1. Decide on the complexity of the pegboard. One option is a simple 2-inch by 12-inch by 6-foot board that's vertical, horizontal, or angled. Others include multiple 2-inch by 12-inch by 6-foot boards going in multiple directions—say, an upside-down U shape, or an N shape.

2. Lay out the 2-inch by 12-inch by 6-foot wooden board on top of another piece of scrap wood. Using the tape measure, mark the location for the holes on the board. The holes can be staggered or on the same level, depending on your preference. Regardless, place the holes so that there's at least 1.5 inches from the long side edge of the board to the edge of the hole (or 2.25 inches from the long side edge of the board to the center of the hole) to ensure that your board is strong enough to support your weight. Put the first set of holes 6 inches from the short

side edge of the board. If you're using a non-staggered design, space the holes 8 to 12 inches apart depending on the desired difficulty level. With a staggered design, space the holes 6 to 8 inches apart.

3. Drill the holes in the board using the 1.25-inch drill bit on the marked locations. Remember, be sure to have 1.5 inches of wood from the edge of the hole to the edge of the board, and use a scrap piece of wood below the main board so you can drill all the way through the board. Blow off excess sawdust.

4. Mount the pegboard to the wall using the stud finder to ensure you are not just drilling into drywall. Use all ten screws to ensure that the pegboard will not come loose.

5. Finally, cut the 1.25-inch wooden dowel into handles that are 6 to 8 inches long. They should fit tightly in the holes. For a looser fit, sand the sides of the handles, uniformly removing thickness from the edges.

Test your weight on the board by hanging prior to beginning training. Now that everything is mounted and tested, you are ready to start training. Add more complex variants if you like by building more pegboards and mounting them to the wall.

Building Your Personal Fitness Mecca

If you decide to purchase your own gym, buy fitness equipment, or build your own training area, here are some recommendations. Everyone's personal gym will be different, so be sure to adjust it to your needs.

Home Obstacle Training Area

If you have a garage or a backyard with plenty of space, you might consider building a modified version of an obstacle course in your house or yard. The simple obstacles described above can be used to build a training area that provides a decent workout. Within the garage, items like a pegboard and hangboard can be hung from the ceiling or walls. You can also purchase premade hanging grips to create your own rig from the ceiling. I primarily use grips from companies like Sinergy Sports or Three Ball Climbing because of their high quality and unique variations in grips. If you don't want to pay for grips, you can create your own. This is limited only by your imagination, so be creative. Adding in things like a horizontal pipe, short hanging ropes, or a baseball hanging from a chain provide variation and challenge your skills. Just be sure to secure everything safely.

Another option is purchasing a playground for your children whose frame can serve double duty for your training. This is not cheap—it will most likely cost around $1,000 or more. The higher-quality playground sets that are made of wood can support an adult hanging from the cross-beam for training. Rock climbing grips or other homemade handholds can be added to provide an additional obstacle for your training.

Home Speed Area: The Cardio Room

My cardio room is actually my family room or TV room. I have my TV set up on one end of the room with the couch in front of it. Behind the couch are my treadmill and bicycle trainer. This allows me to watch TV while training.

Treadmill: When purchasing a treadmill, don't buy the cheapest one. Usually if you stick to a middle-of-the-line model, you will have something worthwhile. This typically costs around $1,000 new. If you want a slightly used one, deals are available on various websites that resell items. The cheap treadmills are lightweight and do not provide a stable running platform. Try using a cheap treadmill in a hotel and you will find out what that feels like. The entire machine shakes with each foot strike. If you leave a remote on the console, it shakes and falls off every couple of steps. Save yourself the aggravation and buy something decent.

Stationary bike: I prefer not to buy a stationary bike but a trainer. This is a machine that hooks up to your regular bicycle so you can ride it indoors. There are several different types that provide resistance through various means, including mechanical, magnetic, and fluid. I personally recommend a fluid trainer (at the high end of the three price-wise). They provide the smoothest resistance and are the quietest. (Even as the "quietest," of course, it still makes some noise.) This is nice if you have family members sleeping in another part of the house—you don't have to crank up the TV volume.

Home Strength Area: The Weight Training Gym

This can cause a rapid depletion of your bank account. I purchased my home gym for somewhere around $700 brand new, because I shopped smart. I purchased my weight set from a local home improvement store. It provided a barbell and 300 pounds of weights for about $200. Then I purchased a bench and rack separately from the same store for another couple hundred dollars. These are not top-of-the-line pieces, but they do the job since I mostly use this home gym on the weekends so I can still work out but not waste family time.

I looked into purchasing adjustable weights, like those sold by Bowflex—you can vary the weight on these from 5 to 50 pounds or 20 to 100—but I decided against it. If you have money to spend, those are great items that make weight adjustment easy. The only bad part is they are expensive and fragile. Do not drop one of those weights after a set—you may break a plate off. If I had money to burn, I would have purchased these to enhance my home gym. Another option is buying a full rack of weights or individual fixed-weight dumbbells, but this is also not cost-efficient. To get the required weights you will end up spending hundreds of dollars—and that does not count having a rack on which to place the weights.

For dumbbells, I recommend buying the kind that look like miniature barbells. Make sure they take the same weights as your barbell. Be aware that some have different-sized holes in the center of the plate. I purchased weights that fit on a standard Olympic-sized barbell to keep things simple. This allows you to create your own dumbbells using the same weights that you put on your barbells. For under $100 I purchased two dumbbells and an EZ curl bar that I can use with my barbell weights. It can be annoying to switch the weights from the barbell to the dumbbell, but it saves a significant amount of money. If you end up using your home gym as your primary gym, consider upgrading to one of the adjustable-weights systems for ease of adjustment.

Finally, don't forget a frequently overlooked item for your home gym: the mirror. Yes, I have two large mirrors in my garage gym. I purchased both from a large home improvement store for about $40. They are several feet wide and several feet tall with no frame. I have them just leaning against the wall. If you are going to put the gym in a room in your house, I recommend hanging them. You want mirrors 24 inches above the ground and 18 inches from the nearest weight to prevent accidents. Mirrors are important to ensure you have proper form but also because who doesn't like to watch themselves workout? Working out while looking in the mirror helps reinforce that mind–muscle connection that is important to building strength and targeting muscles.

Home Strength Area: Olympic Lifting Platform and Weights

If you are into Olympic lifting or CrossFit-type training, I highly recommend going to a gym. However, if you are insistent on having your own personal gym, be prepared to spend a lot of money. The rubber plates, the rack, and the wooden platform will cost hundreds if not thousands of dollars.

I have several friends who've built their own platforms. If you're looking to save money, this may be a good alternative. The bumper plates are expensive no matter where you buy them, but different companies charge different prices. Shop around to find the best deal. I still recommend putting mirrors into your gym for Olympic lifts. Having a mirror in a gym where only you are present will help you identify weaknesses in form that would be hard to see without someone else watching you. Just be sure that dropped weight will not roll or hit the mirrors.

Chapter 10

MORE WAYS
TO GAIN AN EDGE

To maximize your performance, take advantage of everything you can within the rules of OCR. A lot of the techniques, suggestions, and methods I recommend produce tiny improvements. However, if you do a hundred things that cause tiny improvements, the end result can be quite astounding. To win or compete at your best, I believe you have to use every advantage you can—with the exception of rule breakers, like performance-enhancing drugs.

Mental Training

The main edge that most people do not take advantage of is mental training. It is proven that when you watch someone perform an activity, your brain mirrors it by firing the same neurons. This mirror neuron activity looks the same in those that are performing the sport and those that are watching the sport. Therefore, when you watch someone run, your brain is firing as if you are running.

There was a famous study done by Alan Richardson involving training to shoot free throws at a basketball net. He organized three groups of people. One group practiced free throws, one group visualized free throws, and one group neither practiced nor visualized. In the end, the visualization group showed improvement and was almost as good as the group that actually practiced throwing the basketball. The group that did neither was the worst of the three. What does this mean for you, since your sport of choice may not be basketball? By combining actual practice along with time spent visualizing or watching OCR, you can increase performance even more.

How can we use this to our advantage? There are several ways. The first way is through visualization. Prior to going to the gym, track, road, or trail you should know what exercises you will be performing. You don't need to know *every* exercise, but you should have a general idea of the important ones, like "Today I will be doing 4x800m repeats with monkey bars and muscle ups." Either prior to going to your training site or on the drive, visualize yourself absolutely crushing your exercises. Imagine hitting your goal times and achieving your target repetitions with no problems. If you want to help yourself get motivated, you can watch a couple of videos online of others doing whatever your exercises are for that day. This will get those neurons fired up and ready for activity.

The second way is to watch videos of whatever your fitness goal is. You can do this this not only to motivate yourself right before you go to the gym, but also on your free time. Watching the videos will keep your neurons firing as if you're doing the exercise. In 2014, obstacle racing started to get television coverage, which will hopefully continue. If it does not, there are always YouTube videos available. *OCR Warrior* is the primary source and best one for visualizing OCR training and techniques. This is especially useful if you have a weak obstacle such as completing monkey bars. By watching others successfully complete the obstacle, you are helping create the same pathways in your brain. Just make sure you are watching good obstacle racers instead of fail compilations. Essentially, you are training even in your downtime.

Another mental training tip that you can use is a mantra. Repeating a saying over and over again can help motivate people. I personally usually don't use this technique, but I know some racers who do. If you are going to use a mantra, be sure it's something positive. An example of a negative mantra might be "Don't quit." Repeating the word *quit* in your

Evan Dollard versus Evan Perperis in Knockout Round 1 of
OCR Warrior, hosted by Brett Stewart.

mind over and over can have the opposite effect of what you want. A
positive mantra is "Keep going." This echoes positive thoughts throughout your mind.

Drugs

I am all about taking every advantage I can to win, with the exception
of drugs. As a lifetime drug-free athlete, I discourage drug use in others.
Performance-enhancing drugs (PEDs) are illegal and banned by most
obstacle course races. They have no business in elite/competitive OCR.
Even if not explicitly banned on smaller races websites, if their race is a
qualifying event for the OCR World Championship, by affiliation they
are banned. They provide an unfair advantage to the athletes using them
and are not only a violation of the rules but also a violation of the spirit
of the sport.

Performance-enhancing drugs is a broad term that includes EPO (erythro-
poietin), HGH (human growth hormone), steroids, various stimulants,
and anything else banned by the World Anti-Doping Agency (WADA).

The physical benefits many drugs provide allow for a faster recovery, which allows an athlete to train harder again the next day. When compared with a clean athlete, this means the drugged athlete will be able to improve at a faster rate. The drugs do provide short-term positive effects but most studies also indicate long-term damage to the heart and other organs. EPO improves performance by increasing your red blood cell count, thus allowing your body to process oxygen. EPO is safer in one regard because it is less likely to do long-term damage to your body, but it's more dangerous in another because there is a chance you could die if your blood becomes too viscous.

Whenever you are taking supplements, be sure to check their label against the annual list produced by WADA. If you want someone to do this for you, a company called Aegis Shield will check any supplement and report if it is clean, banned, or may contain banned substances based off analysis of the label. This takes the guesswork out of analyzing your supplements. You should pay special attention to fat burners, testosterone boosters, and pre-workout supplements. These are the most likely to contain banned substances because of the stimulants they often contain. However, Aegis Shield does not actually test the substances it just checks the label, so be sure to use reputable brands to avoid purposeful or involuntary contamination.

If you know drug users who are racing at the elite level, encourage them to quit using or quit racing at that level. Drug use, includes things like hormone replacement therapy, provides an unfair advantage. If you think this is a victimless violation, think again. There are plenty of athletes who bust their ass year-round trying to place overall or in their age group at every event. Even if drugged athletes aren't winning prize money, they're stealing a place away from a clean athlete. I have heard elite athletes refer to drugged athletes as not only stealers of money but also stealers of dreams. For smaller events, the placement in a competition often has more intrinsic value than the actual prize purse. You never know what dream you are stealing. Maybe a drugged OCR World Championships finish in twentieth place bumped out a clean athlete, crushing their dreams. Everyone, please do your part in this anti-PED campaign. Let's work together and keep mud runs clean.

Motivation

Everyone has their own motivations for competing in OCR. For some it's all about placing; others are looking to set a personal best, and still others are just there for the experience. Whatever your main motivation is, sometimes that starts slipping. Don't be concerned if this happens to you; the ebb and flow of motivation is completely normal. I have a few techniques I use to help keep motivation high. These include the trophy wall, meeting famous athletes, surrounding yourself in a positivity, and the pilgrimage.

The Trophy Wall

When I finished my first marathon, I received a medal at the finish line and was very proud of it. The more races I finished, the more medals I received. While earning more medals isn't my main reason for racing, seeing my medals displayed helps reinforce good feelings of positive accomplishments. I recommend finding a shelf, wall, or other area to display all your medals.

I have two sections: a spot on the wall for my race medals, and a bookshelf for my trophies. The bookshelf also has all my fitness books stored underneath it. These both sit within sight of my stationary bike and treadmill. It provides a positive environment/reminder during those last couple of weeks before a race or competition when motivation starts slacking.

At a minimum, I recommend keeping all your medals or trophies in a box. While it may not seem important now, there may come a time when you look back on all your physical accomplishments with great fondness. It may not occur until a decade or two down the line when you've stopped working out, but it will come eventually. Finding your box with all your previous accomplishments may be the spark that reignites the competitive flame.

The Famous Athlete

Besides having all my medals hanging on a wall, I have several autographed pictures from my favorite athletes. If you are looking to get an autograph from a famous football or baseball star, this might be challenging. The OCR community is a different story. All you have to do is ask them at their next race. Some post all or part of their race schedule online as part of social media. Due to sponsorships, many are aligned with companies like Spartan or BattleFrog and will therefore be present at a majority of those events. Don't be afraid to ask for autographs; the majority of elite racers are very friendly, and I've yet to have a bad experience interacting with one. As the sport continues to grow, expect athletes to use self-marketing to sell autographed products online, which will provide an option if you're not going to be attending the same race. Nothing says *Stop being lazy* like a world champion or elite athlete addressing you by name and telling you to put in the hard work.

Multiple World's Toughest Mudder champion and the winner of too many races to count, Ryan Atkins is a great source of motivation for elite-level performance.

Surrounding Yourself with Positivity

Obviously the people around you will affect the way you behave. If you are spending your time with folks who are constantly going out drinking and not working out, then your behavior will most likely mirror theirs. I am not saying you need to leave your current group of friends; just be aware of how their behavior is affecting you. Having another athlete as one of your friends can help keep motivation high.

If you surround yourself with people who eat healthy, you are less likely to go get a burger and fries on your lunch break. If you're the only one currently eating healthy and you maintain that, you will be surprised at how it can spread throughout the group.

Social media, magazines, and television also influence your behavior. If you don't follow a few famous athletes or organizations on social media, you probably should (assuming you are on social media). The bombardment of positive messages will help reinforce positive behavior.

While we are at it . . . check out the Strength & Speed main page (www.teamstrengthspeed.com) along with our Facebook page (www.facebook.com/teamstrengthspeed). Additionally, be sure to follow me on Facebook (www.facebook.com/evan.perp) or you can find me by searching for my name Evan Perperis That page is completely public and completely OCR-focused. My athlete page, which I created before I got involved in OCR, tends to focus more on my multi-sport endeavors. Find it by searching for "Evan the Fastest Bodybuilder" or by going to www.facebook.com/evan1234567890.

The Pilgrimage

With OCR growing every year, several permanent obstacle courses have shown up across the country. If your motivation is low, plan a vacation that passes by one of these places so you can train. While I don't think OCR has a mecca for training yet, one day it will. Most likely it will be a place that has a permanent obstacle course and a decent-sized pop-

Athletes from numerous teams including Strength & Speed, Mid-America Obstacle Course Racers, Team Fugitive Run, and The Battle Corps begin the hundred-obstacle, 5-mile Fugitive Run.

ulation of elite athletes. In the meantime, you can use some of the existing endurance and strength meccas for motivation. On more than one vacation, I have visited some of the greatest places in strength or speed training. A visit to one of these helps keep motivation high and allows you to connect with the sport. Here are some places I recommend visiting to jump-start motivation:

Permanent Obstacle Course Racing Sites

• In Oregonia, Ohio, the Kings Domain permanent obstacle course is found near the Cincinnati home of the inaugural Obstacle Course Racing World Championships along with other popular events like Mud Guts & Glory and BattleFrog Cincinnati.

• In Benson, Vermont, Shale Hill permanent obstacle course site hosts several races a year.

In Binghamton, New York, Viking Obstacle Course at Sunny Hill permanent obstacle course site that hosts several races a year and is co-located on a golf course

• In Wright City, Missouri, The Battlegrounds at Cedar Lake permanent obstacle course near St. Louis hosts several races a year.

• In Greenville, New York, Viking Obstacle Course at Sunny Hill is a permanent obstacle course site that hosts several races a year.

Marseilles, Illinois: Dirt Runner: A OCR race and training venue located just outside of Chicago with some challenging, unique obstacles along with significant elevation change per lap that hosts OCRs in addition to strength focused competitions

• In Las Vegas, Nevada, you'll find Camp Rhino indoor obstacle racing and CrossFit gym.

Marc Tiernan of The Battle Corps racing at the Fugitive Run permanent obstacle course, located in Rolla, Missouri.

Bodybuilding / Weight Lifting Sites

• Venice Beach, California, offers Gold's Gym Muscle Beach, aka The Mecca and former gym of Arnold Schwarzenegger.

• In Syosset, New York, Bev Francis Powerhouse Gym is the East Coast mecca of bodybuilding.

• In Birmingham, United Kingdom, check out Temple Gym, Dorian Yates's gym and training site.

• In Las Vegas, Nevada, Gold's Gym Vegas is home to Jay Cutler.

• In Arlington, Texas, Metroflex Gym is home to Ronnie Coleman and Branch Warren

• In Austin, Texas, visit the Museum of Physical Culture.

Running Sites

• Flagstaff, Arizona, is home to several elite marathoners.

• Boston, Massachusetts, hosts oldest marathon in the United States.

• Baltimore, Maryland, is the home of the Under Armour brand store and campus.

• Eugene, Oregon, is home to Steve Prefontaine and Nike.

Incorporating one of these locations into your vacation also increases the probability that you will work out. For example, I am not going to travel all the way to Gold's Gym in Venice and not hit the gym once. It may only be one workout session over a one-week trip, but having it right in the middle of the trip can help prevent muscle atrophy, fat gain, and fitness loss.

Chapter 11

FINDING YOUR IDEAL RACE

If you're looking to place high at your next obstacle race, part of maximizing your performance should be selecting the ideal race. This involves considerations of length, difficulty of obstacles, and location. Luckily, it's pretty easy to tell which races are harder—the race length often corresponds with its difficulty level.

Part of racing is finding a cost-efficient way to do so. Many of the race series have single race fees that can be quite expensive. Your best bet to funding your addiction is to find a series that has several races close to you. Once you do, purchase a season pass to get the best value for your money. Following the different series on social media can also help you save money. The companies often post discount codes for different events, especially the weekend after Thanksgiving. Otherwise be sure to check TeamStrengthspeed.com and MudRunGuide.com for the latest coupon codes, upcoming races, and latest news.

The Different Race Series

Below is a brief explanation of some of the major race series in obstacle racing. Listing every race series would be impractical, repetitive, and incomplete. This is largely due to the number of companies that appear and disappear every year. However, the website Mud Run Guide, which I contribute to, is a great resource for the most up-to-date information on OCR. They have descriptions and reviews of every race along with event calendars searchable by date or state.

Short Course Series

I use the term *short course* to describe any race that is approximately 5 miles or less. These typically include Warrior Dash, Rugged Maniac, and some Savage

Another of the thirty-plus yearly Warrior Dash events begins.

Race events.

Warrior Dash is a good race series for beginners. The short course, about 3.1 miles, and easy obstacles make for a great introductory race for new OCR athlete or those who specialize in short-distance speed. The obstacles require minimal upper-body strength. If you have a strong running background, this race series will suit you very well. They also offer a season pass for a reasonable price that provides access to a huge number of races across the United States every year.

Other races such as Rugged Maniac and Savage Race are a good next step beyond Warrior Dash. They provide more challenging obstacles but at distances typically ranging around 3 miles for a Rugged Maniac and around 5-7 miles for a Savage Race. If you're looking for slightly harder obstacles but not much more running, move on to one of these race series. Savage Race will provide the most challenging obstacles for the short course multi-state race series, with the exception of Conquer The Gauntlet.

Conquer the Gauntlet

A rising star in the OCR industry is the Conquer the Gauntlet race series, run by the Mainprize family. Started in 2012, their family-run event offers a small-venue feel with the high-quality obstacles seen at the larger events. To snag a spot on the podium, obstacle completion is required. Their events are often challenging enough that the women's podium is missing between

Randi Lackey scales one of the five 8-foot walls that make up Walls of Fury on her way to first place at Conquer the Gauntlet Wichita.

Finishers' podium at Conquer the Gauntlet Wichita (left to right: Evan Perperis, Nathan Palmer, Randi Lackey, Nikki Call, and Bryce Robinson). Notice the empty spot for women's third place; only two women finished all the obstacles. A year later, all of these members would be part of the founding of the Conquer The Gauntlet Pro Team.

one and all three placers. Their signature obstacle Stairway to Heaven—
sometimes called The Devil Steps—involves a 17-foot climb up and then
down the underside of stairs. Additional challenging obstacles are often present, including More Cowbell (rope climb), Walls of Fury (five 8-foot walls
in a row), Pegatron (pegboard), Tarzan Swing (ring traverse), and Dead Man's
Drop (horizontal beam). Although currently based mostly in the Midwest,
the company expanding every year. This is one race series that is definitely
worth making a trip to from several states over.

BattleFrog

Although it's not yet a permanent fixture among the obstacle racing scene,
BattleFrog has certainly made an impact in a short time. The company typically runs races longer than short courses—they're around 8km long or 5
miles for open-wave competitors and around 16km or 10 miles for elite competitors. They also have an option for long-course athletes: BattleFrog
Xtreme, a multi-hour competition in which athletes complete as many laps
as possible during the designated time. In 2015, each competitor had around
six and a half hours to start his or her last lap of the course. Although their
elite waves have mandatory obstacle completion, their Xtreme version requires exercises like eight-count bodybuilders for failed obstacles. If you are
looking for some of the hardest obstacles outside a world championship
venue, then BattleFrog is the way to go. Mandatory obstacle completion
helps avoid domination by pure runners. Due to the prize money, the winners
are still very fast, but they also display strength. At many BattleFrog races,
simply finishing with an elite wristband is a point of pride for many athletes
regardless of how many hours they spent on the course.

Spartan Races

Spartan has a variety of races ranging in distance from 3 miles to 26-plus.
Their races are typically more upper-body-focused than many others. If you
have a strong lifting, CrossFit, or gymnastics background, this is a good race
series for you. Obstacles typically include rope climbing, heavy bucket carries,
rock or tire drags, and sizable vertical walls. Some races place a strong emphasis on suffering—they're located at high elevation or run up ski mountains. If getting muddy isn't something you're interested in, their stadium
sprint series is a great option: It offers the benefits of a sprint course located

Corinna Coffin leaps from an obstacle in a BattleFrog race.

in a major city without all the mud. BattleFrog is one of the few race series left where you can fail an obstacle and still be eligible for the podium, assuming you complete the thirty-burpee penalty.

Tough Mudder

Tough Mudders are advertised as experiences and not races. They aren't timed, with the exception of World's Toughest Mudder (the ultra-distance OCR World Championships), and provide an interesting mix of obstacles designed to play on your fears. They typically average around 10 to 12 miles each. If you're a beginner but looking for a longer distance, Tough Mudder is a good choice. Elite obstacle racers should note that you cannot win a Tough Mudder—they don't keep time. That's exactly what makes these races a great way to train for long slow distance mileage with obstacles. The lack of timing means you will get a better aerobic-focused workout running an even pace. It also means that you can continue to train the day before and/or after the event without worrying about your race performance. These are great preparation for World's Toughest Mudder, Spartan Ultra Beast, or BattleFrog Xtreme. The company often hosts back-to-back days on the course.

If you complete multiple laps each day, you can rack up 40-plus-mile weekends with obstacles.

The Various Obstacle Race World Championships

There are numerous race series claiming to be the world championships for obstacle racing, but which is the true championship? The major world championships in obstacle racing are, in order from shortest to longest, Warrior Dash World Championship, Obstacle Course Racing World Championships, Spartan World Championship, and World's Toughest Mudder. Before discussing the true champion, let's learn a little about each event.

Day 2 of Tough Mudder Kentucky begins and Multi-Lap Legionnaires are off again for mud.

The start of the first Warrior Dash World Championship.

A view of the terrain, which was harder than any obstacle, at the inaugural Warrior Dash World Championship.

Warrior Dash World Championship: Warrior Dash first held its championship in 2014 (and possibly their last in 2015) offering an insane cash prize of $30,000 for first place. At $10,000 per mile for a first-place victory, this is one of the largest cash prizes for any 5K race. This is just a fraction of the $100,000 total the company gave away for the top five men and women. The race, held in mid-October, changes locations; its 5K length features twelve obstacles over mountainous terrain. The inaugural course held outside San Francisco, California, has such steep gradients that at points it required crawling on all fours to make it up the mountainside. Although the terrain proved extremely difficult, the obstacles were the opposite. The majority barely caused a break in stride. Climbing over old cars, crawling under barbed wire, walking a balance beam with guide ropes over water, and a slide left much to be desired. The only obstacle that significantly slowed competitors was the final mud pit, which was like traversing a pool of peanut butter.

Obstacle Course Racing World Championships: The OCRWC was first held in 2014 and is considered by many to be the true championship of obstacle racing. The 8.9-mile race—held on the grounds of the Mud & and

Glory race just east of Cincinnati, Ohio—challenges you on every level. The race draws an international crowd. In 2014, a Swedish woman, Siri England, and a British man, Jonathan Albon, were the winners. The most unusual aspect of this race is its lack of affiliation. Entering the OCR World Championships requires qualification from another race series; usually you must place in the top twenty. Which races feed into the OCRWC? Pretty much any legitimate one. This makes it a strong contender to be the true championship. Add in the requirement to complete every obstacle and the course suddenly becomes much more difficult. Fail to complete an obstacle and there is no penalty; instead your wristband is cut off, leaving you ineligible for prizes and automatically below every competitor who finished all the obstacles. The terrain does not make things any easier with a cramp-inducing 4,000-plus feet of elevation gain and ground so rocky that it's hard to ever get into a strong running stride. The obstacles truly test upper-body and grip strength, including monkey bars, large V-shaped monkey bars, a Tyrolean Traverse, a pipe traverse, the Weaver, and the dreaded Platinum Rig. The latter is a series of rings, rotating bars, extra-wide monkey bars, and vertical beams that can be configured in an infinite number of combinations. The Platinum Rig was so difficult in the inaugural year, it decimated 46 percent of the men and 86 percent of the women. OCRWC effectively tests cardiovascular fitness, obstacle proficiency, strength, endurance, and mental fortitude.

The Beast—Spartan Race World Championship: The Spartan championship started in 2011 and is typically held in Killington, Vermont. How is the terrain in Killington? Well, it's home to the steepest and longest mogul trail in the East, called the Outer Limits. The course is 13-plus miles in length with elevation gain of 5,000-plus feet. Spartan events typically have more strength-based obstacles than some of the competing courses. With obstacles like heavy tire flips, rope climbs, bucket carry, sandbag carry, and a hoist (pulling a weight up a rope using a pulley), it can favor those with a better balance of strength than the pure runner. The 13-plus-mile length make it one of the longer world championships. As of December 2014, Spartan announced that to qualify for the 2015 World Championship, you must have placed in the top five of an elite wave at any Spartan Race. The other big news is that the championship is moving to Lake Tahoe, California. Spartan also has the best media campaign due to its partnership with NBC Sports, which televises the championship along with major events.

World's Toughest Mudder: World's Toughest Mudder started in 2011 in Englishtown, New Jersey. It was held there for three years and in 2014 it moved to just east of Las Vegas, Nevada. By far the most extreme of the obstacle racing world championships, it is twenty-four hours in length and requires multiple laps of the twenty-plus obstacles per lap. The winner historically reaches 90-plus miles and completes a total of four hundred obstacles. The conditions are so extreme that racing requires a wet suit. World's Toughest Mudder also draws a large international crowd especially from countries like Canada, Great Britain, New Zealand, and Australia. Out of all the competitions, it is the most difficult based on length and environmental conditions.

Other nominations: Some may argue that other races should be in contention for the obstacle racing world championship, such as the Death Race or Primal Quest. Death Race is a multiday event that involves obstacles and random tasks designed to break you physically and mentally. Primal Quest is a multiday adventure race that is making a comeback after a six-year hiatus. It involves extreme distances with a variety of tasks and modes of transportation. I would argue that these two races and others like them are not obstacle races. Primal Quest is part of adventure racing, and Death Race to Assessment and Selection Events (ASE). ASE include things like GoRuck, Green Beret Challenge, SISU Iron, and The Brutality. By not having a fixed course or specific obstacles, they fall into a different world and are thus ineligible to be picked as world championships.

So which is the real championship? The winner is clear: the OCRWC. This is based on its non-affiliation, the international crowd it draws, the difficulty of the obstacles, and the length, which is about average for most obstacle races. However, I would add that there isn't just one championship but rather there are multiple championships reflecting the many distances of OCR. In running, the 10K world championship is not the championship for all of running. Having just one race for every distance doesn't make much sense. Each distance has its own championship:

- **Warrior Dash World Championship:** Short-course world championship (5K). (As of 2016 Warrior Dash ended their event but entered a partnership with OCRWC and the OCRWC added a short course 3k race to their event in addition to the ~9 mile championship race. Thus, OCRWC also holds the short course world championship too.)

• **Obstacle Course Racing World Championships:** Middle-distance world championship (9 miles) and the most prestigious.

• **Vermont Beast—Spartan World Championship:** Long-distance world championship (13-plus miles).

• **World's Toughest Mudder:** Ultra-distance world championship.

The terrain at 2014 World's Toughest Mudder, held near Las Vegas.

Warning sign at World's Toughest Mudder.

An Interview with the Founder of the OCRWC: Adrian Bijanada

For more insight on the sport of obstacle racing, the world championships, and the future, check out this interview between Adrian Bijanda (the founder of the OCRWC) and Strength & Speed.

S&S: The OCR community has spent the last couple of years arguing over the "true world championship." It is great to see someone actually take the initiative to establish the OCRWC. What was the breaking point for you where this thing turned from a concept into an actual race?

The idea has been floating around for a while but I would say I first seriously considered setting it up in 2013. However, there was never one big moment where I thought we absolutely have to do this. I always daydreamed about creating something that highlighted the athletes because there are so many races out there that are brand-heavy. All the races series seemed to be going in favor of the race companies and forgetting what was important, the athletes. The way I view my company, which is behind the world championships, is that we are an athlete company first. If we focus on the athletes, we focus on delivering a really good experience. We want to make sure the athletes feel special, their families feel special, and their friends that come watch the event feel special. Everything else falls in line after that, like financial concerns and getting volunteers. If we do everything in a respectful way, then everything is going to turn out okay.

Some of the things that I saw were happening, which I did not like, were things like races charging for spectators, exorbitant parking prices, or expensive entry fees. To me, these things were a warning sign of the way things were going. If I am training for a race and I go to the race, why should I have to pay for my wife to come watch me. I paid my entry fee and I paid my dues in training—that is where it should stop. This all led to the creation of the OCRWC and I thought, *What other time in sporting history do you have the opportunity to create an independent world championship for a brand-new sport?* I launched the OCRWC and it was immensely stressful. We had to battle a lot to overcome issues around credibility, marketing, and even our position in the community. Overall, I think we pulled off a really successful event for the inaugural year.

S&S: What made you decide to setup the OCRWC the way you did?

Regarding the distance, I thought the 7.5-to-9-mile range would be a good happy medium between the shorter races that are typically around 5K, and the longer distance races that are around 13 miles. The 8-mile range did not play to one specific type of racer, sprinters or the long-distance athletes. The mandatory obstacle completion was a no-brainer for us. The sport is called obstacle course racing, so there is no reason obstacles should not be the deciding factor. Doing alternative exercises as a way to get around an obstacle does not feel like a pure obstacle course race. By requiring athletes to complete each obstacle in order to podium or be eligible for cash prizes, it prevents someone who is just a fast runner from skipping all or multiple obstacles and still winning. For example, we had some athletes who spent nearly two and a half hours at one obstacle, and ended up finishing first in their age group. That was because mandatory obstacle completion. To think that another athlete could have shown up and thought, *I just do not want to do this*, and then [gone] to do some jumping jacks in the corner instead, just sounds silly to me.

S&S: At the inaugural event, twelve countries were present . . . How were you able to draw such a diverse crowd from around the world?

[laughs] I do not know, we are still trying to figure that out. I think it came from our willingness to work with other races. We are not a race series and we never will be. This means that many of the other companies we work with are not threatened by us because they know we are not going to be their direct competition. I think they also realize that we bring value to races and their athletes. For example, if you are organizing a race in Sweden and you are trying to get yourself on the map, being able to say you are a qualifier for the world championships is a cool thing. The qualification also helps add traction along with publicity to each qualifying race and is a nice feather in your cap. That status will draw in competitors who are trying to qualify and will help increase registration. It is a mutually beneficial relationship, and the more athletes a qualifying race can get, the larger a net we can cast to get people to our event. This also helps identify a true world champion. Bottom

line is that when they do well, we do well.

S&S: Any plans for adding an award for the fastest country, similar to the way cross-country races are run? (That is, the top three times on the individual race day count for the country time.)

I have not thought about that, but I love that idea. I am going to launch that as soon as possible. [It was launched in 2015 for the first time.]

S&S: Setting up this event must have been a ton of work. Were you able to race the course on the day of the event, or were you too busy taking care of backside support ensuring everything ran smoothly?

I went through it beforehand multiple times during the development of the course, but I was unable to run through it on race day. The way we decided on obstacle spacing was [that] I would do a loop of the course; if my mind started to wander and I was not engaged in what I was doing, it was a place we needed another obstacle. If I am no longer engaged, I need something to draw my attention to the task at hand.

S&S: Where do you see the future of the OCRWC going? Are we going to see a change in venue or is Ohio going to become the mecca for OCR just like Kona is for triathletes and Boston is for marathon runners? Can we expect an increase in difficulty?

I think there are pros and cons to having it here in the US. However, long term, I think we do need to take it internationally. I do not want it to become like baseball's World Series, where we say it is a world championship but it is only held in the US and only draws US athletes. That is not what I want. The issue is: Can I ensure we deliver just as good an experience outside the US? It is a matter of finding a venue and then having the ability to build on it four months before the event. Do I have the ability to go out there and manage that site? I would love to say in a year or two it is going to be in the UK, but it is a matter of: Can I set up the infrastructure there? Can I put a team on the ground to execute the vision? Right now, we are lucky because Kings Domain, the site of the Ohio venue, is fantastic. Normally, I would have not pictured that type of event in Ohio, but I think everyone who has raced there would agree it is one of the most beautiful race courses available. So the question is: Where do we find a venue like that, which gives us the ability to build an 8-mile course seven months before the event, then spend time tweaking the race and making adjustments before race day? Finally, it comes down to where the qualifiers are. If 90 percent of our qualifiers are from the US, I do not think I am going to be able to convince people to travel to New Zealand for an event due to the cost of travel. It is a balance of having the right infrastructure with enough participants to keep the event viable. It is probably not shocking to hear that there is not a lot of money to be made from a single event. The way we have this event keep on going is through athletes and sponsorships.

Regarding difficulty of the course, I think it will remain relatively constant. [The year] 2015 brought the addition of a second Platinum Rig. In 2014, the Platinum Rig took out a lot of people, maybe more than I had hoped for. However, the difficulty in 2015 is designed so it is not one obstacle that is going to break people. The difficulty should come from a complete body-wide exhaustion. We are looking for the perfect all-around athlete, not just the great runner. We want the great runner who is also a great climber and has great upper-body strength. We want someone with great agility, strength, and speed. The approach in 2015 was not to have one obstacle narrow down the pool, as it did in 2014. The idea is to have more obstacles that play to the all-around athlete. When you cross the finish line, your arms, back, forearms, and abs should be just as tired as your legs, quads, and calves. You should hurt all the way around if you did it well.

S&S: The Boston Marathon had to lower their qualifying times a couple of years ago due to overwhelming demand. Do you see qualification getting stricter as the sport grows?

One hundred percent absolutely. Stricter qualifying standards are already in the works for 2016. We have criteria now that [are] pretty balanced, but as our popularity grows, we are going to have to have stricter standards. Maybe we will move to a percentile system per age group rather than the top X number of racers. For example, taking the top 5 percent as opposed to the top five in an age group, which would make sense in age groups where there are fewer competitors.

S&S: What standards do you have to ensure that qualifying races meet the legitimacy of an event worthy of feeding into the

OCRWC?

We have a set of standards that are getting stricter by the year. We have a questionnaire that goes out to all the races that want to apply. The questionnaire has things such as making sure they have sufficient technology for timing the athletes, accurate reporting of results, and ensuring there is a marshal at each obstacle to ensure completion. Additionally, we look at the size of the athlete pool and we check their reviews online to ensure they are maintaining their standards. We have had to pull qualification status from events in the past due to not meeting the prerequisites. We have also denied plenty of events because they were a poor fit or did not have all the boxes checked. You will probably see a shift in those as well in the future.

S&S: Many others and I would classify you as a visionary in the OCR community. As a visionary, what do you see for the future of OCR?

I think it is going to move toward a pure athletic endeavor and a pure athletic competition. I think the days of "badass this" and "epic that" are going away. We go for a very clean and very professional feel to the event. We hold our employees to high standards and want our entire staff to be professionals while they are out their representing the OCRWC. The atmosphere of our event should have a vibe more in line with the Olympics rather than a testosterone-fueled type of event. First and foremost, we are looking for athleticism. For example, we were the first event to start drug testing and we are very proud of that. Drug testing will continue for our athletes in future competitions.

Overall, the sport needs to grow into more of a professional sport. For example, when triathlon first started it was viewed as a crazy endeavor. People could not understand why you would swim, bike, and run all in one event or why you would be willing to complete an Ironman. However, it exploded in popularity, but in a relatively responsible way where the focus remained on the athletes. There is branding in triathlon with major companies like Ironman but the focus is still on true athletic performance.

Suffering definitely goes into OCR, and how long you can suffer is important, but other aspects should play a major role like pacing, strategy, and intelligence. Athletes that are winning should have a smart, strategic approach to the race. I would also love to see athletes that are doing their training periodization better. Things like having an A race for the year along with B and C races, which are practice for the main event. I think all that stuff will be sorted out over the next year or so.

S&S: You are also an accomplished endurance athlete. Anything you want the world to know about Adrian Bijanada the athlete?

I come from a triathlon background and have completed a few iron-distance triathlons. Those were long and miserable days. The thing I like about those races is while you are doing them, you are absolutely miserable. I think there is a time where every athlete is racing and thinking, *Why am I doing this?* You are in such a dark place, but looking back on it now, those are transformative moments. They provide a different perspective to daily life.

For example, my first Ironman was a miserable experience. During the race I tore a hamstring. The ten-month training period before the race seemed to go down the drain because I was not going to hit my goal time. However, in the following week, I went back to work and things around the office that would normally cause me to freak out or I might view as impossible were no longer daunting. I hope that the OCRWC brings a similar experience to those that race at the event.

S&S: Anyone, person or company, you wish to thank or mention?

First, I would like to thank my wife, Kristine, because she puts up with a lot. Next, I definitely need to thank my team, Brad Kloha, Brett Stewart, Kevin Jones, Garfield Griffiths, and Brian Tumbler, because they have been great. We are pretty small, but to think of what we pulled off with such a small team has been absolutely incredible.

S&S: Thanks for taking the time to talk to us. You will go down in history as someone who is willing to look beyond a company logo and establish something that the community needed. I would like to say thank you on behalf of myself and all the other obstacle racers. I look forward to seeing you at the next OCRWC.

Chapter 12

INTERVIEWS WITH ELITE OBSTACLE RACERS

Every athlete is different, and every athlete has a different training background. The sport of obstacle racing is only a couple of years old, so none of us grew up with it as our primary sport. This means that athletes are coming into OCR with various backgrounds, including running, lifting, gymnastics, or team sports. This means every athlete has different strengths and weaknesses. Furthermore, each athlete has his or her own opinion on how to maximize performance.

What follows are interviews from some of the top athletes in the obstacle racing community. Some will echo many of the principles from this book; others may contradict some of statements you've read in the preceding pages. The important thing is to evaluate yourself as an athlete, identify your weaknesses, and fix those weaknesses, creating a better overall racer. If you can discover athletes here who are similar to you, try mimicking some of the techniques they've used to achieve success. Make sure you check out these amazing athletes on social media as well; many of them provide training tips and motivation to help you.

Marc-André "Marco" Bédard

Age: 29

Height: 5'9"

Weight: 160 pounds (70kg)

Year Started Obstacle Racing: 2011

Biggest Accomplishment in OCR: Killington Beast 2011. Besting the undefeated Hobie Call at my first experience in OCR was both unbelievable and eye opening.

Other OCR Race Highlights:

30 podium finishes in 36 races in 3 countries

2014 Spartan Race and XMAN Race Canadian champion

6th place 2014 Obstacle Course Racing World Championships

6th place 2012 Spartan Race World Championship

11th place 2014 Warrior Dash World Championship

Strength & Speed: What was your athletic background prior to OCR?

I have been on the Canadian national team since 1999 in biathlon (skiing and shooting). I have dreamed of the Olympics since age eight and finally achieved this goal on home soil at the Vancouver 2010 Olympic Games. I have had numerous World Cup starts and I have won four international medals over the years. I still race biathlons in addition to obstacle course racing. Additionally, I have many national titles in biathlon, cross-country skiing, winter triathlon, mountain biking, and most recently obstacle course racing!

S&S: How has your athletic background hurt or helped you for OCR? What things did you have to adjust to become a successful OCR athlete?

Biathlon is a truly amazing sport: It combines the full body endurance, power, and speed required to cross-country ski with the focus that precision shooting demands. You have to know your body and adjust accordingly while your heart is going 180-plus beats per minute to aim at targets 150 feet away. After hitting those targets, you need to go back to cross-country skiing at maximum effort—all within twenty seconds. This and the fact that I have been pushing my body to race ski races since I was little are the reason I can do well at OCR. I believe it has a lot to do with your mind-set. International-level athletes are the most focused people on the planet, and they would never dare to take a risk trying something that is not going to help them achieve greatness in their own sport. I have always been curious of other sports and their challenges. OCR is one sport where I never know what to expect. It might be a suffer-fest one day, where I am really challenged in ways I did not expect, but I will always have a great time doing it. OCR is also new enough that I never know everyone that shows up, which means I am not sure if I am going to win or not even make it on the podium.

S&S: What is your biggest recommendation for OCR athletes who want to improve?

Train smart, surround yourself with positive people, know your body, know your own limitations and try to push them little by little. Beast mode is a myth; keep your inner beast for race days. Any high-level athlete will tell you that training is a way of life and there are no shortcuts. In order to improve, you need to go through hell and back. You need to stay clean and injury-free so that every step forward is earned and only time will tell where you will land. Patience is key, along with a smarter approach to training. Finally, remember that hard work always pays off!

S&S: What is your daytime job?

I have been a full-time athlete for the past fifteen years but in Canada, like many countries, it is a plus to have a cushion in order to train better and race more. So I have kept a part-time job year-round at the Hilton Hotel, where I can work [few] hours every month and earn enough to cover my needs if I do not make enough from racing.

S&S: How do you balance your job and family with training for OCR?

Sports have always been my whole life. My best half is a champion herself [Claude Godbout] and the reason I can still live the dream after all these years. We share the same love for a healthy life and we both know and understand what it takes to reach high goals. We support each other when we are on top but especially when we hit lows. Making it through those bad times is what is most important for long-term success!

S&S: What does an average training week in your life look like when preparing for a race?

Ski racing is a lot different, yet has many similarities to OCR. For biathlon, we have always focused on one season [one 4-month racing period per year]. OCR is basically nonstop racing year-round, and since we are still racing in the winter, we need to take breaks to put in hours in order to survive the longer races or prepare for shorter ones. In this year's case, we signed with team BattleFrog and will race all of their events, plus probably every championship. So we figured we would concentrate the first couple months of the spring [and] summer on building strength, endurance, and agility without thinking too much about results. Every race is a workout, and this is always where you learn more. Every hour we put in is to perform during championship season. We will concentrate our efforts on OCRWC, Spartan Race World Championship, and BattleFrog Championship, but might race Warrior Dash and WTM as well depending how it goes!

Therefore, for a couple of months, we work in four-week cycles at a time depending on the location of the races. The four-week cycles have three weeks of loading hours and intensities and then one lower-intensity week. We focus on building hours and technique first; then the more the season digs in, the more we will focus on speed and agility. The bigger weeks in skiing get close to thirty hours of pure training, with rest weeks going around ten hours. I do not focus on running, only because I like other sports a lot and also believe that cross-training (not specific) is the base of happiness at any level.

S&S: How high is your peak mileage when preparing for a race?

Not sure! My whole career I have been counting in hours, intensity zones, and types of workouts, so to me pure mileage does not mean much. These days I seem to be running around 30 to 40 miles per week, and a little less when I need to travel to races. However, I do still put lots of mileage on wheels (mountain bike, road bike, roller skis, et cetera).

S&S: What was one of the hardest workouts you have ever done when preparing for a race?

Weighted stairs intervals are the ones that feel the hardest when you do them, but damn they feel good when you go to bed! I run mostly on mountains, but when I am not, I love long staircases, and there are lots of them around Quebec City. At Chutes Montmorency Falls in Quebec City, there is a good set of four-hundred-plus stairs that I like to use for training. I either do ten to twelve intervals, repetitions carrying heavy stuff, or simply [go] up and down at maximum intensity. As a bonus, on hot days you get a free "shower" from the falls on every rep!

S&S: What was your hardest or worst racing experience?

My worst racing experience would be an injury I had during a 25K trail race in Mont Sainte-Anne, or the one time in over a thousand races I DNF [did not finish] a sporting event. At the Houston BattleFrog, I was not ready and I had open wounds on both my hands from the mining ladder. This was the first race of 2015, so in order to recover and be better prepared for the season I did not even finish the race. For me, I do not feel right failing an obstacle at BattleFrog and getting a medal, so I walked off the course. Best kick in the butt I have ever had!

Hardest racing experience would be my very first OCR, which was the 2011 Spartan Beast. I ended up winning the whole thing but I lost a little bit of myself in Vermont that day. I could not walk right for a week, either, and still had to show up for biathlon training like nothing happened because my coach would not have allowed me to race that!

S&S: Could you have done anything different to prepare for that?

Yes, yes, and yes, but I would not even if I could. I am a strong believer that failure is the base for success in life, and without failure you do not make it very far. I learned from my own mistakes and I get stronger every time I make one.

S&S: What is the most common question you receive as an OCR athlete?

Did you win a medal at the Olympics? Hahaha! The answer is no! That one is not OCR-specific, though. For OCR, it is usually training-related questions. So questions like *What do you think of CrossFit?* or *What shoes do you wear?* I am just happy to see so many people enjoy a sporting activity and to see more and more high-level athletes every season!

S&S: Do you follow any specific dietary restrictions (such as vegan, gluten-free, vegetarian, Paleo)?

I will eat everything my beautiful girlfriend makes! Not only she is a beast, but she loves to cook super-healthy food! Seriously, though, the answer is no, I do not follow a diet, but I do avoid any fast food because it makes me sick.

S&S: How do you think that affects your performance?

It is a no-brainer! To me, stress is your worst enemy, and to be chill about food but staying aware of how you fuel up and what makes you feel good is the best way to deal with food. I see many people seeking the shortcuts that are supposed to make you faster. Simple is key here. Eat and live simple and you will be happy and healthy!

S&S: Are there any people or companies that you want to thank publicly?

I am not sure where I would be without my girlfriend Claude, so she is the main person I need to thank. I would also like to thank my team, Team BattleFrog, the best team ever, along with our friends at Platinum Rig. We have it all covered to be the best we can be! Spartan Race Canada has a great place in our hearts, too, and so does XMAN Race in Quebec! OCRWC is our favorite and the only true-feeling championship, so we cannot thank them enough for making it happen!

S&S: What do you see in the future for OCR?

I think OCR is already changing. Most people I know have been around and are losing interest, but I think if companies like BattleFrog, Toughest, and OCRWC, for example, keep pushing the sport toward the competitive aspect, we will see more and more legitimacy in the sport. I predict a long life to it as a sport and not just a weekend activity. It should always stay possible to run it for fun, like any other sport, but it still has a long way [to go] to gain more legitimacy as a sport.

Hobie Call

Age: 38

Height: 5'9"

Weight: 145 pounds

Year Started Obstacle Racing: 2011

Biggest Accomplishment in OCR: I thought about this, and honestly, I could not point to one race and say that is my biggest accomplishment. My biggest accomplishment is my consistency since 2011. To be able to race well so many times in a row is my biggest accomplishment.

Other OCR Race Highlights:

2011 Spartan World Championship in Texas

2013 Spartan World Championships

Won Spartan points system and Super Hero Scramble points system along with both of their championship events all in one year

Strength & Speed: What was your athletic background prior to OCR?

Growing up I was involved in endurance running. In high school, I ran the 1 mile and 2 mile. In college, I ran the 5K, steeplechase, and cross-country. I was barely good enough to get a scholarship at a junior college. I was always told, "Figure out what you want to do in life, because you are not going to run 10Ks for a living." I really was not that good in my high school and college days. After college, I ran everything from 5K to the marathon, with the longer the race, the better. I performed best at the marathon.

For three years prior to obstacle racing, I started doing odd personal records. For example, I broke the world record for lunging the fastest mile. Afterward, I trained myself to run a 4:40 mile with a weight vest on. I started focusing on odd strength- and stamina-type events. With these types of challenges, there are no formal events, so it is hard for people to understand how difficult they are.

S&S: How has your athletic background hurt or helped you for

OCR? What things did you have to adjust to become a successful OCR athlete?

If I would have been a really good runner, I probably just would have stuck with running. Realistically, I would have never shown up to my first obstacle race. The OCR industry has a hard time getting professional athletes from other sports into OCR because they do not take it seriously. Add in the possibility for injury and it scares them away from the sport. An injury in OCR would jeopardize their other goals in running or racing. I probably would have been in that same boat, but I am an adventurous guy, and was not going to make it as a runner anyway.

I do not know if you believe in destiny, but I do. I believe I was meant to do what I am doing now. By chance, I just happened to be running three days a week doing power/strength work. Specifically, things like lunges, weight vest running, and upper-body workouts three days a week. I was living in Salt Lake City and it was smoggy. During the wintertime, I had to run in the dark, so I supplemented this training doing upper-body workouts down in my basement three days a week. To avoid building a lot of muscle, I was doing lots of high-intensity circuit-type training and working all my muscles at a high cardiovascular rate. This type of work just happened to be perfect for obstacle racing. At the time I did not even know what obstacle racing was; I just happened to be training that way by circumstance. Luckily, once I started obstacle racing, I did not have to change my training.

S&S: What is your biggest recommendation for OCR athletes who want to improve?

My biggest recommendation is still running. In order to be successful, you have to be a strong endurance runner. Specifically, a good trail and/or mountain runner, because most races are still 80 to 90 percent running-based. So first, be as good an endurance runner as you can be, because those are the people still winning all the races.

On top of that, work your grip strength and pull-ups. Ninety percent of what the upper body needs is grip strength and pull-ups, with an emphasis on grip strength. There are many other little things but that is the vast majority of the equation.

S&S: What is your daytime job?

I am full-time in the OCR industry as a consultant and sponsored athlete. I am currently working with Atlas Race. They sponsor me and I get good prize money from them, so I manage to make it work. Overall, I persevered and made running my full-time job despite what I was told in college.

S&S: How do you balance family with training for OCR?

Prior to working in the OCR industry, it was not easy. I was very dedicated but I was not making any money doing it. Your family and neighbors look at you as if you are crazy and think, *Why don't you go and get a real job?* It was tough especially with five kids and a wife. Balancing training with family and working a full-time job was not easy. It takes a lot of dedication, and you do not waste your time watching TV or playing video games for four hours a day.

Ever since I started obstacle racing, it has been really good, because the family is interested in it, too. They want to go to races, they want to train for it, and they want me to go to races to see how I do. Now that I do it for a living, it is not that hard because everyone understands that it is my job. It definitely helps that they are a part of it, too, and they get to experience the fun.

S&S: What does an average training week in your life look like when preparing for a race?

I train six days a week, with three days a week focused on lower body and three days a week focused on upper body, alternating days. The lower-body days are mostly running. I honestly do not do much obstacle-specific training. Instead, I just work the muscles I need to get through the obstacles. For example, I have an 8-foot wall in my backyard and I rarely go over it. I actually have not been over it in about four months. I do have a Weaver and a rope in my backyard, so I will occasionally use those as part of my upper-body training. I find working the muscles I need more efficient for training for OCR than actually practicing the obstacles repeatedly.

S&S: How high is your peak mileage when preparing for a race?

I am running such a variety of races throughout the year that it gets hard to adjust your training. One week you are running a 5K distance Atlas race and the next week you are running a 9-mile Spartan Super; it becomes hard to specifically prepare for each race . . . Instead I focus on what I want to specialize in . . . As long as my races are not too much shorter or longer than what I am training for, I do pretty good. I actually train for shorter events. If races are 10-plus miles or take longer than one hour and thirty minutes, I struggle because I do not train for that type of endurance.

I am still figuring out where I want to specialize. I am actually a real low-mileage guy with high intensity, and right now I am not real structured. For 2011, 2012, and 2013, I was only running 10 miles a week. However, that is deceiving because I do a forty-minute warm-up in addition to many body weight exercises. For example, I do a lot of lunges and running with a weight vest. For me, this is a flawed question because I do so much more than just count mileage for the week. My training program got me through the Spartan Sprints and Supers well but I was hurting on the Beast-length events. Those longer races took me a long time to recover.

S&S: What was one of the hardest workouts you have ever done when preparing for a race?

Each workout is hard for its own reason. If I had to pick one, it would be my high-intensity workouts, which are also the shortest. In some ways, it is the most painful and in other ways, it is not. I will answer this, though, because it is a fun one. Here is a workout from 2011 and 2013 that I thought was particularly hard:

40-minute warm-up consisting of calisthenics, plyometrics, and dynamic movements

Treadmill: 6x 1-minute intervals at 4:50 mile pace while wearing a 30-pound weight vest (with a 20-second rest break between each)

Lunge Pyramid: 90 pounds of weight walking lunges for 100m

30–40 pounds of weight walking lunges for 100m

Body weight "lunge sprints" for 100m (lunges done at max speed) (the lunge sprints are repeated a couple of times prior to ending the workout)

S&S: What was your hardest or worst racing experience?

Regarding OCR, the worse the race, the better the experience—it is kind of funny how that works. My most favorite, most memorable experiences and the ones that I will enjoy the most when I look back ten years from now [are] the races where I did not run well. In OCR, I would never equate the hardest with worst.

My worst and most painful experience was a marathon I did in 2002. The week before a marathon, I did a 5-mile race in a canyon with an 8 percent downgrade all on pavement. I was so sore, I actually could not run the entire next week. Finally, on Friday, the day before the marathon, I was able to run a mile and it hurt just a little bit. However, I had to run the marathon because I was running the Utah Racing Circuit that year. In order to win the circuit, running the marathon was required. I showed up and the first 5 miles felt comfortable. Then from that point on every step hurt. My shins, my knees, my quads, my hamstrings, my glutes, my stabilizers: Everything hurt on every step. At the 10-mile mark, I wanted to just quit and walk. However, I could not walk because I was leading the race. I told myself, *As soon as I get passed, I am walking.* However, no one ever passed me, so I had to run the whole race. Especially after 16 miles, every step was agony. It was one painful race, but I made it. If I had not done that 5-miler the week before and my body was well rested, it would not have been so awful.

S&S: What is the most common question you receive as an OCR athlete and your response?

What should I expect? There is a lot of unknown in OCR because it is not on mainstream television and there are not a lot of good videos explaining the experience. Even with all the information, people still do not know what to expect. Ninety percent of newcomers have envisioned something else in their minds, and it is often worse in their imagination. My advice is to remember two things. One, you signed up for a challenge . . . Two, if all else fails, keep your sense of humor and have fun. Eventually, most people are going to hit a point in the race, especially the more difficult races, where people are going to think, *What did I get myself into?* Just keep your sense of humor, keep smiling, keep moving, and remember, *I signed up for something tough.*

S&S: Do you follow any specific dietary restrictions (such as vegan, gluten-free, vegetarian, Paleo)?

I like to think I take the best of all worlds. I have done raw foods before and I try to take some of the benefits I learned from that. Previously, I was a vegan for six and a half years, so I can see the benefits of that. Now I eat with many aspects similar to that of a bodybuilder. I eat every three hours on the dot and end up eating about six or seven meals a day. This provides me with a steady energy level. I also eat a lot more protein now than I used to eat when I was a vegan. That is one of the main reasons I switched off veganism, because it was so hard to get enough protein. Overall, I generally eat clean and natural foods. I do take some supplements, like protein powder, but when I buy protein powder it is just plain whey with no flavoring, no additives, or any of that other garbage. When I buy meat, I try to purchase meat made from grass-fed cows. I stay away from almost all processed foods, minus some supplements, and try to maintain clean eating. I probably eat more green leafy vegetables that anyone on the planet. Overall, I eat clean by eating a lot of healthy fats, a lot of healthy carbs, and a lot of healthy protein. I am not very restrictive, because if you try to go too restrictive for too long, it starts to drive you crazy. In general, I eat to stay healthy and have lots of energy but I am not super crazy about it. After all, I am not a figure or bodybuilding competitor.

S&S: How do you think that affects your performance?

It makes a huge difference in performance. I would not have won half the races I did without eating healthy. Genetically, I am a mess and I have all sorts of joint problems so if I am not eating healthy, I am not staying healthy. It is funny because many people do not understand how to eat healthy. They stop eating a burger and start eating a salad and two weeks later, they do not see results so they conclude that eating healthy does not work. However, they do not realize they are not eating that much healthier. When you are truly eating healthy and not the typical American diet, it makes all the difference in the world. Healthy eating has to be a consistent thing, it cannot be just 90 percent of the time; it has to be all the time to truly get the benefits and results.

S&S: Are there any companies that you want to thank publicly?

I would like to thank Pines Wheat Grass (www.wheatgrass.com). I always loved their products and always will. I use their products to help fuel my training as part of my healthy diet.

S&S: What do you see in the future for OCR?

For the future, I think there will be a lot of the same as what is currently ongoing. It has become popular for a reason and that is the current formula, which works. However, what is going to give it longevity is [that] we need to turn it into a professional sport; otherwise it is just a fad. What we need is a standardized format that is designed for television in addition to what we already have. Once we do that, it will be great marketing for the rest of the world that does not know OCR exists. This will also boost the popularity and awareness of the sport. There is also something about professional sports that create longevity. Otherwise, it will just be a fad like *American Gladiators* was and *American Ninja Warrior* is. Those are the big changes I am working on, making it professional and creating a format that is consumable for television.

Corinna Coffin

Age: 22

Height: 5'5"

Weight: 130 pounds

Year Started Obstacle Racing: Summer 2014

Biggest Accomplishment in OCR: 2nd place 2014 Spartan World Championship

Other OCR Race Highlights: 1st place Coed Team OCR World Championships (OCRWC) with Junyong Pak, Claude Godbout, and Marco Bédard

Strength & Speed: What was your athletic background prior to OCR?

Growing up I played on the travel soccer team. Then I ran cross-country and played lacrosse in high school. Starting my junior year in high school, I joined SEAL Team Physical Training Inc. along with my twin brother.

They are an outdoor fitness group that is run by former Navy SEAL John McGuire. Every day before school, we would work out from 6 AM to 7 AM at a different outdoor park. It was kind of like boot-camp-type training with a lot of cardio mixed with body weight exercises and calisthenics. The group has everyone from your average Joe to those training for the military. That was huge for developing both leadership skills and my athleticism heading into college. Even today, I still work out with them when I am back in the area.

Once I entered college, I played club lacrosse freshman and sophomore years. Then in my junior year and part of senior year, I became involved with the club triathlon team and started CrossFit. The majority of my senior year, I started focusing on OCR, so I did not do as much triathlon-specific training.

S&S: How has your athletic background hurt or helped you for OCR? What things did you have to adjust to become a successful OCR athlete?

My athletic background has definitely played a huge role in the development of both my character and my overall athleticism. It helped create a competitive drive that has been with me my entire life. I grew up with three older brothers and I was the only girl. I would always try to keep up with my brothers and try to do everything that they were doing. We were always involved in physical and outdoor activities, and everyone was always trying to outdo the others. All the sports I have done in my past have relied on running, which is a key part of obstacle racing. In addition, the CrossFit and the SEAL Team Physical Training has helped develop my strength. Since speed, strength, and endurance are all important for success in OCR, the combination of triathlon training, my love for running, SEAL Team Physical Training, and CrossFit served as an excellent gateway and solid foundation to getting started in OCR.

Now that I've been focusing mainly on OCR, I have been trying to find a balance between strength training and running. I have so much fun with CrossFit, lifting, and all the strength-based work, but your running takes a big hit if you overemphasize the strength aspect. I am still working on getting strong, but more of a slimmer strong. Now I am looking for an increase in strength without adding much weight or getting bulkier. Right now, my challenge is striking that perfect balance between running and strength work. I do not feel like I fit the mold of a runner because I have more upper-body strength. This is especially true when you compare me with road racers, marathoners, or ultra-marathoners. It has been fun playing around with the different aspects of training but it can also be frustrating at times.

S&S: What is your biggest recommendation for OCR athletes who want to improve?

You are not going to be a successful OCR athlete without running. Running is huge, and you will not be able to hang with the top athletes in the sport if you cannot run. That should be your first priority.

Then strength work should come second. I'm always interested to hear what my fellow OCR athletes do for their strength workouts since it's an area of incredible variability. My friend and BattleFrog Pro Team member Ryan Atkins says he does only two big strength workouts a week. When talking with Jonathan Albon (2014 OCRWC overall winner), I found that he, too, spends the majority of his time running, incorporating strength training about two or three times a week. The key is to gain strength without extra bulk. For this, I recommend a lot of body weight exercises. While some races have strength obstacles like bucket, sandbag, or Wreck Bag carries, many obstacles involve pulling your own body weight up and over a wall, across a traverse rope or monkey bar rig, et cetera. In my opinion, being able to lift your body is going to get you a lot farther than doing a bunch of heavy lifts. I think there is a lot to be said for body weight movements. That being said, I think I need to practice what I preach a little more. I have been trying to focus more on body weight movements such as pull-ups, push-ups, body weight squats, et cetera, and less on weights and barbell work, although I do see the benefit of their use as well.

Finally, be sure to work on grip strength. I have also added that into my training the deeper I get involved in OCR. So be sure to do things like towel pull-ups, not just regular pull-ups, farmer's carries, and rock climbing.

S&S: *What is your daytime job?*

I have a degree in nutrition and exercise as well as Spanish, and just recently accepted a full-time job with BattleFrog Race Series as lifestyle director, creating content for their web page in addition to racing for them on their pro team.

S&S: *How do you balance your job and family with training for OCR?*

When it is the middle of race season, certain things definitely take priority over others. When I was a student in college, I had my fun socially during freshman and sophomore year. After meeting my boyfriend Kevin [Righi], it turns out we both had a lot of the same priorities and strong common interest in fitness. Both Kevin and I are very motivated and we were not looking to spend our weekends partying. Instead of going out on the weekends during junior and senior year, we used that time to get in really good training. Since we had no classes on the weekends, we would do Cross-Fit, running, and/or long endurance training like cycling. During the weekdays, my schedule was jam-packed, taking seventeen credits, teaching five fitness classes a week, and giving school tours to prospective high school students in addition to finding time to train twice a day.

During race season, it really got crazy with flying every other weekend and then coming back for 8 AM class Monday. On the weekends, if I did not have a race, I would work to catch up on my schoolwork or try to get ahead to make race weekends less stressful.

As stressful as it can sometimes be, when I have a busy schedule it forces me to be more disciplined. A tight-packed schedule means you have to be efficient to get everything done. Furthermore, it puts me into work mode and forces me to efficiently manage my day and time. That's part of the reason why I want to have a job on top of training, because it makes me more efficient, plus I feel like I'm contributing to something more than just enhancing my fitness.

Having a partner, like my boyfriend Kevin, has been a huge help and contributing factor to my success so far in the sport. We motivate each other to work harder, and hold each other accountable so there's no slacking! Having someone along with you, that not only challenges you but also provides a great support system [that] is so important to success in any field.

S&S: What does an average training week in your life look like when preparing for a race?

For a non-race week, I run about four or five times a week. I typically do several types of runs including long-distance runs and track workouts. For the long runs, I usually will not run more than 10 to 12 miles. I will do some long slow distance runs that I like to do on trails and not pay attention to pace but rather just go off time. I started incorporating more track workouts into my routine and am currently doing about two to three track workouts a week, switching off between 200m, 400m, and 800m repeats. Right now, I feel like my endurance is good but I need to work on my speed, so I am in the process of making adjustments to my training regimen. I typically do at least an hour of strength training every day, usually CrossFit, although I like to incorporate more OCR-based movements as well such as bucket, water jugs, and sandbag carries, tire flips, rope climbs, and sled pulls. During OCR season I have realized that a lot of heavy barbell work is not going to contribute a great deal toward my success in OCR. I try to focus my strength training on more body weight movements now, with a greater emphasis on muscular endurance. The SEAL Team Physical Training group

I participate in also does a great job of combining body weight strength training and running.

I've also built some OCR-specific training devices in my backyard. At my parents' house, I have a set of monkey bars hanging from chains on the rafters in one of our barns. The bars also rotate, which helps me work on grip strength and monkey bar technique. There many little things that are super easy to make that you can keep around the house. I have a Lowe's bucket with 50 pounds of concrete inside to practice bucket carries. I have a spear, since I have failed so many spear throws for Spartan Races. These training items are especially useful if you are preparing for an event where you know there is going to be a bucket carry or a spear throw. Next on my list is definitely buying a Wreck Bag.

Even without equipment, you can do OCR-specific training via body weight movements. I like to find a steep hill and do crab walks up the hill. With each step, you really have to dig your heels into the side of the hill, which provides a killer leg workout in addition to your core and shoulders. Doing a couple of rounds of that in between 400m repeats on the track is a really good workout. This also works with backward bear crawls. Instead of going up the hill headfirst, you turn around so your butt is going up the hill first and your head is facing downhill. The beauty of this is all you need is a hill and you can incorporate these exercises into your training. It turns out to be pretty killer exercise.

S&S: What was one of your hardest workouts you have ever done when preparing for a race?

I am going to go with a workout I did with Kevin Righi in spring 2015 that is a variation on a CrossFit workout called the Devil's Mile: 400m walking lunges, 30 pushups, 400m overhead plate carry (45 pounds for men, 25 pounds for women), 30 sit-ups, 400m bear crawls, 30 pull-ups, 400m of broad jumps, 30 burpees.

You can set the plate down during the carry, but you are not allowed to make any forward progress unless the plate is overhead. It is great workout and takes a little under an hour to finish. After I posted some pictures to social media, I got a lot of positive feedback. I have done this a couple of times and what is great about it is that you can pretty much do this wherever you are because the only weight you need is a single plate (and you can always substitute the plate for another heavy object such as a rock, textbook, weight vest, bucket, et cetera). You will definitely be sore for a while because 400m is long for all of those exercises. I definitely recommend a buddy for the Devil's Mile.

S&S: What was your hardest or worst racing experience?

My worst racing experience, but also a day I learned the most, was the individual competition day of the 2014 OCRWC. The Platinum Rig was really hard and it eliminated so many racers, myself included. I went into that race with high hopes, especially after my second-place finish at the Spartan World Championship a couple of weeks earlier. I was looking forward to a rematch with Claude Godbout. Claude and I were in first and second coming up to the Platinum Rig and we had put a pretty good gap in the rest of the field even though it was only 2 miles into the almost 9-mile course. I came up to the obstacle and fell off toward the end on the fat swinging monkey bars. I tried again and again and again—probably close to twenty-five times—but just could not get through it. It was very discouraging and disheartening for the majority of the field, but especially for myself and Claude, who arrived first and watched as almost the entire elite women's wave caught up to us. With such a high failure rate, it basically turned into whoever made it through the Platinum Rig was guaranteed a top-ten finish. Nevertheless, I discovered a weakness there and put a lot more emphasis on rigs and monkey bars in my training. I think it actually scarred me a little [laughs], so now anytime there is a rig-type obstacle it weighs on my thoughts the night before the race. I think that was my worst experience mainly because it was such a big race and I had high hopes coming in, but at the same time I'm grateful to have experienced something like that so early on in my racing career, because it exposed a weakness and helped me improve my training to prepare for more technical obstacles.

For the 2015 race year, my worst experience was the Spartan Sprint in Breckenridge. I had traveled to Colorado early to get in some good mountain training and get acclimated to the elevation, but I think I may have overtrained during those two and a half weeks leading up to the race; my legs were absolutely shot by race day. I think my timing was a bit off as well in terms of properly acclimating. By the time I got to a high enough elevation (8,000-plus feet), I was only one week out from the race (they say two to two and a half weeks is the minimum to gain any benefits). I had high hopes of competing well, particularly with such a stacked women's field, but my body just wasn't feeling it. The beauty of these kinds of situations, though, is you learn a lot from them and it usually pays off down the road. Even when I have good races, I try to take away a couple of lessons learned to make the next race even better.

S&S: What is the most common question you receive as an OCR athlete and your response?

Usually it is about how to properly prepare or train for OCRs. I also am asked a lot, *What race are you doing next?* I think that is a lot of fun, to always have another race that you are preparing for on the horizon. The answer to that changes a lot because I will base my races on how I am feeling, so my race schedule is always up in the air a little. If I am feeling exhausted from all the racing I have been doing, I will take some time off.

S&S: Do you follow any specific dietary restrictions (such as vegan, gluten-free, vegetarian, Paleo)?

I do not follow any dietary restrictions because I feel life is too short not to enjoy certain types of food. I do love eating, though, and since I work out so much, I get to eat a lot. My diet is very health-conscious, though. I like to know what I am eating, so I stay away from processed foods. I generally stay away from anything packaged and try to stick to simple ingredients. If I am eating something packaged, I look at the ingredients to make sure I know what everything is before putting it into my body. I am not a vegetarian, but I do eat a heavily plant-based diet. Regarding protein, I typically eat meat a couple of times a week, and I also eat eggs frequently. I do take protein powder but it is organic and made from whey from grass-fed animals. I am definitely a fan of good healthy fats, so things like avocado, nuts, and various nut butters are a staple of my diet. I would not say I follow a high-fat diet, but I do not restrict the amount of healthy fats I ingest. I do make a pretty elaborate fruit and vegetable smoothie every morning that contains fruits such as banana and mixed berries, and vegetables such as spinach, kale, avocado, tomato, carrots, broccoli, peas (just to name a few). I'll add hemp, chia, and flaxseeds, as well as a little nut butter, plain Greek yogurt, coconut water, and a scoop of protein powder to top it off. It's *usually* quite delicious, but it's always a little bit of a taste experiment depending on what ingredients I have in the fridge. Regarding other carbohydrates, I typically eat sweet potatoes, quinoa, and oatmeal. I also eat bread but it is usually Ezekiel bread. If I am running a lot, like twice a day, my body will often crave more carbohydrates, and if that's the case I listen to my body and give it what it wants. I am not going to fight my body, especially if I am doing a high volume of training. Kevin and I have recently become fans of lentil pasta as well as black bean pasta, made strictly from beans and water. With regard to dairy products, I have no restrictions but generally do not eat a lot from this food group, aside from plain Greek yogurt in my smoothies and eggs, of course. I've switched from dairy milk to almond and coconut milk.

S&S: Are there any people or companies that you want to thank publicly?

I definitely want to thank BattleFrog Race Series for supporting me this past year and flying me to all of their races. They have such a great team of people working for them, and they put on some of the best races in the entire industry. Even though they are a young company, they have already made a strong name for themselves in the OCR community and I truly believe they are here to stay.

Above all, I'd like to thank my family. They are my rock and foundation, and always keep me grounded through the good times and the bad. I want to thank my parents for their endless love and support as I chase my dreams, as well as my three brothers who mean the absolute world to me and have helped shaped me into the person and athlete I am today. Of course I would be lost (and most likely frail) without my boyfriend Kevin Righi, who has been both my boyfriend and my coach for the past two years. Those are two sometimes-conflicting roles that he plays beautifully. Lastly, I would like to thank John McGuire and SEAL Team Physical Training Inc. for the training as well as leadership and teamwork skills they have provided me with since I was sixteen.

Claude Godbout

Age: 29

Height: 5'6" (167cm)

Weight: 132 pounds (61kg)

Year Started Obstacle Racing: 2011

Biggest Accomplishment in OCR: 2014 and 2012 Spartan World Champion

Other OCR Race Highlights:

As of summer 2015 (around 30 races total), undefeated in OCR at any distance in Canada

2014 national champion for Spartan Races in Canada

Strength & Speed: What was your athletic background prior to OCR?

I started doing sports when I was six years old, doing cross-country skiing in the winter and soccer in the summertime. Eventually, I had to choose between the two sports once training became serious because I did not have time to do both; cross-country skiing became my priority. At around sixteen, I started to train seriously as a cross-country skier; I slowly built my way to the top to finally get on the podium at the national level. Then at eighteen years old, things really changed; my boyfriend Marco Bédard made me try biathlon and I thought it was the nicest sport ever. From that point forward, biathlon was basically the only thing I was talking about. A year later, I was on the National Canadian Biathlon Team training full-time to go to the Olympics. Even though I was really close to making it to the 2010 and the 2014 Olympic Games, I still managed to be one of the best biathletes in Canada.

Biathlon and cross-country skiing training have been a large part of my athletic background and even though I am not racing as seriously as I was before in biathlon, I still put my cross-country skis on and go shoot some targets a couple of times a week. Why? I love biathlon and it's one of the best training you can get to be ready for the OCR season. Plus, I feel like racing biathlon in the winter and OCR in the summer is the perfect match for me.

Biathlon is an endurance sport so in order to reach your goal, you have to cross-train at some point. I feel lucky that I'm feeling comfortable doing pretty much any sport from cross-country skiing to mountain biking to swimming.

S&S: How has your athletic background hurt or helped you for OCR? What things did you have to adjust to become a successful OCR athlete?

Biathlon definitely helped for OCR because, like I said earlier, we do a lot of cross-training including strength training, running, biking, swimming, and cross-country skiing. Not only my cardio is good but my upper body is really strong if I compare myself with pure runners, which helps a lot in the OCR world.

Also, biathlon involves a lot of stop and go since we have to stop periodically to shoot targets before continuing on the loop with our cross-country skis. This stop and go is a lot like OCR with the obstacles and running; constantly stopping to complete obstacles and then going back to high-intensity running is definitely a challenge in OCR. Luckily, biathlon gets me to put multiple hours into mastering this aspect.

I still had to adjust my training in order to get ready for OCR. One of the biggest things I had to do is grip strength work, and believe me, I still have work to do! I have also added in more running to help with speed. Additionally, I changed my strength training sessions for OCR to include things like farmer's carry, grip strength training, and more pull-ups (a lot of pull-ups).

S&S: What is your biggest recommendation for OCR athletes who want to improve?

My number one recommendation is to find a way to train that you enjoy. Believe me, the reason I am still involved in sports after all these years is that I enjoy it! If training starts to get boring, you won't get better or last long in the sport world. Try to find trainings that keep you focused and entertained.

That being said, OCR involves trail running and obstacles. So you have to hit the trails a couple of times every week and master the pull-up exercises in order to complete most of the obstacles.

S&S: How do you balance your job and family with training for OCR?

I currently work as a bartender for banquets at the Hilton Hotel, which I think works well for OCR training. I do not have a regular schedule; the hotel calls me when they need me. I'll sometimes work a lot but other times, I can go a month without working. I also always know a week out if I am going to work, so it is important for me to adjust my training plan based off my work schedule.

Working night shifts has its ups and downs: I get to train during the day when I'm fresh, but training can be hard when you went to bed at 3 AM the night before. Occasionally, balancing work and training can feel like too much so you need to know when to adjust your plan. This is call training smart!

Kids? Project on hold for the moment since I feel like I have too much things to explore and races to attend!

S&S: What does an average training week in your life look like

when preparing for a race?

If I have a race coming up at the end of a week, my training load for that week will be lower. However, a regular training week will look a lot like two strength training sessions and two speed training sessions in a six-day period for a total of roughly twelve to fourteen hours per week (having a day off every week). I do not run every day but I will still run a total of six or seven times each week (sometimes doing two runs in one day). In addition, I do a lot of cross-training including kayaking, swimming, roller skiing, mountain biking, and road biking. I try to do my hard workout in the morning and an easier/recovery workout in the afternoon.

The other thing you have to know about my training habits is that I don't get ready for a race a month prior to it. It's a full-time commitment and you have to build your shape six or seven months in order to get good results.

S&S: How high is your peak mileage when preparing for a race?

I do not keep track of mileage during the week and I am also not big on technology, but I do keep track of the hours spent training. Tracking hours is what I have been doing since I [was] fourteen or fifteen years old. Every week (especially during building week), I will set a goal of a certain number of hours that I want to reach.

I would say that my average training volume for a week is twelve or fourteen hours. My lower-volume (tapering) weeks are usually around six hours of training, and my loading week will be around twenty hours.

S&S: What was one of the hardest workouts you have ever done when preparing for a race?

Before the Spartan World Championship Race in Vermont, Marc and I trained on a set of stairs in Quebec City that is right next to the very touristic Montmorency waterfall. Marco and I climbed the 450 stairs about eight to nine times doing a different routine or exercise each trip up the stairs: speed, jumping, 40-pound sandbag carry, et cetera. At the top of the stairs, there was a kids' playground with monkey bars and such so we managed to destroyed our upper body by doing some grip exercises, pull-ups, and burpees. I think the total routine took about an hour and a half.

S&S: *What was your hardest or worst racing experience?*

Although the 2014 OCR World Champs were amazing, I had one of the worst individual racing experiences ever. I was feeling strong and fast so I took the lead early on the race. About 2 to 3km after the beginning of the race was the Platinum Rig obstacle. I have to be honest, the way it was set wasn't the hardest I have done, but the two-by-four monkey bars at the end proved to be quite difficult for most of the women. Despite being confident, I fell close to the end. Still in the lead, I quickly tried to do it again (obstacle completion was mandatory at the OCRWC), but I realized how bad things were: My upper arms and my grip strength were smoked after the first try. I tried and tried over and over again, getting more frustrated, sad, and tired at every try. Roughly twenty-five minutes later, I had to make a decision. A couple of girls managed to cross the rig and they had about a fifteen-minute lead. I decided to give away my wristband, which meant that I wasn't racing elite anymore.

S&S: *What is the most common question you receive as an OCR athlete and your response?*

[laughs] *Do you do CrossFit?* No, the answer is no, I do not do CrossFit.

S&S: *Do you follow any specific dietary restrictions (such as vegan, gluten-free, vegetarian, Paleo)?*

I do not follow any dietary restrictions but I try to keep it simple. I love to cook, so I do not eat any processed food at all and I eat a lot of vegetables and fruits. I think traveling a lot in countries that didn't provide the best food out there helped me to get accustomed to everything without getting my stomach upset and my energy extra low. When you travel it is not as easy, but you have to do the best you can and I try to be laid-back about it. I typically eat breakfast, lunch, and dinner and a ton of snacks in between. When I do intensities or strength training, I will make sure to get my recovery and/or protein shake afterward to help me recover. I do not really do anything different than most of the athletes. I generally follow my hunger: as simple as that.

S&S: *How do you think that affects your performance?*

This question is a little hard to answer for me since I have been eating clean for my entire life. I do not know what would happen if I ate differently; let's just say that I'm happy with how I feel right now. If I ate junk for a month, let's say, then tried to race, I am not sure what would happen. I have never eaten like that and honestly, I don't want to try it.

S&S: Are there any people or companies that you want to thank publicly?

I definitely want to thank my boyfriend, Marco Bédard; we have been training and racing together for so long. Having a boyfriend who is heavily involved in the same activities has helped a lot. I would also like to thank my parents for getting me involved in sports when I was young. Additionally, I want to thank Team BattleFrog because they have been supportive of Marco, our races, and [me]. Finally, I would also like to thank Platinum Rig for their support and providing a great training tool.

S&S: What do you see in the future for OCR?

I think the future will be more of the same as it is right now because I think most of the money is already in the sport. Therefore, I think it will either continue along the same path or possibly slow down a little. However, there are definitely more and more serious athletes getting involved. In the future, I see many really fast athletes getting involved, making the competition more fierce.

Also, with so many OCR companies in the market right now, we are beginning to see a really fierce competition between all of them in order to get their piece of pie, and I'm a little scared about the future in that matter. Hopefully, the OCR world will survive long enough so we get to see a unification between all of them.

S&S: Anything else you want your fans to know?

Why I train and race? That's simple: because I love it! I did biathlon for so long because I enjoyed it and I still compete in it even though not as seriously. It is the same with OCR. I think that describes me pretty well. I mean, why would a girl roll in the mud, break her nails, and put bruises all over her body if it's not fun?

Evan Perperis

Age: 33

Height: 5'6"

Weight: 157 pounds

Year Started Obstacle Racing: 2012

Biggest Accomplishment in OCR: 13th place overall (7th American) 2014 World's Toughest Mudder (WTM)

Other OCR Race Highlights:

Ranking 9th in the world on the OCRWC leaderboard

Four podium finishes in 3 weeks in summer 2015 (2nd overall Fugitive Run, 1st overall Mud Run Guide's Summer Splash, 3rd overall Conquer the Gauntlet, and 2nd Overall Shale Hell 24-Hour OCR)

1st place BattleFrog Xtreme Cincinnati as the only competitor to finish 4 laps of the course

Strength & Speed: Why are you being interviewed if you wrote the book?

I wanted to give the readers a better understanding of who I am and my background in athletics. Furthermore, although I follow 95 percent of the information recommended in this book, I alter small parts of it because I, just like you, am my own unique athlete with specific strengths and weaknesses. The plans and information provided in the book are great for any athlete to improve, [but] if you want to maximize your results, you will have to modify small portions of it to suit yourself as an athlete.

S&S: What was your athletic background prior to OCR?

Growing up I was fairly un-athletic. If you have ever seen the TV show *The Goldbergs*, the main character Adam Goldberg is so similar to me growing up it is scary. However, I did play soccer and baseball on and off growing up. In high school, I ran cross-country but was bad, having only scored points for the team once. My peers from high school are usually shocked when they find out what I do for fun now. In college I started exercising three to five times per week doing some running and some weight lifting. My senior year I became a little more serious and signed up for my first couple of races including a marathon, half Ironman, and full Ironman. I was definitely slow, but I finished all of them despite minimal training.

From 2004 to 2010, I raced in a variety of events, mostly marathons and triathlons. Over the years, I developed my own method for improving both strength and speed. I typically spend four months focused on a sport before switching to another one. This has given me the unique ability to be fairly fast and strong. In May 2014, I won my weight class in a natural bodybuilding show, qualifying for the Drug Free Athletes Coalition World Finals, and did a triple-body-weight deadlift (465 pounds at 155 pounds body weight). Three months later in August 2014, I qualified for the Obstacle Course Racing World Championships and ran a 2:57:33 marathon. Other notable accomplishments include third overall at 2012 Andrew Jackson Marathon, sixth overall at 2014 Marquette Marathon, two Iron-distance triathlons, and a handful of ultras between 40 and 100 miles in length. I have also run a marathon on a treadmill, twice . . . which I do not recommend.

S&S: How has your athletic background hurt or helped you for OCR? What things did you have to adjust to become a successful OCR athlete?

The lack of serious training in high school and college definitely hurts me as an OCR athlete. I have found that my top speed tends to develop slowly. I feel that missing those years where many of my peers were seriously racing for their high school or college teams has put me at a disadvantage. I try to make up for it by finding a training group with someone who can push my pace for track/VO_2max and lactate threshold workouts.

However, my mix of strength-based sports and speed-based sports later in life created a smooth transition to obstacle racing. At some races, I have trouble understanding why others have trouble on certain obstacles because my body already possesses the strength required to complete them.

To adjust to become a better OCR athlete, I have to work more on my speed. By adding in harder lactate threshold and VO_2max workouts, I try to bring my speed to a new level every year. Additionally, due to my extensive weight training background, I plan losing some upper-body muscle to create a faster racer.

S&S: What is your biggest recommendation for OCR athletes who want to improve?

Sit back and conduct an honest assessment of yourself as an athlete. Everyone has positive and negative aspects. Identify your weaknesses and then actively work to improve those. If you have a strong running background, your weakness is probably upper-body strength. If you have anything but a running background, your weakness is probably running-related.

S&S: What does an average training week in your life look like when preparing for a race?

I typically train five days a week and take two complete rest days. My rest days are usually on Wednesday and Sunday. Monday, Tuesday, Thursday, and Friday I run in the mornings and lift at lunchtime. I tend to follow a bodybuilding-type lifting routine but incorporate movements that are similar to actions performed during races. Additionally, I use a lot of alternative handles like chains or ropes I attach to the pulley machine and Fat Gripz for most barbell or dumbbell movements. I even built what I call the Aluminum Rig. It is basically a bunch of rings, climbing holds, and ropes attached to the crossbeam of a pulley machine. I then go back and forth along the crossbeam. I get a lot of questions in the gym because it produces a bit of a scene. Saturdays are typically my long run day since it eats up such a large portion of the day. When preparing for an ultra-distance race, I will often change my rest days to Monday and Friday then use Saturday along with Sunday for long runs. These double long runs on the weekend stimulate the body for long-distance running without causing as much damage as a single ultra-distance run.

S&S: How high is your peak mileage when preparing for a race?

My mileage typically peaks at 70-plus miles a week. Typically, that is only for one to three weeks. Most of my serious preparation weeks have mileages between 50 and 70, with varied intensities depending on the required distance of the race. Running more than that really requires me to sacrifice family time and significantly reduce any cross-training. This is peak mileage for all my serious races. That being said, I try to hit a new peak weekly mileage at least once a year to try to spur growth. I have found that I am fastest at short-distance races when preparing for longer races and doing a lot of aerobic training. Even for ultra-distance races, my mileage does not go much over 70. The big difference for ultra-races is that I do back-to-back long runs on Saturday and Sunday. Sometimes I use races as training events like multi-lap Tough Mudders or back-to-back marathons on a weekend.

S&S: What was one of the hardest workouts you have ever done when preparing for a race?

I think my hardest workouts are back-to-back long runs. Things like running 20 on Saturday and 15 on Sunday. I actually think they are mentally harder than physically. The ability to wake up and block out a good portion of your day to running is mentally exhausting, but then to repeat it again the following day takes a lot of willpower. To me that slow grind is harder than doing repeated intervals and maxing out your heart rate, which typically will not last longer than an hour.

S&S: What was your hardest or worst racing experience?

I am going to list two that stand out as particularly painful. My first marathon was very hard because I was not physically or mentally prepared. I did not have proper training, proper fueling, or proper mental preparation. Prior to the race, I think my longest run was 12 miles. Around mile 20, I hit the wall and hit it hard. It was a struggle to finish and, limping away, I thought I would never run another. Fast-forward a decade and I have run 17 marathons plus a whole bunch of ultra- and long-distance triathlon races.

The second one was my first 100-miler. I raced that one month after World's Toughest Mudder (WTM), which was a mistake. My body had not fully recovered from WTM. I was doing well until mile 78, when I managed to pull both of my internal hip muscles. The next 22 miles were agonizing. I ran the first 75 in fourteen hours but the last 25 took me ten hours. I limped my way across the line eventually after a long night. The next couple of days were equally painful since I was incapable of walking forward. I ended up walking backward for two days because it was faster and less painful than moving forward. People at work thought I was legitimately crazy.

S&S: Could you have done anything different to prepare for that?

For my first marathon, training and nutrition would have fixed that problem. I used an approach of *Do minimal training and suffer immensely on race day*, which can be used to finish a race but I do not recommend it if you care about your performance.

For my first 100-miler, I believe I raced too close to World's Toughest Mudder. With only four weeks between the two, I was not back to 100 percent. Based on my fitness level in 2014, I recommend waiting at least two months between serious ultras if you care about performing well.

S&S: What is the most common question you receive as an OCR athlete and your response?

What is the best way to improve as an OCR athlete? My response is usually to improve as a runner. To improve as a runner, I recommend high-volume training. Most of the time spent in an obstacle race is running and not completing obstacles. Once you get faster and get rid of excess fat, the obstacles will become easier.

Why would you do that? Specifically this is referencing ultra-distance races like World's Toughest Mudder. I do it because the feeling of accomplishment I get from crossing the finish line is something that cannot be replicated any other way. Buying something or eating a certain food provides short-term satisfaction for many, but it can easily be replicated and loses its enjoyment. The struggle of finishing something very hard that requires months or years of preparation is irreplaceable.

S&S: Do you follow any specific dietary restrictions (such as vegan, gluten-free, vegetarian, Paleo)?

I generally follow a bodybuilding-type diet. This means I eat five or six meals a day in smaller portions. Each meal contains a mono- or polyunsaturated fat, a low-saturated-fat protein, and a low-glycemic carbohydrate. I try to eat healthy 90 percent of the day at least but allow for some cheat foods. Any sugary food I try to only ingest directly after a workout to maximize the insulin spike effect. My diet often looks Paleo to many people but that is not really accurate because I do eat minimally processed foods like sprouted grain bread. Other than that, I keep my red meat intake low, about once a week. I will eat some processed foods but only in small quantities.

S&S: How do you think that affects your performance?

The constant grazing provides me with a steady stream of energy. The high-protein diet also keeps my muscles and strength high despite lots of cardio. Realistically, I think I can reduce my protein and increase my carbs, but I have not determined the perfect balance for my long-term goals yet.

S&S: Are there any people or companies that you want to thank publicly?

I would like to thank my wife Amy. On the 2014 World's Toughest Mudder she was six and a half months pregnant but still came out to spend the night in a windstorm even though it was her birthday. She is supportive of my obsessive, often crazy lifestyle, and I could not do this without her. She is also my photographer, so you can thank her for the majority of pictures in this book.

I would like to thank my sponsor Hammer Nutrition for providing me with the best fueling products available. They are one of the few supplement companies that really provide a holistic approach to training. They provide products that can be used at all points of the day from Insurance Caps (multivitamin) to REM Caps (nighttime sleep/recovery aid). Their fuel, specifically designed for endurance and ultra-endurance performance, allowed me to gain ground at every lap at the World's Toughest Mudder.

I would also like to thank Under Armour, which sponsored me for 2014 World's Toughest Mudder and has supported my racing efforts by providing high-quality products. Without them, I would not have been standing on the starting line at World's Toughest Mudder. They provide awesome clothing and amazing gear, and have workers who truly understand fitness. Thanks for all you do and for all of the unseen charity that you give back to the Baltimore area along with military veterans. There is a lot more people to thank who influenced me along my journey, so check out the acknowledgements in the back of the book.

S&S: What do you see in the future for OCR?

Some people talk about the Olympics, but I do not see that happening anytime soon. Maybe in about twenty or thirty years I think that might be a possibility if the sport is still going strong. I believe there are several other sports that have been around for much longer that will become Olympic sports first, including Iron-distance triathlon, trail running, and ultra-distance running.

S&S: Anything else you want your fans to know?

Your results are a directly tied to your effort. Whenever I think I have hit my maximum ability or workload, I meet someone who shows me more is possible. I push myself harder or add more volume, and the results speak for themselves. While I love being extreme in my diet and exercise regime, it is all about finding what makes you happy. For me, this is what makes me happy. Try to find your balance. Just understand that what balance looks like for me may not seem balanced to others.

Kevin Righi

Age: 25

Height: 5'9"

Weight: 170 pounds

Year Started Obstacle Racing: 2014

Biggest Accomplishment in OCR: 2nd place Spartan Citizens Bank Sprint 2014

Other OCR Race Highlights:

1st place Civilian Military Challenge at Bryce Resort 2014

4th in age group at OCR World Championships 2014

Strength & Speed: What was your athletic background prior to OCR?

I played lacrosse and football in high school and went on to play lacrosse in college. I finally gave up lacrosse and found CrossFit a year before I got into obstacle course racing.

S&S: How has your athletic background hurt or helped you for OCR? What things did you have to adjust to become a successful OCR athlete?

It's been a little bit of both. I wasn't a natural athlete when I was younger. Far from it, but . . . playing a vast array of sports growing up has allowed me to pick up on new athletic activities pretty quickly, such as CrossFit and OCR. It has hurt me because although sports such as lacrosse require a good amount of running, it is nothing compared with the amount of running you need to excel at OCR. Another challenge has been adjusting to being a solo athlete. I was also always on a team and never competed in an individual sport competitively—such as cross-country, triathlon, tennis, golf, et cetera— growing up. The mentality that goes into competing with no one on your side except for you has been somewhat of a challenge. Another challenge has been the fact that I compete in CrossFit and in CrossFit I'm considered a smaller athlete, whereas in OCR I'm considered a larger, stronger athlete for my size. So it's been challenging to try to excel in both sports simultaneously as strength is my weakness in CrossFit and running is my weakness in OCR.

S&S: What is your biggest recommendation for OCR athletes who want to improve?

To really excel in the sport the way it is right now, you have to be able to run. If you want to be an elite and be on that podium, you need to be shooting to run sub-7 splits between obstacles at the very least. However, if you just want to get in better shape and improve as an athlete overall, I would recommend a combination of high-intensity training such as CrossFit and long-distance running. A great program to check out is CrossFit Endurance, which combines CrossFit with an endurance running program.

S&S: What is your daytime job?

I am the business development manager for LifeFuels, which is an emerging tech company in the health and fitness space. Our mission is to optimize human performance. Come check us out at www.lifefuels.co

S&S: *How do you balance your job and family with training for OCR?*

It's hard to balance everything in life. A typical day looks something like this.

6:30 AM–8 AM: Morning training session (usually a Metcon or two and a 5-mile run)

9 AM–6 PM: Work

6:45 PM–8 PM: Strength training session and activity recovery for the next day

There isn't much time during the week for rest or downtime. In order to be at the top of your game, you have to dedicate the time to it. My girlfriend Corinna Coffin, who is one of the top elite women OCR athletes right now, has been at school finishing up her senior year at Virginia Tech, so we usually catch up in the evenings on each other's day and talk about training ideas for the both of us for the following day.

S&S: *What does an average training week in your life look like when preparing for a race?*

Preparing for races is something that I would say I really don't do for the most part. There are some races I am looking to peak for, mainly the world championship races, but in a typical week my training will look something like this.

Monday: AM: CrossFit metcon [metabolic conditioning] workout and a 5-mile run

PM: Strength work (usually front or back squats), core work, and mobility

Tuesday: AM: CrossFit metcon workout and a 0.5-mile sled drag with 100 pounds added to the sled

PM: Olympic lifting work (cleans or snatches), strength work (usually some press movements such as strict press, push press, or jerks)

Wednesday: AM: CrossFit metcon workout and a 5-mile run

PM: Strength work (usually deadlift work), core work, and mobility

Thursday: AM: Rest

PM: Olympic lifting work and swim 1600 to 2000m

Friday: AM: Strength work (lower body) & long CrossFit metcon workout (usually a thirty-plus-minute session)

Saturday: Midday: Olympic lifting work, skill work (muscle ups, handstands, handstand walks, et cetera.), metcon session, and end with a 0.5-mile sled drag with 100 pounds on it

Sunday: Long endurance run (10-plus miles)

S&S: How high is your peak mileage when preparing for a race?

A high week for me miles-wise is anything over 25. I usually hit 20 with my two 5-mile runs during the week and long run on Sundays, but depending on my CrossFit metcon sessions I can get as high as 30 some weeks if there is a lot of running that week in my CrossFit sessions.

S&S: What was one of the hardest workouts you have ever done when preparing for a race?

There are plenty of hard workouts that I have done such as the Devil's Mile, Murph with a 20-pound weighted vest, and many others, but a workout that I regularly do to see where my muscular endurance and cardio [are] at is below.

This is an EMOM workout (every minute on the minute) broken into three-minute segments. Perform the given move at the start of each minute then rest till the next minute and perform the next move; keep repeating that pattern.

Minutes 0, 3, 6, 9, 12, 15, 18, 21, 24, 27, do 3 man makers with 45-pound dumbbells for men, 25-pound for women

Minutes 1, 4, 7, 10, 13, 16, 19, 22, 25, 28, do 15 wall ball shots 20 pounds for men, 14 pounds for women

Minutes 2, 5, 8, 11, 14, 17, 20, 23, 26, 29, do 10 burpee box jump overs (24-inch box for men, 20-inch for women)

I've taken this workout to forty-five minutes a few times before, and after those sessions I was dead lying on the floor. I eventually want to take it all the way to sixty minutes.

S&S: What was your hardest or worst racing experience?

My worst racing experience was probably my very first Spartan Race. I came out of the gate way too fast and definitely redlined early in the race.

Working on my pacing is definitely something I have been working on and hope it pays off this year.

S&S: Could you have done anything different to prepare for that?

Checked my ego at the door and [gone] out at a comfortable pace and waited till I was a good way into the race to see how I was feeling before starting to push the pace.

S&S: What is the most common question you receive as an OCR athlete and your response?

What do your training and nutrition look like? I train mostly with CrossFit, but adding in multiple run sessions throughout the week. As for nutrition, I have a green smoothie every morning and make sure my diet is heavy on vegetables, with carbohydrates around my training, and usually some lean protein for dinners. Try to limit the animal protein to only one meal a day.

S&S: Do you follow any specific dietary restrictions (such as vegan, gluten-free, vegetarian, Paleo)?

I don't follow any dietary restrictions per se. I do try to avoid dairy (except Greek yogurt in my smoothies), bread and other grains (except quinoa and certain types of rice), and any packaged foods. I eat a lot of vegetables and nuts, moderate amount of fruit and meat.

S&S: How do you think that affects your performance?

My diet has a huge impact on my performance but also a large impact on my recovery. It allows me to perform at a high level day after day. That combined with quality sleep really does make a difference.

S&S: Are there any people or companies that you want to thank publicly?

I would like to thank CrossFit for everything it has done not only for me, but for millions of people worldwide. I will never go back to a typical workout routine and truly believe I will train with a CrossFit methodology for the remaining amount of time that I am an athlete and even beyond that. I'd like to thank OCRWC for helping to grow and unite an amazing budding sport that needs an event like the OCRWC to bring together all the organizations to a central venue and pit all the best athletes against each other. I'd like to thank LifeFuels for being an amazing company with an awesome mission to go out and help optimize people's lives. They are a great employer and offer me the ability to train and compete at the level I do. And finally, I'd like to thank my training partner, motivation, and amazing girlfriend Corinna Coffin for getting me involved in a sport that she has taken by the horns and has excelled at since day one. We always joke with one another about how we are going to beat each other at this race or that race, but at the end of the day I want her to win every event she enters—and if that means she has to beat me that day in order to do that, then that's what I want.

S&S: What do you see in the future for OCR?

It's a cloudy future right now. I see a bright future some days and a dismal future on others. OCR started as a way to get people up and moving. It wasn't about prize money, elite athlete status, or these championship events. I think OCR needs to realize that, yes, there are these elite athletes and they should be rewarded for their amazing performances, but the focus needs to shift back to how we can make these races and events enjoyable to everyone. To the mother of four children, to the father that wants to see how much he has improved after getting back in shape, to the athletes who competed despite certain disabilities, to the kids that just want to get out and play in the mud. Those people are the heart and soul of the sport and without them, there wouldn't be Spartan Race, Tough Mudder, Warrior Dash, or OCRWC.

S&S: Anything else you want your fans to know?

If you haven't participated in an OCR event, you definitely need to. They are a great way to get up and be active. It can help give you something to work toward, which always makes training more enjoyable. There's a whole community of like-minded individuals and you will leave every event with more friends than you showed up with, I promise.

If you have competed in OCRs, I would say keep competing but don't lose sight of why you fell in love with the sport from the start. It can become very competitive but I would say your only competition day in and day out is yourself. Your goals should always be to get faster than you were yesterday, get stronger than you were yesterday, and get fitter than you were yesterday. If you can accomplish that, you are a winner each and every day.

Cassidy Watton

Age: 26

Height: 5'9"

Weight: 145 pounds

Year Started Obstacle Racing: 2013

Biggest Accomplishment in OCR: My biggest accomplishment in OCR is my overall record. Over the last three years and approximately 30 races, I have only missed being on the podium twice, once at the Spartan World Championship and once at a Spartan Race in Pennsylvania when I was recovering from an injury.

Other OCR Race Highlights:

My record in Spartan Sprint and Spartan Stadium Races. I have won all the Spartan Stadium Races that I have raced in the US and came in second in Australia.

I have also beaten almost all of the great women of OCR, including Rose Wetzel (in 2014 Malibu) and Amelia Boone (in 2014 Florida at the Tampa Special Operations Stadium Sprint).

I finished 11th at the 2014 Spartan World Championships, despite getting lost and despite distance not being my strength.

I also won the 2014 Spartan Sprint World Championship.

Strength & Speed: What was your athletic background prior to OCR?

My background is in basketball, but I grew up playing every sport I could get my hands on. I was a little tomboy growing up, always playing with the boys like [in] kickball, softball, soccer, and footraces, but basketball has always been my main sport. In high school, I ran cross-country and track to stay in shape for basketball. I always said I hated running and that I was just doing it for basketball, but secretly I liked it a little bit. I was the captain and MVP in every sport I participated in throughout high school.

When I got to college at Pepperdine University, I trained with the track team for a semester, but I got sick and eventually ended up quitting. By my sophomore year of college, I was done with organized sports and I let the dream go. Later in my sophomore year, I discovered and got involved in CrossFit for the next four years. Then I discovered Spartan Racing about two years after I graduated. I did my first race and it went well, so I just continued racing from then on.

S&S: How has your athletic background hurt or helped you for OCR? What things did you have to adjust to become a successful OCR athlete?

My background has definitely helped me. I was just having a conversation with some people about the most athletic sport, and I would say it is arguably basketball. Basketball requires explosive strength and coordination. Add these skills from basketball to the physical improvements I made from being involved in track and cross-country in high school and it definitely helped. However, you could see how my background sets me up better for the shorter races like the sprints and the stadium races. I do better at those compared with when I go up against other girls that are endurance junkies. I do not have quite the running background that they do, but my sports from high school at least give me some experience.

I definitely had to make some adjustments when I switched from Cross-Fit to OCR. Previously, I had a large emphasis on strength, explosive power, and keeping my engine going for short bursts. At first, I added a little more running and a little more volume. It took about a year before I started committing to being more of an endurance athlete. What I have changed now is I add in three quality run workouts a week minimum. Sometimes I get more but I at least get the three important ones in each week. They are one long slow run, one long interval run, and one short interval run. Ever since I forced myself to add in those three quality run workouts a week, I have enjoyed running more. Now I will also do recovery jogs, which is something I had never done prior to training for OCR. I also make sure to have fun and keep my strength up. I am really passionate about strength, speed, and having that really powerful engine capable of short bursts so I make sure to include that in my training routine.

S&S: What is your biggest recommendation for OCR athletes who want to improve?

My biggest recommendation is [to] structure your training. Adding a little bit of structure goes a long way. I think many novices just follow a trend of doing more and more, without a plan. Doing things like 1,000 burpees in a day and thinking it is really cool to beat yourself into the ground is not the right answer. However, you are never going to get anywhere without some structure. Structure has allowed me to plan my strength and running training, which are two very complicated things. You can get structure from reading books like this one, training guides like *Obstacle Dominator* by Hunter McIntyre, or hiring someone like me or Rose Wetzel for online coaching.

S&S: What is your daytime job?

My daytime job is a personal trainer and group fitness instructor. I work at a gym called Epic in Miami, which was started by Alexander Nicholas and Karlee Whipple. Alexander is big in the OCR world also runs a gym called Epic in New York City, which is obstacle-course-racing-focused.

S&S: How do you balance your job and family with training for OCR?

Being a personal trainer makes balancing training with personal life not that difficult. I feel a little spoiled sometimes because my personal life, OCR training, and job are all fitness-related. A typical day at work involves waking up early to train a couple of people, then getting in my first workout after finishing with my clients. Typically, my first workout is strength- or metabolic-conditioning-focused. Then I eat a lunch, take a nap, and get ready for my second workout. Sometimes this might just be surfing, paddleboarding, or mountain biking, or it will be conditioning-focused such as my long run or some intervals. Finally, I teach a couple of classes or train a couple of clients later that night. So overall, it is a pretty good life.

S&S: What does an average training week in your life look like when preparing for a race?

A training week would include three structured running workouts like I previously mentioned (long slow run, long intervals, and short intervals), three raw strength training sessions, and three hybrid workouts. The raw strength training sessions are as heavy as possible with sets of no more than five repetitions, and it is typically barbell-focused. The hybrid workouts combine strength and conditioning lasting anywhere between five and forty-five minutes.

I typically work out one to four hours a day and then I take a day off when I feel like I need it. Sometimes I need it after two days, other times it is not until after five days. I am getting better at resting and focusing on being smart and efficient. This way I am not working less but getting better results. Even on days off, I go to the gym and do an hour of mobility or a short rowing session. So during off-days, I spend a lot of time working on my body, which is another really key part of my training.

S&S: How high is your peak volume when preparing for a race?

I typically do not keep track of exact volume or mileage each week. As long as I complete those three key run workouts a week, along with my key strength training sessions, that is what's important. Based on my daily workout volume lasting for a cumulative total of one to four hours, I would say I typically hit around fifteen hours of training a week.

S&S: What was one of your hardest workouts you have ever done when preparing for a race?

Two workouts come to mind. The first is:

(30 seconds max effort on the Aerodyne followed by 90 seconds rest) x 20

It does not sound that crazy but it is surprisingly hard. When I first heard about the workout, I was thinking, *That is so much rest*, but when you are trying to hit maximum watts or calories burned it is very difficult.

The second is a CrossFit workout called the Sevens. It is seven rounds for time of: 7 handstand pushups, 7 thrusters (135 pounds men, 95 pounds women), 7 knees-to-elbows, 7 deadlifts (245 pounds men, 165 pounds women), 7 burpees, 7 kettle bell swings (70 pounds men/ 52 pounds women), and 7 pull-ups. It is a good gut-buster. Combining other exercises with deadlifts really makes this hard, especially when adding in bodyweight exercises while your heart rate is jacked.

S&S: What was your hardest or worst racing experience?

Hardest racing experience was in June 2015, [when] I did the Vail GoPro Mountain Games. I did four events in two days. The first day had a 3-mile downriver paddleboard race followed later that day by a 21-mile mountain bike race. The second day involved a 10K mountain run, followed by a 10-mile uphill road bike time trial. However, I will isolate it to that 21-mile mountain bike race, which was the hardest thing I have done in my whole life. The mountain bike race was three laps of a 7-mile loop, and the first 3 miles of every loop was a straight uphill climb. I was also going against the best mountain bikers in the world and I am definitely a novice compared with them. Biking has allowed me to add a lot of volume to my training without as much impact to my body as running. At the time, I had only been mountain biking for nine months, so more training and more experience would definitely have made that easier than it was. I had improved a lot by the time I got to the race, but was still well below the pros.

S&S: What is the most common question you receive as an OCR athlete and your response?

The most common questions I get regard nutrition. People want to know how to have a muscular and lean body. The short answer is a diet consisting of whole foods, so a lot of meat, fruit, and vegetables. I eat as many calories as I want in healthy fats, consisting of peanut butters, nut butters, almond butters, and grass-fed butter. I will also eat sweet potatoes and some grains. The important thing is [that] if you are eating whole foods, you cannot go wrong. My only restrictions are indulgences, such as dessert or alcohol. I typically eat a couple of cheat meals a week. The big thing is to stay away from processed food.

S&S: How do you think that affects your performance?

Food literally fuels my performance. When I am eating high fat and low carbohydrates, I am primarily burning fat as my fuel source. When I am doing more endurance exercise, I will typically eat more carbohydrates because that is what my body is craving. No matter what I am doing, nutrition is directly correlated to performance. Every day is an experiment to figure out what works for my body and what makes me feel good for workouts. I definitely think about it a lot, though, and try to eat purposefully with the goal of recovering from my last workout and fueling my next workout.

S&S: Are there any people or companies that you want to thank publicly?

I am a member of the Spartan Race Pro Team, so I would definitely like to thank them for all the support I receive from them. I would also like to thank my boyfriend and Spartan Pro Team member Hunter McIntyre. He is the one that got me into OCR; we train together, and he is definitely responsible for a large [part] of why I am involved in OCR. He is also a large part of my training, sort of like my coach.

S&S: *What do you see in the future for OCR?*

It is hard to say. I think it is at a point where it could go either way. It may keep getting bigger or we may have reached the peak. However, I do think it is gaining traction, especially with more television coverage and more race series showing up, like BattleFrog. That is definitely helping legitimize it and make it better. As long as the companies are funded well and making money, I think it is going to pull in more big-name athletes from triathlon, trail running, and other endurance sports. I hope that from that point it will keep snowballing with more sponsorships and more TV coverage. Additionally, I think there will be more TV coverage utilizing shorter races for easier filming. I do not think it is going to happen, but I would like to see stadium races succeed more because they are viewable and spectator-friendly. We are going to have to bring OCR to the people so it can be viewed. Some have already tried to do that with short races in open fields such as Extreme Nation, some are currently trying it like *OCR Warrior*, and Spartan Race has been trying to do it with their coverage from NBC Sports. Overall, I would say that OCR is going to get bigger and I am hopeful for the future.

S&S: *Anything else you want your fans to know?*

Make sure you check out my website www.cassidywatton.com. I put up blog posts and do online coaching for both exercise and nutrition plans from the website. Information about me, what I am currently doing in OCR, and how to get better can also be found on the site.

Lindsay Webster

Age: 25

Height: 5'5"

Weight: 115 pounds

Year Started Obstacle Racing: 2015

Biggest Accomplishment in OCR: I've been referred to as the dark horse in the sport right now . . . It's my first year participating in OCR, but I managed a gold medal at 2015 OCR World Championships, and a silver medal at 2015 Spartan World Championship.

Other OCR Race Highlights:

2014: 4th place Spartan World Championship (my very first OCR race!)

2015: 1st place BattleFrog series; 1st place Savage Race Maryland and Pennsylvania; 2nd place Spartan Palmerton NBC Super and New Jersey NBC Super; 3rd place Spartan Breckenridge NBC Sprint

Strength & Speed: What was your athletic background prior to OCR?

I've always been involved in cross-country running and racing, and raced competitively in rowing, cross-country skiing, and mountain biking.

S&S: How has your athletic background hurt or helped you for OCR? What things did you have to adjust to become a successful OCR athlete?

Every sport I've done has been a huge benefit to me as an OCR athlete, both mentally and physically. Rowing uses many of the same muscles that OCR requires (strong forearms, core, back, and legs, not to mention it's anaerobic training). Many cross-country skiers do well as OCR athletes. Not only does skiing develop both upper- and lower-body muscles, skiers are required to race all distances, whether it is a 2km sprint or a 50km distance race. The same is required of OCR athletes. Then of course, 80 percent of an obstacle course race is cross-country running.

Years of racing competitively have taught me how to train properly. They've also taught me race strategies, such as when to eat and hydrate, how to evaluate my competitors, or how my body handles different lengths of races. That's not to say that I didn't still have a lot to learn to become a successful OCR athlete. The mental grit required in this sport reaches a whole new level. Obviously racing is always tough, your muscles are always screaming and you can't seem to take in enough oxygen, but I've only ever had my muscles cramp or be exhausted to the point of complete failure in an obstacle race. I remember in my first OCR, I thought the obstacles would be a nice break from the running where I would have a chance to lower my heart rate . . . I was in for a surprise! Instead my heart rate spiked at obstacles, and I had to dig really deep mentally just to get myself to start running again.

S&S: What is your biggest recommendation for OCR athletes who want to improve?

I'd have to say that my biggest recommendation . . . is to work on your running. Many people think that obstacle racers only require strong upper-body muscles. That's true, but only to a certain extent. Obstacle races are about 80 to 90 percent running. If you have an excessive amount of upper-body muscle, it's just extra weight that you have to carry around while running (and course designers in OCR love to send you up the biggest mountains they can find)! Find that line where your upper body and grip strength [are] strong enough to get you through the obstacles, and maintain. The rest of the time, pound the pavement or trails. Do hill repeats, try an interval workout once a week, or practice your endurance once a month by running a distance that challenges you.

S&S: What is your daytime job?

I work as a marketing manager for a Canadian mud run called Mud Hero.

S&S: How do you balance your job and family with training for OCR?

My job requires a lot of logistical and computer work throughout the winter months, and the summer is our event season. Event season is busy season. We travel across Canada setting up and tearing down tents and obstacles, living out of a suitcase, and working twelve- to fifteen-hour days of manual labor (we joke around that we're carnies). Thankfully, working for a mud run, I spend so much time around our racecourse and obstacles that it gives me plenty of opportunity for practice. After the long days on my feet, it's really hard some nights to motivate myself to go out and train after work is over. Sometimes this means we don't eat dinner until 10 PM, get to bed at midnight, then wake up before 6 AM the next day and do it all over, but it's great mental and endurance training! We work so much during the summer that our winter months are essentially part-time, so I can build a great physical base during the OCR off-season. I'm lucky that my fiancé Ryan Atkins works for the same company as me, so it makes it easy to juggle family time!

S&S: What does an average training week in your life look like when preparing for a race?

During my race season, an average training week will include two or three strength workouts, around two interval or intensity sessions where I get my heart rate up over 160 bpm, and one endurance day where I'll train for over two and a half to three hours. I always make sure I have at least one rest day. When you train, it essentially breaks down your muscle tissue, and a day off when you're feeling tired will give your muscles the time they need to repair.

I'm a strong believer in listening to my body. If I've planned a high-intensity training session for that day but am feeling tired and sluggish during my warm-up, I'll swap my intensity to a different day and do something easy, or take a rest day if I'm feeling really run down. Many days I'll have done a hard workout the day before and will have something easy planned, but if I feel great then I'll take advantage and do another hard workout. I also make sure to keep training fun. My body doesn't handle more than four days per week of running well, so I love to cross-train. I'll mountain bike or road bike, rock climb, go on long hikes, cross-country ski, skate and play hockey, carry sandbags up a hill or drag a tire behind me . . . the possibilities are endless, and they keep training interesting. I believe that cross-training will make you a more well-rounded athlete, keeping all the muscles in your body strong, and keep your race-specific muscles from breaking down or becoming overtired and injured.

S&S: How high is your peak mileage when preparing for a race?

My peak mileage when preparing for a race is probably about 50 miles, or 80 kilometers. This may not seem like a lot to some people, but everyone's body reacts differently to different training volumes. Some athletes are able to train for fewer hours at a higher intensity, and have the same results as other athletes who put in huge training days. I've learned that when you train, your body doesn't fully absorb and react to the training you've done until about a month later. I'll put in a lot of volume in the months leading up to a big race, and make sure I taper off and lower my mileage the week before the race.

S&S: What was one of the hardest workouts you have ever done when preparing for a race?

One of my hardest workouts has to be hill repeats. Course designers in OCR love to send you up the biggest mountains they can find, as many times as they possibly can within a race, or so it would seem! I find doing running hills on a regular basis is really beneficial to my race performance. I'll either drive to a ski hill, or run repeats up the steep trail in my backyard, which is approximately 400 meters of ascent. Usually I'll choose a hill that takes me about six to eight minutes to run up, and ascend it as fast as I can maintain without slowing to a walk. Repeat that four to eight times, and my legs and I are completely worn out. It's a painful workout, but when I go into a race knowing that I'm fully prepared for those mountains it's a big mental advantage. I actually look forward to seeing the hills in races, because I know it's an area where I may have an edge over my competitors, and that my body will be able to handle it!

S&S: *What was your hardest or worst racing experience?*

Spartan World Championship 2014, in Vermont! It was my very first obstacle race and I had no idea what I was in for.

S&S: *Could you have done anything different to prepare for that?*

I should have done more research on the course and my competitors. I knew that the race would be four or five hours long, which having just completed my mountain bike race season I was ready for. However, I had done absolutely no upper-body strength training and I didn't realize how many carries and climbs were involved in a Spartan Race, much less world champs. I was also taken aback by how much obstacle racing had progressed toward becoming a professional sport. I was under the naive impression that obstacle races and mud runs were something that people did for fun to stay fit. I had no idea that there were now sponsored athletes in the sport, who train year-round specifically for obstacle racing. When the gun went off at the start line, I was blown away by how fit the girls were. I managed to hold my own and finish fourth (about three hundred burpees later), but I've never been so completely depleted in my life. My legs were tired and cramped, and my upper-body muscles had essentially given up entirely. After I recovered, I decided I wanted to put myself through more of it, to improve and see how much better I could do if I trained for the sport, and that's how I got hooked on OCR!

S&S: *What is the most common question you receive as an OCR athlete and your response?*

The most common question I receive is probably *How do you train?* Answer: See above question "What does an average training week in your life look like"!

S&S: Do you follow any specific dietary restrictions (such as vegan, gluten-free, vegetarian, Paleo)?

No, but I eat healthy. I consume lots of fresh fruits and vegetables, and I try to buy locally so that I know where my food is coming from, especially where meat is concerned to avoid additives and growth hormones. That's not to say that I don't eat dessert almost every night! I love cooking and baking, and I don't think it hurts after a long training day or race to treat yourself to a bowl of ice cream, for example! You've pushed your body hard, it's burned lots of calories, and you need to replenish them. I'll replenish my depleted energy stores with lots of carbs and healthy foods, but adding a yummy snack to that keeps me sane. It would drive me nuts to worry about every little thing I ate, and I'm lucky to not have any food allergies. If my body has no adverse effects to gluten or dairy, for example, and I've grown up eating them, I see no point in eliminating them from my diet. To me, a healthy diet is eating three healthy square meals a day, exercising, and enjoying treats in moderation.

S&S: How do you think that affects your performance?

If I have a big race coming up, I tend to be careful to avoid fatty or fried foods. However, one time my birthday fell on the day before a race, and I ate about a pound of ice cream for dessert! I worried it would effect my performance the next day, but I felt great during my race and placed first. Since I eat relatively healthy as it is, I think my habit of eating super healthy in the few days leading up to a race is more of a mental benefit than an actual positive physical effect. However, I'm sure if all I ate were fries for lunch and dinner for a week leading up to a race, I would definitely feel some negative effects.

S&S: Are there any people or companies that you want to thank publicly?

I would just like to thank my fiancé Ryan, who has been my biggest supporter throughout my whole journey into OCR. He has provided me with tons of knowledge, training tips, and been a great training partner on top of all that!

S&S: What do you see in the future for OCR?

I would love to see OCR become an Olympic sport! I think it has a way to go before it gets there, in terms of developing a governing body and enforcing regulations in races, but OCR is already a sport that's become extremely popular around the world in just a few short years. We now have sponsored athletes, and it's featured in the media regularly with a massive fan base. I think that it will get there, and will be around for years to come!

S&S: *Anything else you want your fans to know?*

If I have any fans reading this, than thank you all so much for your support! It means a lot. Never forget to keep having fun racing and training. It's better to enjoy the ride and still be racing years from now than to push yourself too hard and lose your love for a sport. Have fun out there!

Elite Athlete Conclusions

If you did not take the time to read all of the athlete interviews, let me help you about by providing some key takeaways.

• **Running is important:** The majority of time in an OCR is spent running, so that should be a priority.

• **Strength train two to four times a week:** Whether that is OCR-specific work or working the muscles required for obstacles, strength training is necessary.

• **Nutrition is crucial:** All of these athletes eat generally healthy foods the majority of the time. If you want to perform at your best, you need good clean fuel.

• **Volume produces gains:** Although some of the athletes have low weekly mileages, many make up for it by doing a ton of other exercise that elevates the heart rate. Furthermore, if you were a collegiate runner, you can get away with less volume since your body already developed many of the necessary systems to perform well from those four years of high-volume training.

• **It's not a hobby, it's a lifestyle:** To compete at this level, you need to commit large portions of your free time to achieving your goals.

• **If you're looking to achieve the pinnacle of the sport, you need a job that supports your goal:** Many of these athletes have jobs that are directly involved in OCR or provide flexible schedules to allow for maximum training.

• **All the athletes interviewed in this book are good, friendly people:** Do not hesitate to follow them on social media and talk to them in person at races. Most of all they appreciate all the support provided by fans of OCR, because they make the sport what it is today.

CONCLUSION

Being competitive at the elite level in obstacle racing requires hard work. The amount of effort you put into your exercise regime will be reflected in your results. When explaining results to people, I often use this equation:

Results = Hard Work + Genetics + Knowledge

Your genetics have already been decided, so there is nothing you can do about that. Now that you have read this book, you have the knowledge to be successful and build on your given genetics. The only thing left is the hard work. Be sure to set goals that include intermediary goals, one-year plans, and a five-year plan. The intermediary goals should be realistic but should not be easy. They provide little checkpoints of motivation along the way. The one-year plan is designed to help keep you on track to reaching your five-year plan. Your intermediary goals and

Erin Brooks, Ashley Samples, and Barbara Bass hug at the completion of the 2015 OCRWC team competition, where Strength & Speed placed tenth in the world.

one-year plan will change every year as you improve. You will know your goals are the appropriate difficulty if your five-year goal sounds a little ridiculous to people around you. I usually keep my five-year goals to myself because they can seem too ambitious for those who don't understand I will get there through a series of small improvements or intermediary plans and one-year goals.

I would wish you the best of luck as you begin your training, but that is nowhere in the equation. Dig deep and get ready to work hard to achieve your goals. Be sure to share your training and results with the rest of Strength & Speed. We love to hear from others on their journey, especially with stories help to inspire other athletes.

Join Strength & Speed

If this book speaks to you, then join our team. We have a large number of athletes that participate in recreational and elite/competitive obstacle races. We are also the only group of athletes serious about improvements on the road, on the trail, and in the gym. Although we have members who are power lifters, boxers, marathon runners, bodybuilders, cyclists, and followers of a variety of other sports, many of our athletes compete in the OCR world. The OCR community happens to be where strength and speed are both valued attributes. Strength & Speed is an organization where your last obstacle placing is just as important as your powerlifting total, where the date of your last ultra-marathon is just as important as your placing in your last bodybuilding show, and where your performance at your last Ironman is as meaningful as losing 30 pounds of fat.

If you are reading this book and think *I cannot join because I am already sponsored by [insert company] or part of team [insert organization]*, that is not a problem. Strength & Speed is a training methodology and social group. However, rather than focusing on purely social aspects, we focus on performance. Many of our athletes have nutrition, clothing, and other sponsors, but they continue to represent Strength & Speed when they can.

If you are reading this but think you cannot join because you live in state *[insert any name]*, that is also not a problem. Our members are spread all over the US; there are even a few in other countries. We utilize online resources to motivate one another and occasionally meet up for a major race. Create your own team of local brand-new Strength & Speed athletes to race together. If you are just getting involved in fitness, that is also not a problem. As long as you have a desire to improve, you are welcome among other Strength & Speed athletes. After all, everyone has to start somewhere.

Check out our website www.teamstrengthspeed.com for more information, apparel, and an online store. The online store offers a variety of shirts, hats, and sweatshirts, as well as personalized training plans from me, the owner of Strength & Speed. Be sure to follow us on social media for the most up-to-date information (www.facebook.com/teamstrengthspeed).

Strength & Speed athlete and age group racer Demetrios "Sty" Karellas at the OCR World Championships.

Think you have what it takes to show the world that you are both strong and fast? Check out the criteria page : (www.teamstrengthspeed.com/criteria) for the most current version of what it takes to achieve the coveted Level 20.

Interested in being a sponsored athlete featured on the website and featured in one of my future books? Then contact us through one of the above websites or email Evan@teamstrenthspeed.com for more information. We are a small private company, so most of the benefits come from being highlighted on our website along with some free apparel. We also provide team sponsorships if you are planning on racing or competing in an event.

Remember: If you are not actively trying to improve, chances are you are slowly sliding backward. So go out and get what you want. Hard things are never easy, and extraordinary results often require extraordinary effort.

If you want something you've never had,
you have to be willing to do something you've never done.

Acknowledgments

There are a lot of people who have had a positive effect on me that enabled me to reach my current fitness level. There are almost too many to name, but I am going to try to thank as many of them as I can in the pages that follow.

First, and most important, I have to thank my wife Amy. She is also my photographer, designer, support crew, driver, and mother of my daughter. Almost every picture in this book was taken by her on our endless weekend trips. I need to thank her for not only putting up with my often selfish training regime but also the endless hours she has stood by waiting for me to finish races. The biggest testament to her dedication was at the World's Toughest Mudder when she braved a windstorm as I ran hopelessly in circles. At the time she was six and a half months pregnant, and it was her birthday. This is representative of a decade-plus of putting up with me and my hobbies. Thank you so much and I love you. Next, of course, is our daughter who makes every day better by her presence. She melts my heart every time I look at her. I love her.

My mom and dad for raising me in a great environment and teaching me that you can work hard to achieve your dreams. They showed me that experiences are worth more than items you can buy in a store. I also need to thank Nicole for being a great sister and an exceptional athlete while we were growing up. Your athletic prowess gave me something to strive toward as I started getting seriously involved in fitness. Having a family that is involved in fitness makes vacationing easier and more fun. I always look forward to our trips to Rehobeth Beach and working out at the Body Shop.

Thank you to everyone else who has motivated me in one form or another along the way. In roughly chronological order, here is my attempt at thanking everyone. If at the end of my athletic career, I have had as much of a positive effect on people as they have on me, I will count it as a success regardless of my placing. Although a couple of first-place wins are always nice.

Glen Mackey for getting me interested in triathlons. Rimas Radzius for motivating me to run faster throughout college and giving me a goal to strive toward. Rohin Shama and Brendan Gallagher for having the idea to run 40 miles unsupported years before I arrived at college. Andrew Woodward for being my best friend at college and always willing to do stupid things with me, including reenacting the 40-mile run. Despite his longest run being 10 miles and mine being a marathon, we still managed to suffer all the way to DC before getting stranded after our ride failed to come pick us up. All the P/Rs of Company E-8 who taught me that your mind is the thing that limits your physical performance. Without learning that lesson, I do not think I would be half the athlete I am today.

Jonathan Grassabugh for being a role model and roommate, and for making the ultimate sacrifice for our country on April 7, 2007. If you are visiting Arlington National Cemetery, make sure you stop by his grave and say hi. Of note, he loves warm Bacardi, so feel free to take a shot and pour one out for him.

Joseph Scott Brannon for being a role model for work and who taught me more lessons that I can list. I also appreciate the amount of trash-talking he did regarding exercise, which is always great motivation. Chris Mayes, Charles Pennington, and Aaron Churchwell for being my lifting partners at one time. It was great working out with you guys.

Demetrios "Sty" Karellas for suggesting I get into obstacle racing two years before my first race. Why didn't I listen to you earlier? Anthony Miale for redesigning the Strength & Speed symbol along with providing advice as an experienced editor. John Schmaltz for flying out to visit me and riding farther then he has ever ridden on his bike two days in a row. Strongman Greg Verderosa who taught me what real lifting is about.

All of my co-workers, past and present, who have ever beat me in a run or lifted more weight than me. Every time I was outlifted, it provided motivation to improve in the future. This includes Stewie, Adam, Joe K., and Joe E. I should also thank Brian Revell, who finally made me show up at my first Warrior Dash hung over after spending all night at an Under Armour party. I had no idea at the time that it would lead to this. I also need to thank my onetime boss John Taft for telling everyone he meets about my accomplishments and being one of the few people I have ever met who was willing to let me go to the other side of the world for World's Toughest Mudder 2015.

Kate Schifani, who motivated me to run a second marathon on a treadmill, helping me achieve my treadmill marathon PR of 3:10:30. Heidi Pruit and Jamie O'Donnel, who kept me amused when my body fat was so low I wanted to pass out as I prepped for qualifying for the drug-free bodybuilding world finals.

Danny Danner and Matt Heiser, the organizers of the various running groups I have used to support my long run training. Without your groups Sunday Runday North in Kansas City and Clarksville Running Club in Tennessee, respectively, getting up on the weekend would have been much harder and less enjoyable.

Jorge Figeuro, who was a personal trainer before me and inadvertently gave me the idea to do the same. The Greek god Papadon, who is a great professional wrestler and my cousin. He showed me that if you have a dream, you should go for it and keep trying regardless of how long it might take. If you are a wrestling fan, make sure you look him up on social media and then tell WWE to go ahead and sign the greatest unsigned talent today.

The famous athletes who have inspired me and whom I've had the pleasure of briefly meeting. For strength training, Jay Cutler, Kevin English, Kai Greene, and Shaun Clarida. For running, Dean Karnazes and Ryan Hall. All these athletes showed that even though you've reached the highest levels of your respective sports, you can still be friendly and receptive to fans.

The other elites of obstacle racing who gave me something to strive for. Without having a target, it would be hard to improve. Thanks to all the elites for participating in interviews for this book. Kevin Righi and Rusty Palmer for taking a chance by joining Strength & Speed for the initial run at the OCRWC. You guys are awesome and helped me realize the options that were available for OCR athletes. Kevin, I need to thank you especially, since your friends and co-workers have helped out in too many ways to name. I also need to thank Troy Bruns along with Sheila and Greg Yocom for welcoming me into the Mid-America Obstacle Course Racing family.

I definitely need to thank everyone at Mud Run Guide, but especially Brett Stewart and Margaret Schlachter. Thanks for giving me the opportunity to be a part of your website and publishing my articles.

I also need to thank Hammer Nutrition for sponsoring me. What people do not see is the dozens of time I applied for sponsorship and failed. Hammer Nutrition was the first company willing to take me on as an athlete, for which I will always be grateful. For a company, making that first move to sponsor a relatively unknown athlete is definitely a leap of faith, and it means a lot to be a part of their team. I also need to thank David Stakel, Sean Sharpe, and Tiffany White, who work at Under Armour. They have helped me out a lot on this journey and I am very grateful to have them as friends. Since then other companies have provided me with varying level of benefits and sponsorships, including Mud Run Guide, LifeFuels, Hardcore Mud Run, Hannibal Race and Conquer the Gauntlet. While I appreciate free stuff, what is more important to me is companies looking at me and then saying through their actions, *We believe in you.*

Finally, a huge shoutout to my Conquer The Gauntlet Pro Team teammates. You guys continue to motivate me and make me work harder everyday to stay ahead of you or try and catch up to the ones that are better than me. Thanks Cody Peyton, Nathan Palmer, Matt Willis, Matt Campione, Bryce Robinson, Lucas Pfannenstiel, Christina Armstrong, Amy Pajcic, Ashley Jeanne Samples, Brenna Calvert, Nicki Bruckmann, Nikki Call and Randi Lackey. But most importantly of all the entire Mainprize family for helping my dream come true. Thank you so much David, Stephen and Courtney.

I know I have missed some people, but if you have ever been a part of my fitness journey, then thank you. Every athlete I compete against helps drive me to be better. If you are ahead of me, it gives me a goal to chase after. If you are behind me, it is motivation not to let up so you don't pass me.

All the people who follow Strength & Speed and me on social media. Your presence and posts help keep me motivated on days when I feel tired. Thanks for supporting me and buying this book. Best of luck on all your training endeavors in the future.

Photo Credits

All photos taken by Amy Perperis of Strength & Speed unless otherwise noted below.

All photos of Ashley Jeanne Samples, Erin Brooks, Devin Roberts, Barbara Bass, and Adam Baylor taken by Demetrios "Sty" Karellas.

All 2015 Obstacle Course World Championships photos taken by Demetrios "Sty" Karellas.

Chapter 1 photos of Skull Valley taken by Demetrios "Sty" Karellas.

In chapter 3 and chapter 8, Alter Ego pictures from World's Toughest Mudder 2013 taken by Sandra Dodd.

Chapter 12 Claude Godbout Spartan Trophy picture taken by Marc-André Bédard.

Lindsay Webster BattleFrog podium picture taken by Brenna "Red Beast" Calvert.

Corinna Coffin picture courtesy of BattleFrog Series, with permission from photographer Heather Riggs.